IMAGINING AMERICA

IMAGINING AMERICA

AMERICA

Peter Conrad

New York
OXFORD UNIVERSITY PRESS
1980

Copyright © 1980 by Peter Conrad

Library of Congress Cataloging in Publication Data

Conrad, Peter.
  Imagining America.

  Includes index.
    1. United States in literature. 2. Authors, English—
Journeys—United States. 3. United States—Description and
travel—History. 4. English literature—History and criticism.
5. British in the United States. I. Title.
PR129.U5C6   820'.9'32   79-14740
ISBN 0-19-502651-9
First printing March 1980

Second printing April 1980

ACKNOWLEDGMENTS

I have been exceptionally fortunate in my editors, James Raimes in New York and Stephen Brook in London, who have been both encouraging and bracingly critical. Helen Armitage and Anne Evers generously helped me to locate illustrations and clear permissions. The copy editing of Leona Capeless and Kim Lewis helped clarify the text, and rid it of numerous errors. I am grateful as well to Pat Kavanagh for her vigilant defense of my interests and to the governing body of Christ Church, Oxford, for its grants of time and funds for travel.

The following persons and institutions have agreed to the use of material in which they hold the copyright: Christopher Isherwood, Methuen & Co. Ltd., and Simon and Schuster, Inc., for works by Christopher Isherwood; the National Trust of Great Britain for works by Rudyard Kipling; the Estate of H. G. Wells for works by H. G. Wells; Laurence Pollinger Ltd. for works by D. H. Lawrence; *Spokesman*, Professor Edward Mendelson, and the Estate of W. H. Auden for works by W. H. Auden; Mrs. Laura Huxley and Chatto & Windus Ltd. for works by Aldous Huxley.

CONTENTS

IMAGINING AMERICA

1

IMAGINING AMERICA

Versions of Niagara

Before America could be discovered, it had to be imagined. Columbus knew what he hoped to find before he left Europe. Geographically, America was imagined in advance of its discovery as an arboreal paradise, Europe's dream of verdurous luxury. After that discovery, the political founders of the United States were its inventors. They too, like the explorers, constituted America as a promised land, a conjuration of the liberal hopes or aristocratic fears of Europe. They saw the new kind of state they were creating not as a fact but as a formula, not a natural growth of history but the actualization of an idea. As the Gettysburg Address puts it, America was created in homage to a proposition.

Since then, it has been successively re-imagined, dedicated to other propositions. Some of the English visitors whose experience is described in this book interpret America as a savage regression from the niceties of European society. Mrs. Trollope and Dickens revile Americans as spitting, guzzling, cursing brutes. Kipling and D. H. Lawrence, however, ethnologically or mythologically admire America's savagery, and find there a primitive vigor which has been bred out of enfeebled Europe. Other writers see Americans not as a shameful vestige of society's prehistory but as a race of the future.

For H. G. Wells they are cerebral technocrats who will inherit the earth; for W. H. Auden they are all anxious refugees, sad citizens of a deracinated modern world; for Christopher Isherwood they are bland Oriental angels. Americans tolerate and even abet this contradictory European fantasizing about them. Loyal to the ideal pretensions of their society, they're as much the prisoners of their millennial self-images as they are of the prejudicial images Europeans continue to inflict on them.

To the European, the enchantment of America is the variegation of its reality. The surprises of the country are an imaginative promise. At home, you are assigned a surrounding world by the circumstances of your birth: you don't invent a reality for yourself but inherit one, and exist in a society which prides itself on having restricted the range of imaginative choices. A civilized society, according to Matthew Arnold, is one in which the center prevails, in which metropolitan standards constrain the regions, and artists club together in a clique at that center. America is centerless, not a claustrophobic, centripetal society like those in Europe which Arnold revered, but a chaos of disparate realities: the rigorous, abstemious New England in which Kipling went to live; the mechanical modernity of New York chosen by Auden; the primeval west of Lawrence, the psychedelic west of Aldous Huxley. The same region can dexterously adapt itself to each new imaginative expectation of it: as the later chapters of this book will show, Lawrence's New Mexico is not the same as Huxley's, nor is Huxley's California the same as Isherwood's. In England these writers would have had to share the same congested, incest-ridden space. America disperses them, relegating each to the location aptest to his imagination.

The reality of America is selective, optional, fantastic: there is an America for each of us. America, E. M. Forster says, is like life because "you can usually find in it what you look for." Forster went there for the first time in 1947, having (like Columbus in 1492) decided in advance what he intended to discover. His demands on America were contradictory, but the country's versatile reality managed to satisfy them. He wanted America to provide him with scenery of two irreconcilable sorts, "gigantic and homely." But American geography is an encyclopedic inventory of nature, and he found homeliness in the snowy Berkshires, gigantism at the Grand Canyon. In America's vast emptiness (which John Locke likened to the amiably receptive infantile mind) there are truths to sustain any fiction.

Because America offers, as it did to Forster, an incarnation of your most recondite and specialized fantasies, in discovering America you are discovering yourself. Europe equips you with a hereditary, natal self. America allows you to invent a self better adjusted to the individual you have become since outgrowing the impositions of birth. The Victorians felt threatened by America for this very reason: it was a society in which people conferred values on themselves, not the kind of society represented by Victorian novels, in which the attribution of character is society's enfranchisement of creatures who have no reality outside it. But once past this Victorian disquiet, the freedom America grants each person to re-imagine himself is, for the writers examined in this book, the country's virtue. Oscar Wilde in 1882 seized on this ingenuous American freedom with a witty unscrupulousness. America for him was a theater, a place in which he could play at being himself and be handsomely paid for doing so. Wilde enjoys America because he can merchandise a self there, turn existence into gratuitous performance. America liberates him from the pieties of the society into which he was born, and changes his outlawry into celebrity. The next subjects of this book, Kipling, Wells, and Lawrence, all rejoice in America's freedom from the finished rigidity of European society. Kipling likes it because it is not yet that kind of society: it is still an epic aggregation of warring tribes. Wells likes it because it is no longer that kind of society: it has become an efficient technological unit, and eliminated the picturesque inequalities treasured by the Victorians. For Kipling, America fortunately has not arrived at the pacified, mannered state corresponding to the European literary form of the novel. For Wells, it has long since rendered the novel obsolete, and its outlandish truths can only be described by science fiction. Lawrence conjoins these two opposed opinions. Like Kipling, he thinks primeval America more atavistically virulent and divine than sedate, secular Europe. Like Wells, he thinks the industrial United States more sterilely advanced than Europe, and he salutes its mechanical death because he anticipates its spiritual resurrection.

So far, the concern of these travelers is with the condition of American society. The final three subjects of this book, Auden, Huxley, and Isherwood, interpret America's freedom not socially but spiritually. For each of them the new self discovered in America is sanctified by religious conversion.

The images of America proposed from the dismayed Victorian survey of indigence and unmannerliness to the different benedictions of the country by Auden, Huxley, and Isherwood are contrary and inconsistent. This book follows the dynamism of their succession. It begins by setting the complaints of the Victorians about the ill-bred squalor of Americans against the missions of Wilde and Rupert Brooke, who play at converting the heathens to a dandified aestheticism. This introduces a series of attempts to explain America's place in history and to define the literary forms which suit its refractory reality. The Victorians assume America to be slovenly and backward, unworthy of the novel's social graces and subtleties of observation. Later writers admit the novel's irrelevance to America, but they suggest alternatives. In Kipling's case the alternative is epic, in Robert Louis Stevenson's it's chivalric romance—epic and romance being the two forms which in the history of literature logically precede the novel. In Wells's case as in Huxley's the alternative is science fiction, the form which is the novel's logical successor. The book concludes with America's transformation from a state of society to a state of mind, and an examination of the new religions practiced there by its adherents: Lawrence's murderous totemism, Auden's existential Protestantism, Huxley's concoction of artificial psychedelic paradises, Isherwood's Vedanta.

As an advance demonstration of America's virtuosity—its readiness to revise itself for different people at different times—the present chapter sends Frances Trollope and her son Anthony, then Dickens, Wilde, Brooke, and Wells, with Henry James and Sarah Bernhardt as fellow travelers, to a single spot, compulsory for tourists: Niagara Falls. Each one perceives and appraises it differently: each one imposes himself on it, but at the same time discovers himself in responding to it; and the variety of their reactions sums up the imaginative metamorphoses of America across the first half of this book.

Frances Trollope's experience of America was a series of disasters. She traveled there in 1827, taking along three of her children. Anthony remained in England at first, under the supervision of his father, an unsuccessful lawyer. The Trollopes lived with blithe disregard for their small means, trusting to a bequest from a rich relation to save them, and Mrs. Trollope's career in America was characteristic of the family's improvidence. It began in mercenary hope and ended in ignominious ruin. The model community near Memphis which she intended to join turned out to be a swampy chaos. From there she retreated to Cincinnati and opened a bazaar to sell European trinkets. Having failed as a shopkeeper, she took up authorship, and by excoriating its inhabitants revenged herself on the America which had refused to enrich her.

Her *Domestic Manners of the Americans* was published after her return to England in 1832, and its account of a visit to Niagara catches both Mrs. Trollope's disgruntlement and her imaginative deficiency. She is unequal to the challenge of the scenic spectacle, but she covers her own incapacity by snubbing the Falls, superciliously neglecting to describe them. She sets out in the sour hope of disappointment. The north of the Hudson has been so praised that she "expected . . . to find reality flat after description," but the scenery for once does justify the advance propaganda. Foiled, she determines on a new tactic. Because she can't blame the Falls for disappointing her, she disappoints herself instead, and finds herself unable to do descriptive justice to them. But her profession of inadequacy is a devious slight to the landscape. The theory of the sublime assumes that the helpless observer will be roused by the splendors of nature and made equal to the challenge of responding and recording his responses. Mrs. Trollope refuses the dare: "It is not for me to attempt a description of Niagara; I feel I have no powers for it," whereas properly she ought to derive those powers from the scene itself. She transfers the duty of description to a colleague, an English literary gentleman encountered at the hotel, who is better equipped for it. For her part, she insists on treating the Falls not as a natural wonder but as a social amenity, and condescends to praise Niagara for being deferential background music. Niagara is not noisy, and you can converse in ordinary tones quite near the cataract, she says, whereas the Potomac Falls are raucous. The challenge of the Falls is for Mrs. Trollope social rather than sublime: you must perch on teetering slabs of rock "or else lose your reputation as a tourist." The Falls test not response but behavior.

She admits her own excitement, but with grudging negativity ("To say I was not disappointed is but a weak expression"—yet it is the only expression she uses) and withdraws at once into disavowal ("I dare not dwell upon this, it is a dangerous subject," and a description "must lead direct to nonsense"). Rather than exultation, she describes her own perhaps unwise intrepidity—the daring she displayed, for instance, in standing at the edge of the gulf—and the strain of the experience, as painful as it is awesome: the nerves "quail at the first sight of this stupendous cataract." Elsewhere she assesses the emotional cost of the adventure, not its excitement. Her pleasure in crossing to explore Goat Island is compounded of "real safety and apparent danger." At the end of four days, she and her family count the damage the landscape has done them: they have been drenched, their feet torn by rocks, their faces blistered by the sun. She concentrates on her weariness and discomfort rather than on the Falls, and even makes the passers-by share this deflection of vision. While she and her companions are out sketching, another group of tourists struggles up the cliffs to the summit and pauses to chatter about the Trollopes, wondering where they're from and what they're up to. The backs of these new arrivals meanwhile are to the Falls, and "not one of them . . . ever turned the head, even for a moment, to look at the most stupendous spectacle that nature has to show." But Mrs. Trollope is blaming them for an obtuseness like her own—a choice of the inquisitive pleasures of gossip rather than the distracting elation of the sublime; a choice of society rather than nature. So intent is Mrs. Trollope on avoiding description that she leaves herself unable, in the cavern formed by the flood, to discriminate between pleasure and pain, unable indeed to respond at all. She wonders why "to stand for hours drenched in spray, stunned by the ceaseless roar, trembling from the concussion that shakes the very rock you cling to" and struggling to breathe in the moist atmosphere, should be accounted a pleasure, "yet pleasure it is, and I almost think the greatest I ever enjoyed." After permitting herself this perfunctory tribute, she hastens from the cavern, overcome by a severe chest pain.

The challenge of lyrical description, evaded by Mrs. Trollope, is shrewdly circumvented by her son. Anthony Trollope first visited Niagara in 1859, during a stopover in New York between steamers on his way back to England from the West Indies. His account in *The West Indies and the Spanish Main* manages to avoid description by concentrating on the paraphernalia of tourism, routes, schedules, accommodations, tips to guides. The business of organizing takes precedence, for Trollope the civil servant, a functionary of the Post Office, over the place itself. If Mrs. Trollope fails to see Niagara because she is too busy transcribing her own symptoms of alarm or discomfort, her son fails to see it because he is too busy arranging an itinerary. But he is less dismissive than his mother. She stresses the inconveniences of the place, its abrasive rocks and soaking torrents; he at least exerts himself to render it convenient. He bureaucratizes Niagara, reducing the experience of it to a matter of administrative efficiency. The tourist is advised to travel up the Hudson by day and save time by traveling onwards from Albany overnight, since there is nothing to be seen. Details of railway sleeping-berths are provided. On arrival, the traveler is warned to alight on the Canadian side and to lodge at the Clifton Hotel, not to wait for Niagara Falls station. Trollope didn't take his own advice, and had to hire a carriage back from Niagara Falls to the hotel, which cost him, he complains, an exorbitant five dollars.

Exposure to the wonders of the scene is cautiously rationed: you should station yourself between the rocks and the Horseshoe Falls after sunset, and remain there for half an hour. Expenditure is required for the enjoyment of the sensation. Guides have to be sweetened with the occasional twenty-five cents, and oilskins for the passage under the Falls cost sixty cents. Instead of a romantic abandonment to emotion, Trollope recommends a prudent calculation of distance from the Falls: "five yards make the difference between a comparatively dry coat and an absolutely wet one." Niagara defeats his mother; but Trollope protects himself from it, recoiling into a pusillanimous efficiency. Like his mother, he moderates his enthusiasm by choosing to express it in a negative locution ("Nothing ever disappointed me less than the Falls of Niagara"), and like her, he reduces the marvel to a social scale. She had called the Falls a murmurous accompaniment to conversation, and he says (apologizing for a preliminary half-day of unresponsiveness) that "their charms grow upon one like the conversation of a brilliant man." He then apologizes for having no more to say on the subject, which he briskly dismisses: "So much for Niagara."

Trollope returned to Niagara during the 1861 tour which he wrote up in *North America*. His approach here is again circuitous and grudging. At the Falls of the Montmorency he introduces a shame-faced disclaimer, pleading that he is ill-at-ease describing waterfalls and supplicating (like a thrifty bourgeois, husbanding resources) to be allowed to reserve "what little capacity I may have in this way . . . for Niagara." He ingeniously excuses his omission by saying that the Falls are best seen when frozen in mid-winter, and then confessing that he wasn't there in that season. He is happier with the Chaudière on the Ottawa River, because it can be domesticated: he explains that its name derives from its resemblance to a boiling kettle. Once at Niagara, he ventures an initial grandiloquent assertion—Niagara, he claims, outdoes the combined achievements of nature and art—which he then can't sustain, for he attributes to Niagara his own officious values and commends it not for sublimity but for efficiency. It is reliable: "the waters never fail," whatever the season, and their volume is unvarying. The bureaucrat is concerned with practical workings, not with atmospheric effects (the aureoles which were to enchant Rupert Brooke in 1913 are prosaically dismissed by Trollope: "I do not care for this prettiness"), and Trollope thinks Niagara technically remarkable, on account of the volume of water it thrusts over so sheer a drop.

Businesslike self-control chastens the vagrant enthusiasm of the romantic. "Power of eye-control," Trollope says, "is necessary to the full enjoyment of scenery." The alarms and impulses of sublimity are calmed into a set of dutifully reverent exercises. Seated on a rail at the end of a bridge, the visitor must practice identifying himself with the rush of water until he feels himself rushed off toward the ocean. Then, having attained this empathetic state, he is abruptly graduated to the next stage: "when this state has been reached and has passed away you may get off your rail and mount the tower." The pantheistic self-identification with the waters which Trollope prescribes for visitors is an emotion he personally reserved for the plenitude of commerce, rather than the prodigies of nature. On this same tour, the granaries of Chicago and Buffalo stir him to an emotional intensity which is absent from his account of Niagara: "I breathed the flour, and drank the flour, and felt myself to be enveloped in a world of breadstuff." The torrent of grain, like the flood of Niagara, is evidence of God's husbandry, for it assures Trollope that provision has been made, by some celestial bureaucrat, for the "increasing millions" of the United States.

As Trollope tells it, even the daring anecdote of the *Maid of the Mist*'s "wondrous voyage" becomes a parable of commercial cunning. The little tourist steamer had somehow offended the local sheriff, who set out to seize it. The captain rescued the boat by making it run the rapids into the whirlpool. Trollope wishes he could conceive "what [the captain's] thoughts were at that moment," but such foolhardy heroism is beyond him, and he resolves the episode into a demonstration of defiant capitalistic courage: "an American would steam down Phlegethon to save his property from the Sheriff." The conundrum is whether the captain was the proprietor, or whether he risked his life for a fee (as Trollope's informant alleges); the conclusion is the sale of the boat, and the triumph not of romantic heroism but of shopkeeping ingenuity.

Just as Trollope turns the steamer's contest with the rapids into a stratagem to protect property, so he is anxious that the visitor should protect himself from the dangers of the place. He estimates risk with the exactitude of an insurance agent. For instance, he calculates the odds against navigating the whirlpool as fifty to one, and advises that, although the steep suspended ferry ride across to Canada is hair-raising, he has made the journey a dozen times without incident, and dares not presume that the reader will be any less fortunate. Nor do accidents ever happen, he notes, during crossings of the river. The advantages of hiring oilskins—to shield oneself from the spray during a descent of the shaft which takes visitors to river level—are computed. Trollope has experimentally made the descent both with and without oilclothes, and decides against them because of their nastiness. But commercial equity makes him add that all the same "the ordinary payment should be made for their use," even if they're left behind, because the visitor's duty is to avoid prejudicing the interests of "those whose trade it is to prepare them." He has advice as well for those whose time is rationed, and indicates a point on the Canadian side which will serve "those who desire to see all at a glance."

Encumbering Niagara with these time-saving routines and commercial scruples, Trollope is at least true to his own drab unresponsiveness. Dickens on the other hand rhetorically muddies his account of the Falls, in the *American Notes* of 1842, because of his anxiety to convince himself that he has felt something. Niagara, he says, is a sacred place, where the initial perturbation of the spirits is placated by a visionary tranquility, which is our assurance of the Creator's presence. Dickens prides himself on never leaving the Canadian side during his ten-day sojourn, preferring nature's sublime solitude to fretful human company. But his is an uproarious urban art, which cannot comprehend the placidity of nature. He therefore sets the rhetoric to do the work of responding for him. Regiments of capital letters—Peace of Mind, Eternal Rest and Happiness, Image of Beauty, Enchanted Ground—inflate emotions into abstract nouns. Tepid feelings are forced to stand to attention as allegorical headlines. Yet the expletives and exclamations are all prudently unsubstantialized: "What voices spoke from out the thundering waters; what faces faded from the earth, looked out upon me from its gleaming depths . . . !" What voices and what faces indeed? The rhetorical bluster appears to be giving but is actually taking away, since it refuses to commit itself to defining the nature of the watery portents. The syntax is as automatic as the emotions. Dickens relies on parallelisms which are mechanical elaborations of a nonexistent feeling: "What voices . . . what faces . . . what Heavenly promise"; "I never stirred . . . I never crossed . . ."; or the series of infinitives which extend an elephantine sentence—"to wander . . . to stand . . . to gaze . . . to climb . . . to linger . . . to have . . . to look." These parallelisms ritualize the absence of emotion, managing to say nothing while sounding imposingly invocatory. They galvanize language, keeping it moving though getting it nowhere: "still do those quiet waters roll . . . ; still are the rainbows spanning them. . . . Still, when the sun is on them, do they shine and glow like molten gold. Still, when the day is gloomy, do they fall like snow." Bemused by his own circuitous and repetitious language, Dickens ends by praising Niagara for possessing those same qualities: it still thunders on, though he is not there to witness it—"always does the mighty stream appear to die as it comes down, and always from its unfathomable grave arises that tremendous ghost of spray and mist which is never laid." His own description has made a machine of it.

Trollope forces Niagara to pander to the comforts of the bourgeois; Dickens has it deliver a moralizing sermon. In both, the pathetic fallacy subdues nature: Trollope makes it serve human convenience, Dickens makes it console human discontent. Henry James, describing his journey there in *Portraits of Places* (1871), adopts an aesthetic version of these Victorian techniques for annexing nature. He treats Niagara as a natural creation aspiring to the superior condition of art. His concern is not to profess a hyperbolically sublime response to it, but to compose it, to rearrange it in accordance with aesthetic principles, which refine nature's coarseness and order its mess. A pitiless aesthetic conscience censors James's sensations. The formal equivocations of art are James's defense against the disarray and disappointment of life, and he works to arrange and isolate an impression of Niagara which must be protected from a vulgar, threatening actuality. Trollope helpfully indicated the best vantage-points. James's concern is not how to see Niagara, but how to make an image of it. He can justify the slovenliness and trash of Niagara village by regarding it "as one of those sordid foregrounds which Turner liked to use," but confesses that it is an aesthetic irritant, encroaching on the integrity of his impression. Even the argument for public ownership of Niagara resolves itself for James into a consideration of aesthetic form. The Falls should be framed, separated from "ignoble contact" with venal human scruffiness, accorded "the negative homage of empty spaces." The virtue of emptiness is that it imposes on the busy tumult of Niagara the austere aesthetic principles of James's own novels, which empty society, subduing the populous affray of Victorian fiction, and silence it, recording not the external uproar but the secret psychological things people don't say.

Looking down from the suspension bridge, James marks a change in perception by describing the scene as "perfect" and "ad-

mirably simple." Niagara for him is not rowdily, incalculably sublime, as it is for Trollope and Dickens, but beautiful, with a small-
scale preciosity. James is alert not to grand effects but to minute
details, like the chromatic ambiguity of "the world-famous green"
water on the precipice, which baffles painters and poets. He emphasizes "the perfect taste of it" and its "grace," qualities of linear
delicacy, not the formless oratorical froth of his predecessors. Refusing to lose himself in a vague, muddy enthusiasm, he analyzes
Niagara into its pictorial constituents, which are line and color. As
a linear composition, "the shelf and its lateral abutments" outdo
Michelangelo by describing an impeccable semicircle. Even the alarming leap of the waters over the precipice is calmed by James into a
geometrical abstraction, "the rounded passage of the horizontal to the
perpendicular," and he approves its perfection as if it were a miracle
of human artistic ingenuity, not an accidental fact of nature, praising it for being so "successfully executed."

Whereas the god of romantic sublimity creates nature in thun-
derclaps of startling force, the god who designs James's Niagara is,
like James himself, a fastidious miniaturist who permits himself no
unpremeditated outbursts. Niagara is, James insists, "thought out."
Its creator was not a fearful cosmic tyrant but an estimable artificer,
to whom James defers: "the genius who invented it was certainly
the first author of the idea that order, proportion and symmetry are
the conditions of perfect beauty."

James turns the vicissitudes of the river, hurled across the terrifying drop and lashed on toward the whirlpool, into the history of
a long-suffering fictional character. The recovery of the stream at the
base of the Horseshoe is "a drama of thrilling interest." The water
resembles an exhausted swimmer and takes on "an air of recent
distress," but it summons strength from the consciousness that the
ordeal of the drop is over, and although its dignity has been battered
its volume is undiminished. At the rapids there is a hysterical relapse.
The waters now have "the air . . . of being forced backwards, with
averted faces, to their fate," and their agitation is a flurry of protest.

James imagines them shrieking, sobbing, clasping hands, and tossing hair. The desolate meaninglessness of the welter disturbs him, and he populates it with these human forms to confer on it some sense of emotional and aesthetic logic. The cozy pathetic fallacy of the Victorians has become for James a matter of aesthetic conscience. Thus for him the spectacle of the rapids "may be called complete only when you have gone down the river some four miles," to the whirlpool, where "the unhappy stream tremendously renews its anguish." The river is now suddenly forced sideways toward the Canadian shore, and it reacts with "surprise and bewilderment," stirring itself into a vortical rage. Its emotions are ingrown, like those of James's own characters, and instead of venting them it turns them into venomous self-punishment. The whirlpool doesn't spray "the offending cliffs" which are the cause of its torment, but recoils toward its own center in an introverted panic, "shaken to its innermost bowels and panting hugely, as if smothered in its excessive volume." James has conducted his character, like the protagonist of a tragedy, from the initial uneventful complacency of the lake through the shocks and reverses of the Falls to this final maelstrom of agony and exhaustion. He has followed the river as it affronts its destiny (to use the phrase he employed of a fictional heroine, Isabel Archer in *The Portrait of a Lady*), and so is "content to ring down his curtain" on "the drama of Niagara."

James calls himself "a scribbling tourist, ineffectively playing at showman," an entrepreneur exhibiting Niagara not as a natural spectacle but as a tragic performance. Ten years later, Sarah Bernhardt made it the setting for one of her dare-devil histrionic performances. In 1881 she was taken to Niagara by a steel and petroleum magnate from Pittsburgh, and she records the visit in her memoirs. To her, the Falls are a monument of Art Nouveau, glazed and ornamental yet swirling and serpentine, like a cabinet of Lalique jewels. Pendants of ice hang on the rock like outsize jagged jewels. The water is "a curtain of silver." Its fluidity freezes into icy fixity, or else it falls in such masses that it seems solid and immobile.

Either way it conforms to the decadent appetite for synaesthetic combinations of opposite qualities. Although it is an assertion of natural force, it looks arty and simulated. The rhinoceros-shaped clump on which Bernhardt mounts is treacherously "smooth and transparent as artificial ice."

Because the Falls are ornamental, Bernhardt is preoccupied with the costume appropriate for viewing them in. She wears a heavy fur mantle on the American side but, tired by it, slips it off to reveal a white dress with a satin blouse. The fur she tosses with vainglorious negligence over the side of the ice-mountain, to reclaim it at the bottom. On the Canadian side she is compelled to array herself in a yellow mackintosh with a hood to conceal her hair, "an enormous blouse much too wide covering the whole body, fur boots with roughed soles to avoid broken legs and heads, and immense mackintosh breeches in zouave style." She is given an iron-tipped cudgel as a prop. The prettiest woman, she complains, is reduced by this uniform to a shaggy clumsy bear, and she rebelliously decorates herself, refusing to cover her hair and pinning roses into her waterproof blouse. But when she checks her appearance in a mirror, she admits that her vanity has merely made her absurd. The silver belt gathering the mackintosh in folds around her hips makes her look obese not svelte.

She looks at herself in the mirror; the tourists gape at her; no one notices the Falls. Sarah's triumph is to upstage Niagara. The sublime indifference of the Falls challenges her to make them the set for one of her performances, to harness them to her capricious egotism. Her Pittsburgh friends have already presented her with a crude glass box containing a mannequin version of herself perched on an ice-hillock in the Falls. She is offended by the coarseness of its execution, and her response is to compete with this ugly model and project herself into the Falls. She climbs recklessly onto the block of ice shaped like a rhinoceros and, shakily poised on the outcrop, momentarily vanquishes the torrent, stilling it into a theatrical tableau. The landscape piques her because it won't acknowledge and applaud her. At first she dresses up for it, as if hoping to change its roar into a thunder of approbation, but she is stricken by shame at her preposterous sartorial vanity. Then she resolves that the way to impress Niagara is to venture into it, to make herself its center.

Her antics amusingly corrupt the romantic theory of how one should respond to the sublimity of nature. The sublime first challenges and exhausts the petty human ego, but then rouses the spectator from his state of disablement, stimulating him to respond to cataracts or mountains with the elation they deserve. Bernhardt's reaction to the importunity of the sublime is not excited bewilderment, as the theory prescribes, but annoyance and a defiant vow to make the vast ignorant natural object take notice of her. Oscar Wilde recommended the same stratagem to another actress, Lillie Langtry. He first advised her against a visit to the Falls, but when she did go he remarked that "she was photographed at Niagara, with the Falls as an insignificant background." The wall of water has become a discreet theatrical curtain. Wilde himself visited Niagara in 1882, the year after Bernhardt, and his fussy aesthetic criticism of it is in part homage to her. He consented to don oilskins for the passage under the Falls only when told that Bernhardt had also worn them.

Remembering Niagara, Wilde mocks the Victorian statistical idyll which made the sheer bulk of water so impressive to Trollope. The might of nature, which the sublime originally celebrated, had become for the Victorians a matter of commercial plenitude, as in Trollope's comment on the granaries. Wilde, in a conversation with Mrs. Langtry, said "they told me that so many millions of gallons of water tumbled over the Fall in a minute. I could see no beauty in that. There was bulk there, but no beauty." Niagara looks to Wilde like the messy contingent clutter which James so disliked in the Victorian novel, and which his own criticism of the Falls refines into logical form. Nothing is necessary, all is random and scatter-brained: Wilde sees "simply a vast unnecessary amount of water going the wrong way and then falling over unnecessary rocks."

Wilde deprecates Niagara as botched art, criticizing the outline as disappointing and the design for lacking variety of line, but praising an iridescence and evanescence which are (according to the aesthetics of Wilde's master Walter Pater) the dearest qualities of beauty: "the dull grey waters, flecked with green, are lit with silver, being full of changing loveliness; for all of the most lovely colours are colours in motion."

Insidious, fluctuant, delicate beauty—which Pater in the 1868 conclusion to his *Renaissance* had compared to a racing stream, a whirlpool, and an overwhelming flood—is invoked as an alternative to the pompous, swollen sublime. Wilde even makes a prurient joke about the tumescence of Niagara, associating his own disappointment with the anticlimactic dismay of brides honeymooning at the resort: "the sight of the stupendous waterfall must be one of the first, if not the keenest disappointments in American married life." The sublimity of America becomes a bullying bigness, which Wilde's epigrams prissily insult. He caused offense on his tour of the country by declaring the Atlantic to be disappointing and by calling the prairies "a piece of blotting-paper."

The Victorians found Niagara sublime. Wilde's aesthetic generation finds it beautiful, winsome, feminine, fleeting, not noisy and vast. Instead of the orthodox demonstration of God's creative puissance or retributive fury which Dickens discerned in Niagara, Wilde sees the place as a tribute to a subversive aesthetic divinity: it is an "embodiment of Pantheism." He is reminded as well of Leonardo's remark "that the two most beautiful things in the world are a woman's smile and the motion of mighty waters," which again relates Niagara to the aestheticism of Pater. The *Renaissance* essays include a meditation on Leonardo's Mona Lisa, which combines a waste of waters with the mesmeric, even vampirish, smile of a woman. Wilde, remembering both Pater and Leonardo, has relocated the Mona Lisa and made her the presence which rises strangely beside the waters of Niagara, the weary, exquisite goddess of the place.

The next aesthete at Niagara, Rupert Brooke, also sees the Falls as a rebuff to the safe Victorian piety about nature. During his American journey in 1913, Brooke sent back dispatches to the *Westminster Gazette*, which were collected, after his death in the war, and published in 1916 as *Letters from America*. Niagara is by now a temptation to the buried, obsolete Victorian in us all, provoking the sort of premeditated, hydraulic uplift discovered in Dickens's account. Brooke laments that "the Victorian lies very close below the surface in every man," and spectacles like Niagara entice this ancestor out of hiding by providing occasions for solemn sermonizing. Writing as a hedonistic Georgian, Brooke turns the cast-off Victorian into a disreputable old Adam, a recidivist who must be restrained by force.

At the same time, he coarsens Niagara into a tawdry, windy, verbose excess, an admission of nature's vulgarity. The nineteenth century had colonized nature, drawing from it consolatory meanings and moral intimations. Brooke, in contrast, insists that "Niagara means nothing." It can't be understood in melioristic Victorian terms: "It is not leading anywhere. It does not result from anything. . . . It is merely a great deal of water falling over some cliffs." Because it has no meaning, it can have no moral. But conversely, because it has no meaning, it can be beautiful. Wilde had made the absence of meaning and the morality the criteria of beauty. The thing of beauty, as the preface to *The Picture of Dorian Gray* declares, is proudly irrelevant and vacuous, indifferent to the crass utility of the Victorians. Acknowledging that Niagara is no more than a fall of water, Brooke adds "but it is very remarkably that." The same rule of pure aesthetic purposelessness is applied to the tout-infested fringes of the Falls. Touting, like the crash of water from a height, is its own end and justification, and the hubbub of the photographers, elevator operators, and postcard sellers means as little as do the Falls themselves. Whereas Trollope might have justified these scavengers as industrious creatures subduing nature to human profit, Brooke refuses to invent a purpose for them, and says they "have no apparent object in the world, but just purely, simply, merely, incessantly, indefatigably, and ineffulgibly to tout."

The aesthetic freedom from meaning and purpose is a prescription for epicureanism. Brooke's Falls are therefore pleasure-bent. The waves are "laughing, springing . . . borne impetuously forward like a crowd of triumphant feasters." The flood suggests to him Pater's claim that life is not a plodding moral progress but a slippery flux of sensation. "Our physical life," said Pater, is an affair of sensuous apprehension immune to the analytic determination of the intellect, a "strange, perpetual weaving and unweaving of ourselves," and the wisdom of hedonism is that it encourages us to succumb to this impressionistic reverie rather than laboring to organize it. Brooke sees the torrent of Niagara, criss-crossing strands of water, in exactly this way: "Perpetually, the eye is on the point of descrying a pattern in this weaving, and perpetually it is cheated by change." Pater had turned the process of impressionistic vision into an inflammatory code of conduct, urging young men to savor transitory sensations and not "to form habits," which are the source of morality and which therefore condemn the aesthete to "a stereotyped world." Brooke finds a similar hectic self-delight in Niagara with its "multitudinous tossing merriment," for water is the image of life unconstrained by precept, unimpeded even by those austere laws of form to which James makes Niagara submit.

Rioting toward the verge, the waters mime a stationary reluctance for a moment, but then embrace their fate with a frenzied hilarity. They are a Dionysian rabble, proving to Brooke "that Greek belief that great crashes are preceded by a louder merriment." But after this frantic dissipation, there is a change at the verge. Just as the Greek tragedies Brooke recalls develop self-destructive passion into resigned calm, so the waters change from the turbulence of their headlong charge to decorative beauty during their descent. The river embraces its fate ("on the edge of disaster" it lifts "a head noble in ruin, and then, with a slow grandeur" plunges into the depths) and, like a tragic character, becomes beautiful by doing so. Its reward is a dazzling iridescence: "violet and green fray and frill to white" as the waters fall, and finally evanesce into a white mist which wanders languidly off over the landscape, like a spirit released from a tortured tragic body.

Turning from the turgid Canadian Falls to the American side, Brooke finds there a fragile decorative effeminacy. Bernhardt dressed up to impress the Falls. Now the Falls themselves are a compound of costumery and ornament, a "long curtain of lacework and woven foam," or "as richly diaphanous as a precious stone." The Victorians emphasize fixity, as in that Dickensian account of the waters still rolling, still shining in the sun, still spanned by rainbows. Brooke sees the opposite quality of flux in the "ever-altering wonder" of the water. The Victorians admire solidity, Brooke impalpability: the aura of rainbows coming and going.

James at the Falls is anxious to guard the integrity of his impressions, and relies on a stern aesthetic conscience to marshall random observations. Brooke's impressions are frailer, more internal, and therefore more relative than James's, and Niagara changes its character as he changes his point of vantage. Above and at a distance the Falls look radiant and transparent, but when he ventures below they turn into a nightmare of ruin and panic. On the journey behind and beneath the Falls, it is impossible "to recognise liquid in the masses that hurtle past." Water is now stony, the noise it makes ominous and overbearing. The same self-delighting purposelessness which Brooke at first delights in is now alarming: behind the Falls he hears a sound "not of falling water, but merely of falling; a noise of unspecified ruin," which anticipates the imagery of a later literary period—the collapsing masonry of T. S. Eliot's *Waste Land,* the echoing cave of Forster's *A Passage to India.* Beyond the base, the river loses its impressionistic ease and fluidity. Whereas James at this point interpolates the drama of the river's recovery, as it repairs its battered dignity and prepares itself to battle on, Brooke sees only defeat. Shattered by its fall, sullied by "scum that was foam," the river slides along "sullenly" until the rapids stir it into excitement again.

Brooke considers the rapids to be "more terrifying than the Falls, because less intelligible," and hears in them voices prophesying war. They are less a landscape than a creature, with a demonic writhing motion which suggests muscular action, and their inhuman power is different from that of the Falls. Their resolute and active "masculine vigour" contrasts with "the passive gigantic power, female, helpless and overwhelming, of the Falls," and for this reason the rapids are "a place of fear." In calling the rapids masculine and the Falls feminine, Brooke has wished on them his own sexual disquiet. The sublime and the beautiful have become warring psychological impulses. (Burke's theory of nature associated the prodigious immensities of the sublime with the authority of the father, and the consoling pleasures of the beautiful with the affection of the mother. Our responses to landscape dramatize infantile fears and desires: we recoil from the punitive power of the father toward the sustaining comfort of the mother.) Brooke has internalized Niagara, and confided to it his sexual uncertainty. The Falls are beautiful and appealing because they are passive and female, the rapids are sublime and terrifying because they are active and masculine. Flinching from the violence of masculine identity at the rapids, Brooke yearns for the soothing helplessness embodied by the Falls.

Brooke's private Niagara is a place of psychological unease. His public Niagara offers a corresponding political premonition, hinting at the destruction in which the world was to immerse itself the following year, and in which Brooke was to resolve his own uncertainties by changing from an aesthetic weakling into a warrior. At first he resists the sententious temptations of Niagara. He admits that "great cloudy thoughts of destiny and the passage of empire . . . are at home" there, but he declines to think them, and instead meditates on Niagara's rainbows as an image of art, beauty, and goodness, chimerically thrown up by "the stream of life . . . but unable to stay or direct or affect it, and ceasing when it ceased." Niagara thus resembles the beautiful, unavailing art of Pater's dangerous conclusion to *The Renaissance*, suppressed because its argument that wisdom consists in the exploitation of chance moments of intense sensation was considered immoral. A flux of impressionism like Pater's life-stream recurs later in Brooke's American journey, when he is watching the Rockies from a railway observation car. Being "perpetually drawn backwards at a great pace" through the grand scenery is, he thinks, an image of life, for "as in life, you can never see the glories till they are past, and then they vanish with incredible rapidity," which Pater warned life would do unless each instant was prized and headily enjoyed.

Niagara conducts Brooke from hedonism (in his first view of the waves as reckless self-indulgent merry-makers) to a tragic impressionism, forcing him to admit (as Pater urged) that there is no reality except his momentary life of sensation, and that even art cannot "stay or direct or affect" the self-wasting instability of experience. Niagara also prepares aestheticism for war. The same torrent which represents to Brooke the evanescence of individual existence also subsumes that single, pitiful life in a multitude of other lives. The river, he sees, has countless waves, but one controlling current, and the process of merging one life in the indifferent many is destructive but also perhaps redemptive. Individually, the stream is the solitary life hastening to dissolution. Collectively, it is an image of men and nations hurtling toward war, and in this inevitable rush to destruction Brooke, who was so soon afterwards to abandon himself to it, found "an almost insupportable but comforting certitude." Niagara is now the "dark flood" of human history, and Brooke's acquiescence in it prefigures his willing sacrifice of himself to the war, which turned suicide into chivalry: "some go down to it unreluctant, and meet it, like the river, not without nobility." Grimacing at his own platitude, Brooke discovers in the self-destruction to which Niagara entices him a peace surpassing that of "the quietest plains or the most stable hills." His volume of dispatches ends, appropriately, with the declaration of war.

The pointlessness of Niagara is for Brooke first its charm, later its fatal temptation. It has no meaning, and can be put to no use, so that it snubs both the moralizing and the materialism of the Victorians. From this meaninglessness Brooke derives that grim certitude which reconciles him to the promise of his own death. Niagara is a place of disintegration and despair. This view of it is challenged by H. G. Wells, who slights the hysteria of romantic sublimity and harnesses Niagara to scientific uses. In planning the journey recorded in 1906 in *The Future in America,* Wells declares that he has no interest in the American present, but travels only to inquire what the country might become in a rational and scientific future. He therefore intends to ignore its spectacular scenery: "I don't propose to see Niagara." However, he does "stop off" there (as he apologetically puts it), and at once insults the landscape, calling the gorge unremarkable and the quantity of water no more stunning than dozens of downpours elsewhere. The waterfall is merely an alibi for visiting honeymooners, a noisy "accessory to the artless love-making that fills the surrounding hotels," as imbecile in its meaningless clamor as (it is implied) the frantic couplings of the tourists.

For Wells, the interest of Niagara lies not in the sublime frothing of the waters but in the "human accumulations" which mark a scientific victory over the cacophonous waste: "The dynamos and galleries of the Niagara Falls Power Company . . . impressed me far more profoundly than the Cave of the Winds; are, indeed, to my mind, greater and more beautiful than the accidental eddying of air beside a downpour. They are will made visible, thought translated into easy and commanding things." Wells's language recalls that of James, who had seen in Niagara a similar transition from the turbulence of emotion to the lucidity of thought, "the passage," as he says, "of body to soul, of matter to spirit, of human to divine." For James, the transition is accomplished by art: the god who made Niagara was a genius who valued symmetrical form. For Wells, the transition is accomplished by science. He reveres the wheel-pit of the power station as a sacred place, where the turbines hum devoutly in a "cloistered quiet." The dynamos are clean and silent, without the filth and fury of the waters and equally without the clatter of early industrial machinery. From the natural sublime of the nineteenth century, which muddies the senses and wastefully disrupts nature, Wells has passed to the mechanical sublime, which regulates the mind and technologically supersedes nature. The Falls are an image of debilitating emotion (hence the jibe about the honeymooners), the turbines of placid and improving thought. The turbid ghost of the Falls now inhabits the sleek machines which remake and perfect both nature and the human body: they are "as silent, as wonderfully made, as the heart in a living body, and stouter and stronger than that."

The power station offended Brooke, who argued that diverting the water for the generation of electricity diminished the Falls by making them prosaically useful, whereas otherwise they thrilled because of their motiveless rush to destruction, "the feeling of colossal power and of unintelligible disaster caused by the plunge of that vast body of water." The eager self-sacrifice of the waters anticipates the reaction of Brooke and his generation to the war, which excited them not because they wanted to defend a cause but because it promised them heroic self-extinction. If Niagara were made intelligible by being harnessed for power, "the heart would be gone," Brooke feels. Wells accepts the loss without misgiving, guaranteeing that "the accidental unmeaning beauty" of savage landscape will be replaced by a scientific "beauty of fine order and intention." Niagara, to Wells, is a laboratory in which America re-invents itself, outgrowing the grandiloquently primitive nature with which it has been burdened. He is unmoved by catastrophe, considering it merely as an evolutionary challenge: he virtually welcomed the news of the San Francisco earthquake because it would enable the city to reconstruct a more sanitary version of itself, and he added that if New York were "a blazing ruin" (as he makes it in his novel *The War in the Air,* published two years after the American tour) the inhabitants would understand the calamity as a beneficent Providence and build a new city worthy of their rational future.

The War in the Air, a romance of this future, returns to Niagara and reports on its technological transformation. After the aerial bombardment of New York, the Germans in the novel seize Niagara "to avail themselves of its enormous power works," and here the first combat between the German and Asiatic air fleets takes place, watched from the ground by the hero Bert Smallways, either in Prospect Park or on Goat Island. The small-minded Smallways is immune to the wonders of the landscape. He is irritated and confused by the gush of the Falls, which mixes "all sorts of sounds, like feet walking, like voices talking, like shouts and cries." Nature now sounds like a chaotic human mob. Bert curses the "silly great catarac'. There ain't no sense in it, fallin' and fallin'," although to Brooke its lack of motive was the source of its symbolic allure, not the proof of its inanity. The Falls render themselves squalidly useful as a sanitary disposal system, washing away the detritus of global war to be preyed on by scavenger birds. The waters swill their refuse to the whirlpool: "Never had that great gathering place, that incessant, aimless, unprogressive hurry of waste and battered things, been so crowded with strange and melancholy derelicts . . . luckless brutes, shattered fragments of boat and flying-machine, endless citizens from the cities upon the shores of the Great Lakes above. Much came from Cleveland." Better a rubbish dump, for Wells, than a sublime vacancy good only to be gaped at.

The German invaders rationalize Niagara, actualizing Wells's technological utopia by force. They exterminate troublesome human life, expelling the townspeople and making a desert of the environs of Niagara "as far as Buffalo." Niagara now exemplifies the world cruelly tidied up, with nature and human society organized out of existence. The streets of Niagara City are empty: "its bridges were intact, its hotels and restaurants still flying flags and inviting sky-signs, its power-stations running. But about it the country on both sides of the gorge might have been swept by a colossal broom." Houses, woods, fences, and crops which might shelter the enemy are wrecked. Niagara ceases to be a resort and is reconstituted as a military depot. The Falls become an aeronautical park, with a gas recharging station at one corner above the funicular railway. The hotel is converted into a hospital. The vaunts of nature are diminished by the mechanical monsters which crowd the sky: in comparison with these murderous flying-machines, the American Falls seem narrow, and Niagara City is an anthill.

These versions of Niagara, ranging from Trollope's prosy estimation of volume and denomination of safe vantage-points to Brooke's lyrical impressionism, from Dickens's rhetorical pomp to Wells's ruthless scientific exploitation of an improvident nature, testify to America's capacity for self-transformation. Objects in America aren't determined by history or enmeshed by association like those in Europe. Each observer sees them as if for the first time. To imagine Niagara is to invent it, to create it over again. Arranged as a series, these images enact a historical reversal which anticipates the progress of this book. The Victorians see Niagara as a prodigy of nature, but their successors either refine that wayward nature into aesthetic form (like James and Brooke) or commandeer it for scientific use (like Wells). Imagining the object comes to mean cancelling it out. This is why the neglect of Niagara by the later writers in this book is itself significant, because it is a consequence of the imagination's meditative withdrawal from observation. The later subjects of this book don't even bother to practice imaginative distortions of America's physical reality, for they are simply uncurious about it. They go there to construct private mental shelters for themselves and in doing so are insulated from their environment. Aldous Huxley deplored spectacles like the Falls or the Grand Canyon as symptoms of nature's gross bad taste, and the only landscapes he could countenance were the featureless deserts of the American Southwest, because their dreariness was for him an aid to and an image of mystical self-concentration. Increasingly, the reason for going to America is not to see America but to contrive a change in yourself which detaches you from your physical surroundings. When Auden and Isherwood migrated there in 1939 they had contracted to write a travel book about the country, but they never did so; Huxley planned a similar book about the west coast, but never wrote it.

America's bequest to all three was a salutary introversion which disjoined them from America itself. A statement by Bertrand Russell, returning to England in 1914 after a term at Harvard, hints at the change. "Niagara," he reports with priggish philosophical rectitude, "gave me no emotion."

2

INSTITUTIONAL AMERICA

Frances Trollope
Anthony Trollope
Charles Dickens

The Victorian novelists are anatomists of society not, like their modern successors, confidants of the solitary, antisocial ego, and their task in visiting America is therefore to explore and explain the constitution of society, whereas later generations in America concentrate on the changes it works—theologically, psychedelically, mystically— inside the individual. The Victorians imperially partition the realm among themselves—Frances Trollope treats American manners, the society's domestic interior; Anthony Trollope and Dickens assess its institutions, the society's political exterior—and their criticisms of it are legalistic quibbles about the proper division and distribution of social functions. American life doesn't make the expected constitutional discriminations between private and public, or between nature and society, and it bewilders the novelist, whose art depends on strictly respecting these boundaries. The incomprehension of the Victorians maneuvers them into an angry, frustrated dead-end. They are imaginatively disconcerted by America, and blame it for not being the sort of society they can write novels about. But their complaints are a necessary preliminary to the justifications of America which follow, for the qualities which are to the Victorians America's disorderly vices become in later generations its startlingly original virtues.

Mrs. Trollope leaves to others the masculine task of institutional analysis, and chooses to consider the democratic political system of America only in its influence on domestic conduct, with the object of reconciling her countrymen to their own aristocratic constitution. She intends, she says, to study "interesting details," which is the novelist's method, depicting the surface of society not institutionally disassembling it. But the horror of America is its obliteration of detail, its bleak uniformity. Mrs. Trollope's first experience of it, arriving in 1827, is the flat, murky, undifferentiated shores of the Mississippi, which are miserable because vacant. She complains that America is dismally uninteresting, even though the objects it contains are bizarre. The Mississippi "presents no objects more interesting than mud banks, monstrous bulrushes, and now and then a huge crocodile." Isn't a crocodile interesting? Apparently not, because Mrs. Trollope's criteria of beauty and interest are genteel and domestic. American nature disgusts her because it is not artificial. On the river banks there is "at no one point . . . an inch of what painters call a second distance." She objects, in fact, to nature's domestic unmannerliness. She takes her domestic standards outdoors. Her predecessor Cobbett the political journalist, who lived in America between 1792 and 1800, had accused nature on Long Island of being too abundant. The English have tamed nature into neatness by making gardening an exterior equivalent of interior decoration. The house extends its rule outdoors, and gardens, Cobbett says, are "kept as clean as drawing-rooms, with grass as even as a carpet." America baffles and rebuffs nineteenth-century visitors by reversing these orderly priorities. Nature now extends rudely indoors, and Mrs. Trollope's Americans swill, guzzle, and spit at table as grossly as if in the wilderness.

The pleasures of discovery, of visual suprise, are inimical to Mrs. Trollope. She has passed from the sublime shocks of the romantics to a Victorian preference for what's already known. In New Orleans, specious novelties—the blacks, the "unwonted vegetation"— "afford that species of amusement which proceeds from looking at what we never saw before," but that amusement, we infer, is a low thing. The city contains "little to gratify the eye of taste," because taste is a cultivation of stock responses. Romantic ingenuousness of vision yields to a sober and scornful Victorian second sight. Walking in the Louisiana forest, Mrs. Trollope admits to feeling "rather sublime and poetical," but instantly disavows that sentiment by criticizing the forest for not being a garden. The trees are stunted because not regularly planted. She censors first impressions, and blames herself for her initial untutored instinctive reaction to slavery. The first slave encountered is an object of sorrowing wonder, but experience chastens this sympathy, and when Mrs. Trollope has learned more about the actual condition of the blacks as indoor servants, she smiles back on her foolish susceptibility. She is vengeful about first experiences of anything. The primary experience, which is everywhere provoked by America since the country is so new and strange, can be justified only if she can repeat it. Walking in the forest near Memphis "made us feel we were in a new world; and a repetition of our walk the next morning would have pleased as well"—because then the experience would no longer be a new one, and would be assimilable. Travel for Mrs. Trollope isn't exploration but the fortification of prejudice. She goes abroad to justify her preference for staying at home. The conclusive reason for visiting America, she argues, is "that we shall feel the more contented" with our own country.

Mrs. Trollope's worry that America has lowered the boundaries between nature and society, between novelty and the decorous habits of taste, makes her obsessively censorious about table manners, which are a symbol of nature instructed, of routine and imitation correcting ravenous impulse. Americans horrify her by gorging their food with "voracious rapidity," poking their knife blades into their mouths, hacking at their teeth with pocket knives, loathsomely spitting. Their table manners bespeak as well a confusion between the categories of public and private behavior which troubles the English imagination, formed by novels which scrupulously segregate these two provinces. During dinner in America, the company behaves as if in private, with a rude disregard for manners. But in conversation there is too little sense of the issues proper to a private gathering, too much glaring publicity, because the talk is exclusively political.

Social cooperation is the product of alcoholic weakness. A squatter is helped to build his cabin by neighbors who are rallied by "social feeling and the love of whisky." On other occasions, sociability is compulsory, and overrules the private life rather than complementing it. At her Memphis hotel, sickened of "social meals" by beastly feeders on the steamboat, Mrs. Trollope longs to eat in a private room, but her landlady would interpret such a proposal as an affront and refuse. The table is not a composed society, but an informal communal trough. All the male inhabitants of the town pour in, gobble in silence, and quit the table immediately they're sated. Or else segregation is calculated to frustrate social relations: the dining-room of the Cincinnati hotel is congested with sixty or seventy men, while a few ladies eat apart in the bar room. Defense of one's privacy is resented as social treason. When, in Cincinnati, Mrs. Trollope makes bold to drink tea in her hotel bedroom, the proprietor rebukes her and orders her to live communally or else leave the house. In Ohio it is considered an offense to fasten a door, so that Mrs. Trollope is "exposed to perpetual, and most vexatious interruptions from people whom I have often never seen." Yet promiscuous exposure doesn't consolidate a society, for these intruders have no conversation and are limited to political or religious controversy, "subjects which custom as well as principle had taught me to consider as fitter for the closet than the tea-table." The gaps in this nonexistent society are filled not by customary institutions but by ugly nuisances: the "ample piazza" outside the Trollope cottage in Mohawk is promptly occupied by a slaughter house for hogs.

There is no consistency in individual histories, just as there is no organization of social functions. Engaging servants, Mrs. Trollope is warned not to request a character reference (as if the applicants were persons without character, which in Mrs. Trollope's unformed America is a plausible assumption: character is society's bequest to the individual, since it is conferred by the opinions of other people and the manner of our dealings with them; but in America society doesn't cohere and therefore it cannot validate individual existences). She engages Nancy Flitcher, who presents herself as an exemplary creature but turns out to be a notoriously abandoned woman.

Cincinnati offers neither public nor private amusements, and women are saved from reclusiveness as prisoners of the private life, condemned "to the interior of their houses," only by "public worship and private tea-drinkings." But public worship is as unseemly as public eating, and women are permitted by their men to succumb to the lewd ecstasies incited by revivalist preachers. With equal impropriety, ignoring the correct adjudication of functions between the sexes, the most dignified men of the town go to market at dawn to scavenge for comestibles. Newspapers are the only literature: American books have the same squalid defects as American manners, printed on dirty paper in slovenly type. The public arena, deserted by the human beings who should occupy it, is appropriated by animals. Cincinnati in Mrs. Trollope's estimation is less a city than a farm. Cows are milked at the house door, and wander off wherever they please when the pail and meal tub are withdrawn into the house. Pigs are the citizens: their snouts, moist from rooting in the gutters, nuzzle pedestrians; their blood dirties the stream from the abbatoir; their amputated tails and jaw bones trip up the feet.

This constitutional confusion between private and public, which fills private houses with rowdy squalling mobs and leaves public spaces to the pigs and the encroaching wastes of mud, provokes other kinds of social illogic. For instance, the lot of the slave, Mrs. Trollope contends, is in some respects preferable to that of the free servant, because domestic slaves are cared for, and accept a condition into which they have been born, whereas hired "helps" resent their voluntary servitude and fret for liberty. Because society is so unorganized, there can be no genuine freedom (the boast of equality coexists with the ownership of slaves) and no modesty either, since

THE BAZAAR, BUILT BY MRS. TROLLOPE, 1829.

Mrs. Trollope the shopkeeper: The Bazaar, Cincinnati. The Cincinnati Historical Society.

both depend on the rights of privacy abrogated by America. Political contradictions deform manners, and Mrs. Trollope points to the moral lapses which follow from the habit of affecting indifference to the presence of slaves. A young lady, so pudic that she edges onto the chair of a female neighbor to escape the contagion of a man seated on her other side at dinner, nonchalantly laces her stays in front of a Negro footman. A Virginian has a Negro share his connubial bed-chamber, in case he or his wife need her to fetch a glass of water during the night. Disrespect for privacy also means that there can be no leisure. The American is a hustling public creature, never off duty. The places of shade and relaxation in Philadelphia are rarely used, because the citizens have no notion of relaxation: "even their drams . . . are swallowed standing," and they reserve their repose for church, where of course it is least appropriate.

Society is a raw and unkempt expanse of nature, while nature is a thronging, pestilential, cacophonous society. America has reversed an order on which the English imagination relies. Society is as awesomely vacant as a romantic landscape: after a theatrical performance in Philadelphia the streets are dark, silent, and empty, with no sounds of human mirth, and "this darkness, this stillness, is so great, that I almost felt it awful." On Sundays, chains barricade the streets to prevent horses and carriages from passing. Mrs. Trollope objects to Sunday observance as suppression of social activity: in Hoboken, the ladies are sentenced to church, while the pleasure gardens are patrolled exclusively by men. While society is depopulated, nature is overcrowded. Describing summer in Maryland, menaced by copperhead snakes and "the petty terrors" of "the crawling, creeping, and buzzing tribes," assaulted by the bullfrog's croak, the tree frog's chirp, the mosquito's hum, and the whistle of the locust, Mrs. Trollope turns this intolerable "insect din" into a mock society. The uproar suggests to her the maddening bruit of American electioneering, in which the candidates are antagonistic beasts, "ready to peck out the eyes" of opponents. Similarly, she remarks that the sordid American preoccupation with lucre is less appropriate to human society than to the regimentation of the anthill. Social deficiencies are supplied by obnoxious, intrusive nature: at breakfast in boarding houses, the only conversation is supplied by a parrot.

Mrs. Trollope limits herself to manners, separating political analysis from social description as is proper, in her view, for a woman, and she appeals to the female guardians of the private life to refine the masculine coarseness of the public life. The opposition between politics and manners coincides with the difference between men and women, and Mrs. Trollope implores American women to become conscious of their intellectual powers and to redeem their tobacco-chewing, whisky-swilling husbands. America is dull because men work so conscientiously, and have no gift for play. Women, the partisans of privacy and recreation, might rectify this: "if the ladies had their way, a little more relaxation would be permitted." In Washington, Mrs. Trollope invokes the feminine arts of social enjoyment to occlude the drab masculine business of government. Declining to understand politics, she takes Washington's status as "the seat of government" to mean that it is "the mirror of fashion, and the model for national etiquette," and in place of political intrigue she sees otiose and elegant social amenity. In the streets instead of men bustling about to sales of dry goods, "you see very well-dressed personages lounging leisurely up and down Pennsylvania Avenue." Politics she imagines to be a prolonged evening party, and she pictures the representatives whiling the sessions away "with no labour but a little talking." Attending the congressional debates, she confesses to having heard none of the arguments, but commends "the extreme beauty of the chambers." The politicians are criticized not for their principles but for their deportment, slouching, wearing hats, and of course spitting. To Mrs. Trollope, the notable difference between the Congress and Senate is that the senators are too elderly and infirm to "toss their heels above their heads."

However, despite Mrs. Trollope's disclaimer that she is a woman and therefore unequipped to "reason back from effects to their causes," she does slip back across the barrier she erects by treating manners as the social effects of political causes. She advises political theorists to take note of the social details she transcribes, which will prove more instructive than "any abstract speculation." The barbarous facts of America are materializations of a political idea. The theory of equality means to her "a hard greasy paw" and "accents that breathe less of freedom than of onions and whisky"; it means gobs of masticated tobacco deposited on a chair by an itinerant preacher, or the men in the lower tier of theater boxes, their sleeves rolled to the shoulder, their heels in the air, their rumps admonishing the audience; it means the crassness of the greasy fellow who accosts President Jackson and inquires about the recent death of his wife. Mrs. Trollope confines herself to social anecdotes, but each of these glimpses of uncivil behavior is a political parable. Though professing only to criticize America for being ill-mannered, she is in truth criticizing it for being ill-constituted. Explaining why religious controversy is not a fit subject for the tea table, she refers to "our own well-ordered land," where such improprieties don't occur. She means by well-ordered not only disciplined but rationally organized, and America upsets her by confusing or reversing the necessary orders of existence: private and public, society and nature. A relentless publicity disrupts the private life; public institutions, on the other hand, aren't central to the society but are recesses of demented privacy. When Mrs. Trollope's American friends prate of their glorious institutions, she can only think that they mean hospitals and penitentiaries. In a visit to one of these, she sketches in anticipation the America of Dickens, in which a personal privacy censured by society takes refuge in prisons or madhouses, an America in which character exists only behind bars. The Asylum for the Destitute in New York, through which Mrs. Trollope is conducted, preserves a mental segregation of the sexes: the male offenders are resilient and ebullient, but the women are crushed and depressed, unable to recover from their shame. This institutional enforcement of an emotional disparity is one more image of America's offense, which is to decompose society.

Anthony Trollope's criticism of America agrees with his mother's by adhering to her categories of judgment. America confounds his expectations as an Englishman and as a novelist because it alters the balance between private and public areas of experience. However, his tone is more conciliatory than hers, and he recognizes that America is not a defacement of the Old World but a phenomenon which is disorienting because new, a warning of a change in history. His *North America* begins, like his mother's book, by separating society from politics, the feminine province of manners from the masculine preserve of institutions. Hers is a woman's book, he argues, because it is concerned with gossip about social pecadilloes; he undertakes the masculine investigation of political arrangements. Her social mockery gives way to his political vindication. But he too sees manners as a casualty of American democracy, and finds an architectural admission of this in Washington. The Capitol building illogically and discourteously turns its back on the Potomac and the city center. It is offensive to the city it was meant to adorn, and demeaning to the statesmen, who have to enter by the back door and then, because the hilltop site places the front higher than the back, toil up a second flight of stairs. Trollope deplores as well the vulgar dorsal wriggle of female deportment, the bowls of viscid grease in which hotel food swims, and the promotion of children to social equality with adults. But he argues in his conclusion that America has succeeded socially, by which he means, not that it is better mannered than his mother found it, but that it has technologically atoned for its native faults by its triumphs in medicine, commerce, mechanics, and the invention of domestic comforts.

Having apportioned America equally between himself and his mother, Trollope goes on to subdivide it between himself and his wife. She travels with him during the autumn of 1861, but returns to England at the beginning of winter when he proceeds to parts of the country where, "under the existing circumstances of the [civil] war, a lady might not feel herself altogether comfortable." This double division—society is female, politics male; the Northeast is suitable for a woman, the embattled South is not—imposes on the bewildering expanse of America the proprieties of personal relationships. Trollope is subduing the country by humanizing it. He has transferred the pathetic fallacy of the romantics from nature to society: they colonized an insentient nature by projecting onto it their own desires and fears; he colonizes an incomprehensible territory by reducing it to the scale of human emotion and social arrangement. Thus he treats the historical and geographical contradictions of America as benign domestic disputes. The novelist translates public antagonisms back into private altercations. The war between the states is likened to an embarrassing squabble between a hypothetical Mr. and Mrs. Jones, "the dearly beloved friends of my family." This twists political principle into a matter of genteel equivocation: Trollope's manners forbid him to say which side is right in the civil war, because both the combative Joneses are his friends. Elsewhere, the southern states become a grumbling domestic servant who is determined to quit, so that "it is of no avail to show him that he has all he can desire in his present place." Secession is represented as a divorce. The South is a husband drunkenly besotted with the vice of slavery, the North an ill-used wife. She should divorce him, but instead he has peremptorily divorced her.

But Trollope acknowledges that American society generally resists novelistic diminution, and this is why it worries him. The hotels in Newport are too cavernous to permit social relations: twelve ladies disappear into the gaping emptiness of a drawing-room intended for two hundred. Trollope's longing for a smallness of scale which guards privacy explains his furious resentment of a remark made in Dubuque, alleging that England has no vegetables. The aspersion infuriates Trollope, and he is prompted to a eulogy of his own abundant kitchen garden. He is enraged because the domesticity of England, for him its dearest quality, has been impugned. England specializes in vegetables, like those grown in "my own little patches at home," which make the household self-sufficient. America, as Trollope realizes on the prairies of Illinois, specializes in corn, which can be cultivated in these vast undomestic expanses. The difference of crop indicates a difference of moral attitude. In contrast with the prudent English husbandry which encourages those cramped domestic patches to bring forth "peas, beans, broccoli, cauliflower, celery, beetroot, onions, carrots, parsnips, turnips, seakale, asparagus, French beans, artichokes, vegetable marrow, cu-

cumber, tomatoes, endive, lettuce," as well as herbs, cabbages, and potatoes, on the American plains corn is harvested with wasteful negligence, because of the very richness of the earth. Trollope declares himself "grieved by the loose manner in which the wheat was treated" in Minnesota: "I have seen bags of it upset, and left upon the ground," because there was no profit in collecting it.

The careless profligacy of American agriculture and the empty infinitude of the midwestern plains warns Trollope that there is no nature in America, since there has been no domestication of the wild. Rhode Island is uncultivated, and "the prettiness of home scenery is a work of art." The Great Lakes are cold, cumbrous, uncouth, and dull, "intended by nature for the conveyance of cereal produce," not for picturesque delectation. American society isn't constituted by a human amelioration of nature but by the contrivance of mechanical alternatives to a nature which remains obdurate and inimical. Hence Trollope's admiration for the mod. cons. which are "patent remedies for the usually troublous operations of life": a ready supply of hot water, elevators, self-opening soda-water bottles, stowable railway beds. Human beings in America cannot perform the operations of life which create a society. Machines have to be imagined and then invented to do so on their behalf. The climate is deadly: central heating is therefore invented to subdue it, creating indoors an artificial tropical paradise in the most freezing weather. Instead of the social complication which sustains the novelist, Trollope finds mechanical ingenuity.

His instincts as a novelist are baffled by the inconsistency of American social rules. Ladies can be flirted with, it seems, on shipboard, but in railway carriages they are sacrosanct, and must not be addressed. On the New York omnibuses, the arrangement for paying the fare through a hole at the driver's back immediately on entering befuddles him, and leads to comic delinquencies: protesting bells are rung at him. The novelist is at a loss to understand the habits and relations which ought to be his speciality. Trollope confesses after the incident on the omnibus that "I knew I was not behaving

41

as a citizen should behave." As America recoils from the persecution of nature to the consolation of machinery, so Trollope gives up the attempt to understand the invisible but inflexible social laws which govern conduct in railway carriages and on omnibuses, and concentrates instead on economic processes—the passage of corn through the Buffalo grain elevators, for instance. And these economic processes he translates into social forms. The Buffalo elevators dispense with sacks and bags, he notes, and the wheat travels in an "open, unguarded, plebeian manner," whereas in England it is handled with aristocratic deference "and travels in its own private carriage" of sacking. The contrast between the brash publicity of America and the courteous privacy of England is replicated even in the career of cereal crops.

Character in America is also constructed so as to perplex the novelist, whose imagination must have a feminine quality of introversion, a capacity to unpick the minutiae of personal relations. "The trade of a novelist," Trollope says, "is very much that of describing the softness, sweetness, and loving disposition of women." American women confound him by being harsh and domineering, not demure and gentle, ungraciously exploiting the chivalry of men and outstaring seated male passengers on the street cars. This is why, in the novels of Henry James, the pushy American woman (like the journalist Henrietta Stackpole in *The Portrait of a Lady*) is such a problem: she upsets the English order of fiction which depends, like the society it describes, on a division between delicate female introversion and ambitious male activism, and the novelist doesn't know how to cope with her. Nor are American men any more novelistically apposite. Their steely acquisitive virtues are too impersonal, and they are "less malleable, and . . . less capable of impressions" than the novelist's English subjects. As observers, Trollope argues, their preoccupations are materialistic not picturesque, and they must be observed in the same spirit. They have no character, while their women have too much.

Trollope even holds the stoicism of Americans against them.

They are patient for hours when delayed on train journeys. Families who have lost their possessions in the Ohio floods don't lament or complain but are "passive under personal misfortune." This virtue of endurance seems to Trollope the symptom of a characterless stolidity, an inability to demonstrate emotion, which deters the solicitous, inquisitive novelist. Trollope's archetypal American is the western loafer, inertly chewing tobacco by the hour, luxuriating in a boredom which, Trollope says, would make an Englishman frantic. The novelist cannot penetrate the minds of American women because he is intimidated by their aggressiveness; he cannot penetrate the minds of American men because they have none.

American morality confirms this erasure of qualities. At West Point, Trollope complains that, as so often in the public institutions of America, there has been a virtuous but (to the novelist) regrettable "attempt to make the place too perfect" by the rigid exclusion of alcohol and women. Such stringent probity simplifies society, and alienates the novelist, whose art depends on lapses and imperfections. For the same reason, Trollope justifies the rabid mercenariness of New York, not only because the desire to earn money is a generally benign human characteristic, but because it complicates social relations, which would otherwise be starkly unsubtle. The greed of New Yorkers at least makes them interesting. It equips them with qualities, since they need "ready wits, and quick hands, and not a little aptitude for self-denial" in order to succeed.

The American habit of separating small-town state legislative capitals from the actual commercial capital worries Trollope, because it is a similar simplification of society. He mentions this often, concluding that "St. Paul enjoys the double privilege of being the commercial and political capital of Minnesota. The same is the case with Boston in Massachusetts, but I do not remember another instance in which it is so." Political capitals are sited at an average distance from the state's various confines, "but commerce submits to no such Procrustean law," and isolates Detroit on the extreme edge of Michigan. The irrational choice of a swampy site for Washington has been belied by commerce, which refuses to second the decision. Only trade makes cities populous, and trade has ignored Washington. Trollope's commentary connects the novelistic imagination with commerce, because commerce ordains those "large congregations of mankind" which are the novelist's material. The separation of legislative and commercial functions bothers Trollope because it segregates powers and interests which mesh and overlap in a metropolis, and from whose interaction the extended Victorian novel takes its form.

Trollope does acknowledge that America makes difficulties for the novelistic imagination because it is a phenomenon of a new kind, a country which has reversed the logic of historical succession. In England, the present is a tentative growth from the past. The tenses of present and future are no more than the all-enveloping past bringing itself reluctantly up to date. The novelist's research into motives and relationships therefore leads him backwards into personal and social history, in quest of lost time. In America, history is not what has happened already (since nothing has) but what will happen in a millennial future. The thrust of inquiry is predictive, not retrospective. America has altered time. Instead of incorporating the present into a retentive, protective past, it cancels the past (by seceding from the ancestral corruption of European history) and hustles the unworthy present into the promised future. Trollope finds evidence of this temporal impatience everywhere—in individual lives as much as in the growth of towns. Cities anticipate their history by laying down ambitious street-plans long before there is a population to justify them. Children likewise anticipate their adulthood. At West Point, Trollope regrets, a youth is not permitted to grow at leisure, but has his adolescence telescoped: "at fifteen he is not to be a boy, at twenty he is not to be a young man" but a gentleman, officer, and soldier.

Similarly, American towns aren't allowed to grow, but are projected into the future by an exercise of speculation. English towns are organisms and never have the "ugly, unfledged" incompleteness of American towns, which strain to live up to the pretensions of their plans for themselves. Hence the partiality for grids, those urban parallelograms which both Trollope and Dickens disliked: they are premature designs for the future. Trollope finds Washington putative and pretentious, its minimally numbered or initialled streets mostly unbuilt, and Central Park in New York is a bare network of roads, "good for what it will be, rather than for what it is." The founders of American cities build for a future which will fill the area up, whereas European towns are built gradually "as they have been wanted." Street plans are laid down with a trusting blankness which for Trollope is an image of commercial aspiration, and America relies on history to replete its vacant spaces. American urban designers anticipate and supersede history by learning from it. Trollope admits that, although the rectilinear plan of Philadelphia is odious to him, "drainage and gas-pipes come easier to such a shape," as do water supply and sanitation. But recoiling from this millennium of right angles, he confesses a preference for the old European vices of involution, waywardness, and deformity: he longs for "a street that is forced to twist itself about."

Because in America history overtakes itself, even the acquisitiveness of the pioneers is presumptive. They don't hoard present wealth, but hasten toward future enrichment. They are characterized by "love of money to come, joined to a strong disregard for money made." Their greed is belied by that immaterial scorn for possessions which Auden was to identify as one of the spiritual paradoxes of America. The pioneer won't pause to enjoy what he has. Trollope, who says that, having built one block of real estate and begun to collect rents, he'd never bother about extending his enterprise, is actually more of a smug materialist, by his own admission, than the arch-speculator Monroe P. Jones, who proceeds at once to repeat his success. As Trollope says of the New York tycoons, the capitalist requires "not a little aptitude for self-denial." The slave of Mammon is an abstinent puritan. Americans are concerned with becoming rich (because the activity is an earnest of virtue) and not with the gross business of being rich. Their self-denial in getting money is equaled by their lighthearted extravagance in spending it. New Yorkers spend as airily and riskily as they get, and Trollope says "there is in this a living spirit which to me divests the dollar-worshipping idolatry of something of its ugliness." Failure is as much a spiritual challenge as success. In Chicago, Trollope notes that after a reverse men "instantly begin again," and their generous provision for the future pardons their lapses: "they make their plans on a large scale, and they who come after them fill up what has been wanting at first."

History has been bypassed (Chicago didn't exist twenty-five years ago, Trollope says; now it has 120,000 inhabitants) or else reversed. Whereas the European industrial present has to do battle with an obstructive past, the American present can freely invent the future. On his tour of Michigan, Trollope reflects that while European agriculture precedes the birth of cities, in America "the cities have come first" and the pioneers have begun by erecting luxury hotels and laying railroads. In the Midwest, the location of towns is actually determined by the railway routes. Railway lines run through the main streets, and the citizens, far from resenting the noise, filth, and inconvenience, are fond of the engines. In England the same jovial cohabitation with the railway couldn't occur, Trollope is sure. America has again turned around a European historical order. In England the land had been cultivated before the railways invaded and sullied it, but in America the railways have been "the precursors of civilization" and in the West "the discoverer of the fertility of the land." There is the same reversal of expectation with hotels as with railways. In incipient settlements, Americans rig up vast hotels on the assumption that eventually people will arrive to live in them: "the hotel itself will create a population—as the railways do. With us railways run to the towns; but in the States the towns run to the railways. It is the same thing with the hotels." Hotels create guests. In Europe, because such accommodations are scarce, careful arrangements are made before setting out, but in Trollope's America it is taken for granted that there are immense hotels everywhere, and this is a cause not an effect of travel.

Trollope understands this reordering of time and historical cause, but imaginatively it depresses him. The novelist's gaze is trained inwards and therefore backwards; America obliges him to become an extrovert and look trustfully ahead. However, a century later Auden was to see this mechanical anticipation of civilization as one of America's unique imaginative freedoms: because industry in America comes in advance of civilization, it doesn't discredit myths but creates them. America makes a mythology from the industrial spoliation of nature—Melville's Ahab hunting the white whale, Auden's own version of the lumberjack Paul Bunyan clearing the forest—whereas in Europe machines are enemies of the imagination.

For Trollope, there can be no society in American cities because they are no more than predictions for a future which has not yet actualized. Nor can there be any society on the frontier, because place is unhallowed by affection. The backwoods settler "has no love for the soil" but values it only as an investment, and promptly relinquishes his land if it threatens to turn into a society: when comfort and amenity catch up with him, he sells his holdings and moves on toward a new frontier.

In place of society, America has institutions. Foiled as a novelist, unable to investigate the detail of human relations and communal habits, Trollope turns into an inspector of institutions. In New York he transcribes his fatiguing official itinerary: "I went to schools, hospitals, lunatic asylums, institutes for deaf and dumb, water works, historical societies, telegraph offices, and large commercial establishments." On the battlefields of the Civil War, he reviews the drilling of regiments, cavalry maneuvers, artillery practice, and the accommodations of the troops. Even literature is considered less as an art than as an institution, for Trollope argues that although Americans may not as yet be outstanding producers of books, they are already conspicuous consumers, and his study of the subject therefore emphasizes not writers but readers and particularly manufacturers, the

tradesmen who in the absence of an international copyright agreement pirate most of their goods from the English market. Literature
is assessed as an item in the national wealth, the "highest produce"
of the country.

Dickens finds in American institutions a malign secretive introversion. The prisons and asylums he visits during the tour described
in *American Notes* are morbid refuges where characters protect a
deranged or dangerous individuality which their bland, uniform society won't tolerate. For Trollope too, institutions cope discreetly
with the dark underside of existence, which cannot be mentioned.
Institutions cleanse the city's bowels, flush away its abnormal human
refuse. Of New York he says, "the drainage . . . is excellent. The
hospitals are almost alluring. The lunatic asylum which I saw was
perfect," though he is startled to find that the most incorrigible inmates are English. Institutions impersonalize, reducing individuals
to patients or statistics, tidying away the scruffy mess of human nature. They simplify society by feeling bound to represent themselves
and their clients as perfect. At the Boston Library, Trollope is assured that theft is unknown. The novelist is automatically suspicious
of human motives, and distrusts such professions of blamelessness,
not only because they are often pharasaical but because they efface
character, making all people seem spotlessly the same. Trollope
therefore protests against those American institutions which boast of
having created a "terrestrial paradise." Such talk, he says during his
discussion of the messianic constitutions of the states, arouses his
most cynical mistrust: when people brag of being better than their
neighbours, "we button up our pockets and lock up our spoons."
The novelist would rather not live in paradise. His subject is not the
inspidity of virtue but the vital complication of vice, which America
wants to suppress. This is why both Trollope and Dickens are uneasy with experiments like the model factories at Lowell, Massachusetts. Dickens emphasizes the thin, shoddy newness of the settlement, its desolate absence of individuality. The factory girls and
their rooms are spotless because characterless. Trollope too notices

at once the fresh clean appearance of the mill workers, and attributes this purity to the protection of an institution. They are not victims of an open labor market but interns of "a philanthropical manufacturing college," a seminary devoted to the conversion of cotton into calico, "a commercial Utopia." It is this exclusiveness and perfection to which he objects. Because it is a Utopia, Lowell cannot be a community, and can make no allowance for natural social growth, being sequestered even from the capitalists of the New England region. It guards its virtue by being fugitive and cloistered. For this reason, it is not even remarkably profitable, and cannot provide work for a large urban population.

Trollope dislikes American institutions because they have dispensed with the natural complications of society and the imperfections of personal character. Dickens shares this perception, but is aware of a macabre institutional privacy which Trollope doesn't penetrate. Dickensian institutions are often the defenses of a crazed, murderous individuality. Trollope's institutions conceal the grubby other side of experience: hence his gratitude for the drainage system and the mental hospital in New York. But it is this proscribed, deviant region which Dickens delights to explore: hence his nocturnal ramblings as *The Uncommercial Traveller* through the labyrinthine criminal quarters of London. Dickensian institutions are sinisterly secret. At Avignon, Dickens was excited to a ferocious prurience by the torture chamber of the Inquisition in the papal palace, and in Italy was fascinated by the institutional perversities of the Catholic Church, its false piety or its imprisonment of youth in enforced celibacy. In *Pictures from Italy* he refers to the "atrocities and monstrous institutions, which had been, for scores of years, at work, to change men's nature." This for Dickens is the error of institutions, and of America—to offer to alter human nature. He cherishes the truculence of human nature, its comically heroic refusal to correct itself. Human nature won't learn: therefore it is racked and tormented, as at Avignon, or sentenced to solitary confinement, as in the prison he visits at Philadelphia. The most innocuous institutions are liable to become places of incarceration for Dickens. The uncommercial traveller shuts himself in a pew in a London church, and welcomes the claustration; the *American Notes* describe the bedrooms in the hotel at Lebanon, New Hampshire, as prison cells, so drearily unfurnished that Dickens expects to be locked inside, and listens involuntarily for the turning key when he retires to bed.

Dickens's American tour is a succession of visits to such places—prisons, hospitals, asylums, orphanages, workhouses, or slave quarters. Trollope remarks that the purpose of travel in Europe is to view scenery and ancient cities, but in America, deprived of the picturesque, the traveler's study must be "the social and political life of the Americans." Dickens marks the same distinction in the titles of his travel books. Italy is pictorial, impasted with associations which the traveler must evoke. Dickens compares the solitude of the Roman campagna with that of the American prairies, but concludes that the former is less appallingly vacant because it retains traces of habitation, whereas western America is a nullity "where men have never dwelt." America changes the traveler from a painter to a bureaucrat. Dickens writes reports of institutions inspected and issues his experiences in the form of a departmental memo: the work's full title is *American Notes for General Circulation*. Trollope is conscientious about his bureaucratic schedule, but Dickens is impatient and scornfully negligent: "one day, during my stay in New York, I paid a visit to the different public institutions on Long Island, or Rhode Island: I forget which." The worst Trollope can say of American institutions is that they are inefficiently constituted, making expansive provision for the future rather than shoring up the cautious wisdom of the past. Dickens more freakishly finds in these institutions a demonic disorder which upsets society. His America is a bad dream. Its open public spaces are wastes: the Mississippi is a vile stream of slime; the streets of New York are abandoned to roving bands of pigs; the streets of Philadelphia are a geometrical desert rather than a porcine sty, so "distractingly regular" that Dickens longs for a crooked line; the streets of Washington are a graveyard of grandiose intentions, mapping out ornamental thoroughfares "that begin in nothing, and lead nowhere." These vacant, haunted places, from which people have fled in fear and loathing, are repopulated with phantoms by Dickens's teeming imagination: he devises a daily routine for the scavenging pigs of New York, and accompanies them in fantasy on their rambles. His own malign magic deforms or insubstantializes the places he visits. In Washington, for instance, he imagines the town to have mysteriously shifted away as if, at the end of the season, "most of the houses [had] gone out of town for ever with their masters." Yet while he is chimerically uncreating American cities, the cities are working their own glum sorcery on him. In Philadelphia he feels himself stiffening into Quakerish sobriety, turned to stone under the influence of the stern rectilinear town-plan.

Outside, in Dickens's nightmarish America, there is emptiness: panic has driven away even the houses. Inside, there is a reclusive privacy, guarding its shame. Even places of public resort are catacombs of separated cells. The oyster bars of New York are doubly fugitive, both subterranean and cellular. They are excavated beneath the ground, approached by "downward flights of steps," and constructed to reflect the ungregarious nature of the oyster eater, who has something to hide. Dickens imagines "the swallowers of oysters . . . copying the coyness of the thing they eat," recoiling into the protective casing of their guilty privacy. Hence cubicles are erected to barricade them from another, and they sit apart indulging their solitary vice "in curtained boxes, and consort by two, not by two hundreds."

The prisons of the city are black pestilential solitudes where rats can half-eat an inmate in an hour's time. The Tombs, in lower Manhattan, contains in the yard at its center a secret place even more dismaying than its foul prison-cells, for here the gibbet is located. Executions are events of indecent secrecy, staged before a select audience: "the law requires that there be present at this dismal spectacle, the judge, the jury, and citizens to the amount of twenty-five." Society is convened only to witness a sacrifice. The hangings are hidden both from the community of the cheerful, careless streets, and from the criminal company within. "The prison-wall is interposed as a thick gloomy veil" which not only separates society from the processes of retribution it ordains but separates the malefactor from his fellows, whose presence might confirm him in "unrepenting hardihood" during "that last hour." If the inmates of the Tombs could witness executions, the condemned man, Dickens argues, might be tempted to affect stoicism to impress them. Instead, he is locked like Fagin in *Oliver Twist* in an oppressive solitude, where his fears can reduce him to gibbering remorse.

Dickensian institutions are deathly, either executing their wretched victims or coolly organizing them into statistical quantities, which is death to the unruly individuality which Dickens prizes. The uncommercial traveller watches this extinction of individuality as a Mormon ship assembles its passengers in London for the voyage to America. The traveller represents, as he says, the house of Human Interest Brothers. His motives are not economic but humanitarian, and he tours institutions like the Wapping workhouse to satisfy an "uncommercial curiosity." Likewise, at the Mormon ship, he prides himself on his "uncommercial individuality." Commerce, as Trollope argued of the homogenized American businessmen, is the enemy of individuality. So, it becomes clear as Dickens watches the Mormons marshaling their converts, is enrollment in a faith. The conscripts to Mormonism have lost all personal independence and become featurelessly institutional. The passage to their American millennium is a fate worse than death, because they have been removed from uproarious, eccentric England to a bland sanctity which suppresses personal will.

Whereas Trollope's America is no more than misguided, Dickens's is malign, the vast death-chamber of English individuality. A disgruntled Mormon agent tells the uncommercial traveller that few Scottish highlanders are recruited because they're too fiercely self-reliant to be interested in "universal brotherhood and peace and good will." They are individuals, and therefore don't want to dwindle into saints. A Wiltshire laborer interviewed by the traveller loses his character when he comes to describe his adopted faith, since to him it is no more than an institutional slogan which he repeats but cannot associate with his own existence: "O yes, I'm a Mormon. I'm a Mormon," he says, and peers about for an excuse to sidle away. The Mormons have a mysterious and (to Dickens) depressing "aptitude for organisation." They subdue a crowd of eight hundred, abolishing bustle or hurry by reducing each party to a list of entries on a ticket. They bureaucratize a jovial, bumptious Dickensian mob by disallowing individuality: the Jobson family group is rebaptized, and allotted the same given names in each of its generations. The inspection of tickets is a rite of passage solemnizing the forfeiture of individuality: at the other side lies the collectivist and polygamous paradise, where not even the most intimate emotional relationships are the preserve of the individual.

This warning that America vengefully unmakes character by institutionalizing it is extended in the novel written after Dickens's first visit there. The monthly installments of *Martin Chuzzlewit* began to appear in 1843, the year after *American Notes*. Martin the picaresque, dispossessed hero resolves to go to America to make his fortune, but is hoodwinked by entrepreneurial sharpers, who send him off to build a city in a swamp. He falls ill in this miasmal waste, and returns to England deploring the greed and vice of America, though perfunctorily prophesying its moral recovery. The novel's nasty animosity toward America caused offense at once, and critics still argue that Dickens's intemperance betrays him into an artistic error: the American section is thin and shrill in comparison with the surrounding English chapters. But this lapse, however drastic, is deliberate, for it is intended to denote an imaginative difference between England and America.

England is the sanctuary of character, of individuals made monstrous by their self-absorption. The egotists who preside over the English section of the novel, Pecksniff the fraudulent architect and Mrs. Gamp the sodden midwife, create autonomous nonsense-worlds from their introversion. Pecksniff the hypocrite devises for himself a supercilious periodic style which is the idiom of his fantasy, and takes up residence inside it. Mrs. Gamp meanwhile conducts a garrulous dialogue with herself and, tolerating no invasion of her private domain, invents for the purpose a nonexistent interlocutor, Mrs. Harris. She turns introversion into absolutism: "Gamp's my name, and Gamp's my nater," she insists. She and Pecksniff monopolistically draw the world into themselves. In contrast with their enraptured self-sufficiency, the American characters of *Martin Chuzzlewit* are noisy rhetoricians whose identity isn't a law unto itself but depends on the approbation of institutions. The Americans boast not of being themselves but of being Americans. The English disease is solipsism, the American counterpart is jingoism. The English monsters are poetic fantasists, their American counterparts prosaic ranters. The English have too much character, and are immured in monomania; the Americans have no character at all, and hope to borrow some from the institutions to which they adhere.

An Englishman may save his life by emigrating to America, but he will lose his character. This is why Martin Chuzzlewit's friends are so anxious to dissuade him. They think of him indeed as a Svidrigaylov, Dostoevsky's character in *Crime and Punishment,* who expires with a gruesome Dickensian jest: he announces to a bystander that he is going to America, and promptly shoots himself. Tom Pinch begs Martin not to go, not to be "so dreadfully regardless of yourself." He speaks of Martin's decision as if it were a threat of suicide, and chooses his words aptly, for to go to America is, in the view of the Victorian novel, to dreadfully disregard the self, to extirpate one's character. The driver who takes Martin to London seconds this fear by reminiscing about a character called Lummy Ned in a doleful past tense. Martin asks, "Is he dead?" But the past tense turns out to mean that "he went to the U-nited States," which is an abrogation as final as mortality. The driver's next remark is intended as a commendation of America, but it twists ironically into a complaint. Ned landed in New York without a penny, but was nevertheless very welcome because "all men are alike in the U-nited States, an't they?" The equality which is the country's social and economic glory is, for Dickens, its imaginative affliction: in making men equal it makes them all alike; it may not recognize hierarchical social difference, but neither does it tolerate individuality. Lummy Ned is doubly dead, lost to England and lost to himself.

Martin's determination to emigrate is "a desperate resolution," like a promise to end it all. The driver can supply no information about the cost or duration or conditions of Lummy Ned's passage, as if this had been the journey which cannot be described because no traveler returns from it. The weeks before departure for America are for Martin a period of disintegration. He pawns his wardrobe and slouches about the streets, having relinquished "his delicacy and self-respect," as if these sacrifices were an initiatic training for the voyage ahead. The Statue of Liberty promises that emigration will be a resurrection, revivifying the "wretched refuse" of Europe; for Martin it is merely a death. As he declines into indigence and dejection, he becomes obsessed with the idea of America, which seems to represent a deathly release from pain.

America has a similar significance for Mark Tapley, Martin's indomitably jolly companion. Mark undertakes the journey as a test of his good humor, an experiment to discover how much his optimism is capable of bearing. Emigration is for him a comic martyrdom. Outfacing death is the proof of faith. Mark calls America "a very likely sort of place for me to be jolly in," like the martyr exulting in imminent destruction. Aboard their ship, the steerage cabin is a congregation of maladies like a communal grave: crammed into it are specimens of "every kind of domestic suffering that is bred in poverty, illness, banishment, sorrow, and long travel in bad weather." Predicting the day and hour of the ship's arrival in New York is like anticipating the moment of one's death: the passengers all make excited guesses, but no one can be certain. The firemen on the steamboat which meets the ship in New York harbor are extraterrestrial visitors, "objects of hardly more interest and curiosity than if they had been so many angels, good or bad." The steamer itself is a disturbing prodigy like something from beyond the grave, working its legs "like some enormously magnified insect or antedeluvian monster."

The resurrection sponsored by America turns out to be a living death. The woman with whom Mark and Martin travel, who is searching for her husband, almost dies when she doesn't find him on the quay in New York. Later, Mark reports, she finds "his remains": he is not dead, but more weakened by "fevers and agues than is quite reconcilable with being alive," a ghost of the man she had known. Even the renewed optimism of the united family suggests to Mark the proximity of the end. They leave as happy "as if they were going to Heaven. I should think they was, pretty straight, if I may judge from the poor man's looks." As they approach the swamp called Eden, Mark explains his resilient good-humor by saying he is "brightening up afore I die." The fever to which he and Martin succumb there is, like their initial act of emigration, a parabolic death.

The purpose of the United States, announces the flatulent General Choke when persuading Martin to settle in Eden, is "the regeneration of man." This is precisely why Dickens abhors it, for his imagination, like his finest characters, is abnormal, improper, comically unregenerate. Growth, change, improvement, and maturity are optimistic faculties of character with which his chaotic, regressive imagination cannot sympathize. Hence, when America reconstitutes paradise, Dickens longs for the fall. This is the significance of the miserable muddy Eden of the novel: it is the paradise from which one craves expulsion. Mark Tapley is pleased by the news that there will be serpents (agents of the fortunate fall) there. He is so elated by this certainty that "a stranger might have supposed that he had all his life been yearning for the society of serpents, and now hailed with delight the approaching consummation of his fondest wishes." Dickens's characters aren't ejected from paradise because they're unworthy of it; they petition for parole from it because it's unworthy of them. Eden after all is a place of regeneration for Martin: the fever compels him to acknowledge his responsibility for and reliance on the loyal Mark, and to admit his own selfishness. But to raise him it must bring him low, close to death. The new world is very nearly the next world.

Dickens's America mortifies its victims by depriving them of their characters. New York newsboys cry the details of crime and corruption through the streets, and Martin objects to the "Rowdy Journal" as "horribly personal." By this he means horribly impersonal, since the paper's fault is its scandalous refusal to respect individual privacies. Major Pawkins, a Pennsylvania politician who is touted as one of the most remarkable men in America, has no mind and no character, and therefore has nothing to hide. Mentally he proceeds "on the principle of putting all the goods he had (and more) into his window." Pawkins brags that in America human nature has been developed by institutions, whereas in Europe it is retarded. In fact, human nature has been obliterated by institutions, punished into uniformity. Dickens objects to the mercenariness of New Yorkers because it is a collective obsession, not a hubristic private dream like Pecksniff's schemes for self-enrichment. Not even vice in America can manage to individualize people: "all their cares, hopes, joys, affections, virtues, and associations, seemed to be melted down into dollars." This uniformity is physical as well as mental. The Americans Martin encounters are without exception listless, hollow-cheeked, tedious, and portentously verbose. The company in the hotel bar endlessly replicates the set of five or six types he has already met. When you've seen a thousand Americans, you've seen one. Their common worship of individualism has ended by effacing their individuality. They all value personality as a commodity, but because it is the same ideal personality which everyone wishes to acquire, the result is homogeneity: every nonentity Martin meets is introduced as one of the most remarkable men in the country. In Chapter 21 Dickens covers a change from England to America by saying that, now Pecksniff is a thousand leagues away, the narrative can again claim "Liberty and Moral Sensibility for its high companions." The sarcasm, heavy-handedly mocking Americans for thinking that liberty and moral sensibility are their national prerogative, is actually a defter irony, for it is literally true that a character like Pecksniff can exist only in the salutary absence of liberty and moral sensibility, since he is a monster of illiberal, amoral imagination. The vaunted freedom of America will not countenance such a being.

America either kills character or institutionalizes it. The windbags of *Martin Chuzzlewit* all lament the backwardness of English institutions. General Choke blames the British for not knowing how their own institutions work (Martin has just contradicted his assertion that the Queen lives in the Tower of London), and says that such institutional expertise is a privilege of "intelligent and locomotive" Americans. As America embroils Martin and Mark, it makes them into institutions. Martin proposes that they should establish themselves in the architectural profession as Chuzzlewit and Tapley, but Mark protests that he can only accept the anonymity of being "Co.": "I've often thought as I should like to know a Co.; but I little thought as ever I should live to be one." Being a company consequently means not being a character, sentencing yourself to dumb inaction, and Mark perceives that he "must be a sleeping partner: fast asleep and snoring." While Mark dwindles into a company, a nameless and vestigial commercial appendage, Martin (when news of his investment in Eden spreads) becomes a celebrity, which is another forfeiture of character. He attracts begging letters and preposterous invitations, and is compelled to hold a levee to receive an inquisitive mob. He is now a public property, and his private letters are published in the "Watertoast Gazette." Reporters anatomize his boots, pimples, and teeth: not even his body is his own. Promotion to institutional status is death to character, and Captain Kedgick is disappointed that Martin and Mark didn't have the decency to die in Eden, as "a public man" would have done, to meet "the public views."

Dickens the celebrity: an American cartoon from the Raymond Mander and Joe Mitchenson Theatre Collection.

America revenged itself on Dickens by making him the victim of his own prophecy. It first made a public man of him, and then killed him. His second trip there, between November 1868 and April 1869, ruined his health and hastened his fatal heart attack in 1870, and it did so because he had allowed himself to become an institution, a commercial property freighted about the country by a lecture agency. He gave readings from his novels throughout New England, in Baltimore, Washington, Philadelphia, and finally New York. The exhausting schedule, the bitter weather, and the nervous excitement of the performances weakened him, and by the time of his farewell banquet at Delmonico's in New York he was faltering and in pain. Selling himself to a delirious public, killing himself in order to bring his novels alive in dramatic readings, Dickens was suffering a morbid American institutionalization. America exacts a penalty from those it celebrates and enriches: it had made a classic of him, and was urging him to confirm his immortality by dying.

When Martin is denounced by Elijah Pogram as an enemy of

American institutions, he decries those institutions as an array of techniques for killing: "Are pistols with revolving barrels, sword-sticks, bowie-knives, and such things, Institutions on which you pride yourselves? Are bloody duels, brutal combats, savage assaults, shooting down and stabbing in the streets, your Institutions?" Institutions are vices armed and aggressive: "a man deliberately makes a hog of himself, and *that's* an Institution!" Martin says of Pogram's gluttony, and he dares Pogram to number "Dishonour and Fraud . . . among the Institutions of the great republic!" People in America are not characters, nor do its institutions constitute a society. Imaginatively offended by America, the Victorians register as deficiencies those qualities which their successors extol as its peculiar freedoms. Mrs. Trollope is horrified by the American abolition of privacy, but it is this which later convinces Isherwood that California is a paradise: there are no boundary fences between properties in the suburbs, because angels have no secrets and no territorial jealousies. The lack of social amenity and historical depth—everything is temporary and makeshift, as Dickens says of the Boston shopfronts, because there is no past to validate it—which distresses the Victorians is later welcomed as a liberation. Kipling admires America because it is not yet enfeebled into a society, but is still engaged in the epic conquest of a hostile nature; Auden and Isherwood value it because it wipes out memory and thus cancels guilt. Even the absence of character comes to seem a blessing. Mrs. Trollope meets only gruff brutes, not people trained and chastened by membership in society; Dickens finds the crowds drearily homogeneous, and Trollope suggests that American virtues tend toward impersonality, encouraging mimicry of an ideal self which is a collective possession, not the cultivation of a private integrity of being. But Lawrence hails in America the dissolution of a stale and obsolete notion of character, the decomposition of that acquisitive personal identity to which the Victorians and their gossipy, circumstantial novels cling. For the Victorians, America is unreal and imaginatively unavailing. For their successors, its unreality is its imaginative attraction.

3

AESTHETIC AMERICA
Oscar Wilde
Rupert Brooke

During his tour, Trollope visited the site of Dickens's Eden, the slushy wilderness of Cairo, Illinois. His purpose was as usual institutional inspection, to survey the troops quartered there, but he found on arrival that the soldiers had moved on, and instead took glum inventory of the hardware of the installation. Describing the wintry mess of the place, he admits to having failed Mark Tapley's test. His joviality is unequal to the desolation of Eden. He escapes in a second-class railway carriage, and rejoices despite the squalor of the car, because he has been ejected from paradise: "we were being carried away from Eden." His joke unwittingly introduces the next image of America, the aesthetic version to be elaborated by Wilde and Rupert Brooke. A character in Wilde's play *A Woman of No Importance* says that America is a paradise, which is why Americans are so anxious to get out of it. Wilde's lecture tour in 1882 hoped to provoke a fortunate fall in this tedious paradise by converting Americans to the sinfully vainglorious values of aestheticism.

Recalling America in a lecture given after his return to London, Wilde at once announces his incompetence as a Victorian inspector of institutions. He is instead an aesthetic observer, treasuring impressions rather than estimating quantities. He boasts that he cannot give the latitude or longitude of America; neither can he "compute the value of its dry goods, and I have no very close acquaintance with its politics." The hustling commercialism of the country bothers him, not as it did the Victorians because it is uncivil, but because it is unpoetic. Romeo and Juliet, he says, would have had no time to spare for lyrical pathos in America, because they'd have been preoccupied with catching trains. The turmoil of the streets jars on the musical sensibility, and the towns of the western plains are offensive not for their unaccommodated lack of manners but for their uningratiating English names. Wilde claims that he refused to lecture in Grigsville, so appalled was he by its ugly name.

Wilde's is a perverse and adversary wit, which challenges the confidence of Victorian morality and normality by exactly imitating the Victorian solemnity about standards and the Victorian finality of utterance. Wilde is as judicially stern about ugliness as the Victorians were about immorality, and it's the fact that he mimics the Victorian tone of reprobation which makes his alteration of Victorian values so dangerous. He is an immoralist appropriating the accents of the moralists. This is why, at his trial in 1895, he so enraged his accusers by first denying that he'd kissed a certain proletarian youth, and then giving as his reason the fact that the boy wasn't at all pretty. His defense began in the language of Victorian indignation, only to change at once into the brazen language of pederastic preciosity. Wilde's wit disrupts morality by being so nonsensically moralistic.

The wit not only subverts morality, but subjugates America by diminishing it. Wilde complained of "the inordinate size of everything" in America, and revenged himself on its preposterous immensities by miniaturizing it in epigrams. The prairie is like blotting-paper, the Mormon Tabernacle of Salt Lake City is like a soup kettle. G. K. Chesterton was to find in American wit a humorous equivalent to the vertiginous exaggerations of American architecture: the tall story is a comic correlative of the skyscraper. Wilde also argues that the drawling loquacity of American speech is language's effort to distend itself to cover the remote reaches of the territory. Geography, he says, has a "fatal influence . . . upon adjectives." Platitudes are the form of speech most apt for the prairies. Flatulence and flatness correspond. Wilde's wit, because it is so small-scale, is a criticism of the hyperbolic manner and of oversize America. The epigram's virtue is its economy, and in Wilde this very concision of utterance taunts the inflated American objects it is describing. All he would say about the Atlantic was that he'd found it disappointing.

Having scaled down and dismissed the vast vacancy of the country, Wilde isolates a few stray, delicate, epigrammatically minute details which he is able to praise: the fragile cups from which he drinks tea in the Chinese quarter of San Francisco, and the steel rods and rhythmic wheels of the waterworks at Chicago. But even these enthusiasms aim to slight the commercial materialism of America. In Chicago, Wilde admires the machinery because it is "lovely," not because it is efficient; and in San Francisco, when his bill arrives in the Chinese restaurant, he admires the calligraphy instead of checking the addition: "it was made out on rice paper, the account being done in Indian ink as fantastically as if an artist had been etching little birds on a fan."

Professing ignorance of institutions, Wilde dissociates himself from the Victorian concern about the composition of American society. Trollope's criticism of institutional purpose bends into an appreciation of institutional finery. Wilde objects to the Independence Day celebrations in Atlanta because they are tattier than the New Orleans Mardi Gras, and says that the pageant is "the most perfect school of art for a people." Institutions now exist only to flaunt their ceremonial trappings. Wilde reported that he had seen only two processions in America: "one was the Fire Brigade preceded by the Police, the other was the Police preceded by the Fire Brigade." When he is taken on institutional tours, he contrives not to respond with the customary Victorian compassion. Taken to a prison in Lincoln, Nebraska, he rejoices to find that the inmates are mean fellows, "for I should hate to see a criminal with a noble face." He criticizes their costume (they wear "hideous striped dresses") and their literary taste (a condemned murderer is spending the weeks before his execution reading novels, which Wilde believes to be "a bad preparation for facing either God or Nothing"), but can summon no sympathy for their miserable fate.

Whereas the Victorian novelists are distressed by America's failure to protect the private life and the consequent absence of domesticity, Wilde commends America because there "the horrors of domesticity are almost entirely unknown." His terms of disparagement are often domestic. When he wants to wound, he invokes a kitchen utensil (the Mormon Tabernacle is a soup kettle, the steam engine which carries him west is "an ugly tin-kettle"). The conditions of social existence in America promote marriage but palliate it by forbidding closeness between the partners, which Wilde acclaims as a blessing. The popularity—the virtual compulsoriness—of marriage ensures that individual matches are neither intimate nor permanent. "The American man marries early," Wilde says, "and the American woman marries often." They get on well together because they are not together very much. Wilde explains the success of marriage by saying "no American man is ever idle" and "no American woman is considered responsible for the quality of her husband's dinners." The promiscuous tables of boarding houses, which Mrs. Trollope deplores, are for Wilde the married man's guarantee of freedom from his spouse. Couples live in company, which "does away with the necessity for those tedious tête-à-têtes, that are the dream of engaged couples, and the despair of married men." Wilde's wit operates to confound smug normality. Paradox is the literary form taken by perversity, so that Wilde is able to maintain that American marriages are preserved only by the easy availability of divorce. When people think they're bound together for life, he argues, they are apt to decline into rankling resentment of one another, but the fragility of the contract actually enforces it, and "reminds the husband that he should always try to please, and the wife that she should never cease to be charming." Wilde sums up his joke against American marriage by calling it "one of their most popular institutions." Marriage, that is, is not a private relationship—the ghastliness of marriage is now precisely its privacy, that "eternal duologue about bills and babies"—but a public arrangement.

As well as disestablishing marriage, Wilde reverses the relations between the sexes. The Victorians made women the tutelary deities of the private life, men the bold adventurers into the larger public world. Ruskin assigned gardens to queens and treasuries to kings. America worried the Victorians because it disturbed this allocation of experience. Trollope cannot write about American women because they are too brashly public, or about American men because they're too retentively private, too absorbed in the pursuit of wealth to have acquired the attributes of character. Wilde welcomes this contrariety, and announces that in America the sexes have changed places. Women are shamelessly public, men shrink into privacy. "The strange thing about American civilisation is, that the women are most charming when they are away from their own country, the men most charming when they are at home."

American women are undomestic cosmopolitans, as ambitious and combative as men are supposed to be. They can even tell stories, Wilde marvels, without forgetting the point. Their vivacity urges them to abandon a tedious home. Lady Caroline in *A Woman of No Importance* criticizes them for being so inequitably pretty, and for carrying off all the eligible bachelors. She argues that they should stay in their country, since they are always boasting that it is the paradise of women. But "that is why," explains Lord Illingworth, "like Eve, they are so extremely anxious to get out of it." Their expatriation, the sign of their rejection of a merely domestic destiny, extends into the after-life. Good Americans go to Paris when they die, Wilde says, while the bad ones are extradited to America. American men cower in the domesticity their women have vacated. They have no "social existence in London," and confine themselves to lolling in rocking-chairs or morosely window-shopping. Their quality is only apparent at home, and in the home: back in America, they are "the most hospitable of hosts."

Because America has altered the character of the sexes, the

American girl becomes an alarming creature, the embodiment of a paradox, for she is a predatory innocent. Hester Worsley, the American visitor in *A Woman of No Importance,* epigrammatically reverses relations between America and England. America has transferred male attributes to women; now it makes bold to compete with England and, refusing to be patronized, claims for itself the privileges which England imagines to be the preserve of its long experience. When Lady Caroline asserts that there can be no country in America, Hester retorts "we have the largest country in the world," with some states the size of France and England combined. Lady Caroline fancies that this must be very draughty, but the vast emptiness of America now opens into a territory of moral freedom and second chances: Hester tells the disgraced Mrs. Arbuthnot that there are wiser and less unjust lands than England over the sea. Innocence goes with confident territorial amplitude, sad experience is the style of English claustrophobia. Hester says, "the world is very wide and very big," but Mrs. Arbuthnot answers, "for me the world is shrivelled to a palm's breadth." America no longer defers to English society and history. For Hester, society is no more than a set of cliques, and when Lady Caroline says that there are no ruins or curiosities in America, Hester replies, "the English aristocracy supplies us with our curiosities. . . . They are sent over to us every summer, regularly, in the steamers, and propose to us the day after they land. As for ruins, we are trying to build up something that will last longer than brick or stone." She proceeds to accuse English society of a shallow selfish materialism which ignores "the unseen beauty of a higher life." American vacancy has become a moral value: the absence of cultured accoutrements is now the mark of transcendental virtue. After this harangue, Illingworth comments, "all Americans lecture. . . . I suppose it is something in their climate." Wilde had earlier reduced the American language to a function of geography: bewildering distance creates the habit of hyperbole. Now he reduces American moralism to a function of the weather.

The American innocent abroad, like Hester Worsley, disarms

and disables her more experienced elders. In this Hester resembles those obnoxious American infants about whom Wilde complained. Because America is a land which has abjured history and determined never to grow up, it follows that the child is accorded social, moral, even gastronomic priority there. Wilde remembers the offensive precocity of the American child, castigating the deficiencies of its parents across the dinner table, and remarks that "in America, the young are always ready to give to those who are older than themselves the full benefits of their inexperience." The innocence of America threatens to turn backwards into infantilism. The simplicity of first childhood becomes the imbecility of second childhood. Illingworth makes this point in the play, saying that "the youth of America is their oldest tradition. It has been going on now for three hundred years. To hear them talk one would imagine they were in their first childhood. As far as civilisation goes they are in their second."

The purpose of Wilde's tour of the United States in 1882 was exactly the opposite of Hester's uplifting crusade in the play. She is the American child who has ventured abroad to correct her elders; he is the European adult who has ventured abroad in order to corrupt his innocent juniors. Hester's purpose is to redeem a sour and cynical Europe, Wilde's was to induce a fall in drearily paradisial America. The paradox is summed up by Mrs. Allonby in *A Woman of No Importance,* when she defines a thoroughly bad man as one who admires innocence. Wilde mockingly admired American innocence, and therefore in 1882 set out to spoil it. His heroine, a decade later, was to travel in the opposite direction to scourge European experience.

Wilde's tour had two objects. One was mercenary, the other aesthetic. Both were aimed against the invincible innocence of the Americans: he took advantage of their innocence by separating them from their money, and meanwhile lured that innocence toward decadence by tempting it with his theories of aesthetic reform. He was sent to America by the entrepreneur D'Oyly Carte, under whose management *Patience,* the Gilbert and Sullivan operetta deriding aestheticism, was being produced in New York. Wilde, the original of the affected Bunthorne of Gilbert's play, was to appear in competition with the parody of himself, lecturing in soulful earnest on the subject the operetta satirized. Wilde's presence was not only a publicity stunt but a prudent contractual maneuver: he acted as *Patience*'s trademark, ratifying the product's authenticity. Earlier Gilbert and Sullivan operettas had been pirated in America. In 1879 D'Oyly Carte had sent the collaborators to New York to supervise the authorized productions, and to threaten the pirates with prosecution. In 1882 Gilbert and Sullivan were occupied in London, and couldn't be dispatched to protect the official New York version of *Patience*. D'Oyly Carte therefore hired Wilde to represent his interests, and to act as a poster for the operetta.

Wilde expected self-parody to be a lucrative business. He told a friend that he hoped to return with a thousand pounds; in another letter he explained to playwright Dion Boucicault that he intended to "gather the golden fruits of America" in order to "spend a winter in Italy and a summer in Greece amidst beautiful things." During the tour, he amassed tribute from the adoring population, chiding the urchins who sold pirated editions of his poems for cheating him of his royalties and nonchalantly accepting treasure like the manuscript of Keats's sonnet on blue, which had been sent by the poet's American niece, Emma Speed: "what you have given me is more golden than gold," he wrote in acknowledgment. America was for Wilde an earthly paradise of credulous generosity, to be mercilessly exploited. In return for inflated lecture fees and unsolicited gifts, Wilde disbursed remembrances of himself. He retained a staff of secretaries to fake his autograph and distribute locks of his hair: the demand for the latter was so great that he declared himself to be in danger of balding. His own unscrupulousness titillated him. He saw that the American admiration for any kind of celebrity licensed the confidence-trickster, and by implication he aligned himself with a romantic outlaw like Jesse James. In St. Joseph, Missouri, shortly after Jesse James's death, he watched the relic hunters scramble to buy James's dust bin, his foot scraper, his door knocker, and his coal scuttle, just as in New York admirers pleaded for Wilde's own leavings. In a letter he comments on this gullibility: "the Americans are certainly great hero-worshippers, and always take their heroes from the criminal classes." Celebrity like Jesse James's or Wilde's own is thus virtue's envious tribute to vice. Timorous, law-abiding Americans nominate as their heroes those who behave with an illegality or an outrageousness which they admire but wouldn't dare to emulate. Wilde's comment is a self-fulfilling prophecy, for his subsequent career confirmed his heroism by making him officially a member of the criminal classes. In 1895 he was arrested, tried for homosexual misconduct, and sentenced to two years' hard labor.

Wilde's first technique for subverting American innocence was to make money both from his own popularity and from Gilbert's calumniation of him. His second stratagem was to introduce into this philistine Eden the unnatural and tainting love of art. The aesthetes thought America would become interesting only if it became wicked, and the purpose of art was to induce this fortunate fall. Max Beerbohm, who first toured America in 1895 as secretary to his half-brother, actor Herbert Beerbohm Tree, described the country in this way, although he marveled that the depraving change had already occurred. Interviewed in Boston, Beerbohm declared Chicago to be beautiful because "it is so wicked and corrupt and vicious." He wondered at its alacrity in becoming "splendid, Babylonish, wonderful": it deserved extra credit for turning decadent so precociously. Conservative critics of America proverbially say that it has passed from barbarism to decadence, bypassing the stage of civilization which ought to come between; but for the aesthetic critic, this is the wonder of it. Like a corrupt infant, it cannot wait to grow up before embracing venery. Beerbohm is amazed by Chicago for this reason: "I cannot understand how a city so young should be so vicious," he told a Boston reporter. Aestheticism turns into a variety of arson, destroying things in order to make them beautiful, and Beerbohm indeed considered arson to be one of the delights of Chicago. He recalls seeing a "splendid fire" there, "beautiful red and white flames," but "soon a lot of men with hats rushed in and threw water on the fire. It was an act of vandalism." The offense was to extinguish the fire, not to set it. Crime beautifies; only the drab enemies of art want to suppress it.

Wilde likewise saw himself as the serpent insinuating itself into an uneventful, virtuous garden. His were the persuasive ethics of the serpent: he always said that he could resist anything except a temptation. The bait to which he hoped Americans would succumb was not knowledge (used by his predecessor in Eden) but art, and his aestheticism is a devilish creed, deriding moral integrity and arguing instead for an elegant, heartless, idle superficiality in life as in art. He explained to a friend that he would be very disappointed to leave America without making "one person love beautiful things a little more." The serpent's justification in Eden was that it had convinced Eve to love knowledge and the freedom of intellect a little more. This diminution of Wilde's aim, which will count it as a victory to have converted a single person, is itself revealing. Mrs. Trollope, upbraiding Americans for their bad manners, hoped to reform an entire society. Wilde more cautiously but more effectually hopes to corrupt a solitary individual. One such victim is located by Beerbohm, who improbably claimed to have "discovered a man of exquisite taste in Hoboken." Wilde jokes about the infernal nature of his campaign to his fellow dandy Whistler in May 1882, after he'd crossed into Canada. Reviewing his progress, he remarks "I have already civilised America—*il reste seulement le ciel!*" Satan too undertook his assault on the earth as a stage in his recovery of power in heaven; Wilde assumes that heaven must be lamentably uncivilized, because art is the prerogative of the sinful.

His encounter with the miners of Leadville, Colorado, comically acts out the contradictions of Wilde's seductive mission. The miners are armed against the incursion of art, like the angels with flaming swords guarding paradise. They regularly execute their saloon pianists, and Wilde is warned that he and his manager will surely be

Wilde's subversive mission: Max Beerbohm's "The name of Dante Gabriel Rossetti is heard for the first time in the Western States of America. Time: 1882. Lecturer: Mr. Oscar Wilde."
Tate Gallery, London.

killed if they dare to appear there. Nevertheless, Wilde goes ahead, determined to bring his luxurious, enervating gospel to these needy men, who have the reputation of being the roughest (and therefore according to Wilde's standards the most inartistic) in the world. Their innocence proves impregnable. He lectures on the early Florentine painters, but the miners "slept as though no crime had ever stained the ravines of their mountain home"—unaware, that is to say, that Wilde's praise of Botticelli and Benvenuto Cellini is a crime, an offense against decent unimaginative normality. A reference to Whistler does succeed in antagonizing them. Wilde describes one of Whistler's nocturnes, and the very idea goads the miners to a righteous fury. Some draw revolvers and leave to see if the renegade artist is "'prowling about the saloons' or 'wrastling a hash' at any eating shop. Had he been there I fear he would have been killed." On this occasion Whistler takes the blame for Wilde's aesthetic sedition.

Mrs. Trollope had hoped to redeem America by making it well mannered. Wilde hoped to redeem it by making it stylish. He was offended by the ugliness of American dress and the discomfort of American interior decoration: the chimney-pot hats and swallow-tail coats of the men, and the cast-iron stoves, machine-made furniture, and white-washed walls of their houses, shocked him. Aestheticism began in Ruskin and the pre-Raphaelite painters as a spiritual revival, but in Wilde evangelicism has given way to dandyism, and moral regeneration to a fashion show. Wilde dressed himself up as an embodiment of his theory, and presented himself to America as a work of art. What he said in his lectures was less important than what he wore to them. His elaborate frippery teased the puritan severity of the American transcendentalists. From Augusta, Georgia, he complained to Julia Ward Howe (to whom we owe "The Battle Hymn of the Republic") about the quantity of his luggage, and added "what would Thoreau have said to my hat-box! Or Emerson to the size of my trunk . . . !" But his wardrobe was his scripture, the elaboration of his mock-infernal creed. In the same letter he resolved not to be "afraid of the depraved luxury of a hat-box."

He was forever organizing the replenishment of his wardrobe. From St. Louis, he wrote to D'Oyly Carte's agent ordering two tight velvet coats with flowered sleeves and ruffs of cambric. The garments were to be supplied by a theatrical costumier: Wilde treated actors as mannequins, and wrote after his return to New York to Laura Don commending her new play and her performance in it, but questioning the lining of a cloak she had worn. Wilde's identification of character with costume recalls an experience of his heroine Sarah Bernhardt on her arrival in New York two years earlier. The customs men rifled her wardrobe, rudely handling her velvets, satins, and laces and eventually calling in a pair of shrewish milliners to estimate the value of the gowns she was importing. Bernhardt called it "a chiffon court-martial": her dresses had been on trial. But then she, like Wilde, was what she wore. Wilde made news in America each time he changed his clothes. He arrived in New York wearing a bottle-green overcoat of otter fur, with a sealskin cap. (This item contrasts interestingly with the fur coats Kipling wore during his residence in Vermont, which is discussed in the next chapter. He was photographed in one of these coats in 1893, standing in a snowy street of Brattleboro. Kipling's furs are the animal's defenses against an inimical climate. To survive the cruel Vermont winter, he had to grow a furry second skin. Wilde's coat, on the contrary, symbolizes nature sacrificed to art: seals and otters have been flayed merely to adorn his precious body.) At New York parties, he wore black velvet. He found an aesthetic vindication for the utilitarian costumes of the Americans. The oilskins at Niagara were acceptable because Bernhardt had worn them. At Leadville, climbing into an underground suit of India rubber for a descent (in an ore bucket) into the mine shafts, he announced that the slack folds of the rubber envelope reminded him of the Roman toga—except that the lining "should be of purple satin, and there should be storks embroidered upon the flaps, with fern embroidering round the edges." Later he adopted the broad-brimmed hat worn by the Rocky Mountain miners, prizing it as the most graceful thing in the world.

This appropriation of local uniforms, which he thus converted

Wilde in his fur coat, photographed by Sarony in New York, 1882.

from use to beauty, is matched by Wilde's transformation of social problems into aesthetic quibbles. In Cincinnati he suggested that criminals should plead the ugliness of the city as an excuse for their misdemeanors, and in San Francisco he admired railway navvies who put aside their picks and shovels to drink tea from exquisite blue and white cups. Moral rearmament or the reformation of manners has been supplanted by aesthetic faddism. Wilde recommended that, instead of aspiring to the republican austerity of George Washington's life, people should dress as Washington did, because his costume was noble and beautiful.

Between Wilde and Rupert Brooke, aestheticism changes, and the change is passed on to America. Wilde wished to civilize the country by dressing it up; Brooke, weary of civilized existence, admires America because it is undressed, pastorally disheveled. Wilde's dandified religion of style, self-admiringly immaculate, has turned in Brooke into a cult not of style but of the image, isolated, empty, inhuman. Niagara was such an image: it means nothing, Brooke concluded. Wilde was at least concerned to reform America, and is as fussily domestic in his criticisms as the Victorians he derides, but for Brooke the continent existed—as the symbolist poets said the world did—only to be turned into a book.

Brooke traveled across the United States and Canada in 1913, on his way to the South Seas, returning to Europe the next year to die in the war. His dispatches to the *Westminster Gazette* were collected posthumously and published in 1916 as *Letters from America*. Henry James contributed an avuncular, uncomprehending preface, which marks the gap between the Victorian social appraisal of America and Brooke's more abstract and aesthetic modern per-

Kipling in his fur coat, photographed in Main Street, Brattleboro, Vermont, in March 1893. Collection of Howard C. Rice, Jr.

ceptions. Brooke was delighted by the garishness of New York, and found in its enskied advertisements a crass equivalent of the vacant poetic images he venerated. James is appalled by this enthusiasm, and can only explain it by imagining that, lost in the pandemonium of the city, Brooke was "obliged to throw himself upon skyscrapers and the overspread blackness picked out in a flickering fury of imaged advertisements for want of some more interesting view of character and manners." The elderly, protective James longs to take the doomed golden youth by the hand and guide him toward a finer, more discriminating view of the subject. But the truth is that Brooke no longer cares for character or manners. These are Victorian concerns: Mrs. Trollope writes about domestic character, her son about the national character as it is reflected in public institutions, and those institutions are also models of national housekeeping, distended versions of the private homes whose economies Mrs. Trollope chastises. Brooke belongs to a new century, which is interested in American cities as images of spirit, and indifferent to those who inhabit the cities and to the workings of institutions.

Brooke's is a poet's New York, not a novelist's. For him the appeal of what James called "the vertical business blocks and the lurid sky-clamour" lies on the outside, in their poetic surface of image and advertisement, not novelistically within. James regrets that Brooke didn't criticize the American "monotony of type." But whereas the novelist regrets this monotony, since it blurs the discrepancies which create character, the poet exults in it, since it reduces disparate individuals to a crowd of identically athletic and attractive bodies, and makes from a chaotic population a single image. Brooke scoffs at the sententious efforts of the Victorian novelists to understand the operations of American society. On a guided tour of Montreal, he is shown only banks and churches, institutions for amassing credits in this world and the next; he regrets that the Ottawa Parliament was built "in the middle of the last century, an unfortunate period."

From the harbor at night, Brooke sees New York as a city constructed of electric lights: "luminous trams, like shuttles of fire" cross Brooklyn Bridge; Coney Island is a remote "low golden glare"; the skyscrapers are cliffs lined with light. As he describes New York, it becomes a city confected of images. Even the perpendicular grid of streets which depressed the Victorians is justified because it is a device for singling out and framing images: the western streets capture and hold iridescent sunsets. The man-made canyons are a canvas for startling distributions of light and shade: after darkness has settled into the streets, the upper heights of the buildings are mellow in the sun. Transforming objects into images, Brooke calls the skyscrapers cathedrals. The process of translation is a mortifying one. The buildings can only become images if humanity is expelled from them, and what remains after the evacuation is intimidatingly abstract. The Singer and Woolworth buildings are raised to a faith "cold and hard and light, like the steel that is in their heart." Brooke can admire them only when they are empty and have renounced their commercial function—when they have become, that is, as serenely vacant as the poetic image is. He argues that the skyscrapers are great buildings because at certain hours of the day they seem to be not merely places of work but structures with "an existence and a meaning of their own." This meaning, like that of Brooke's Niagara, is entirely self-referring, austerely unconnected with human affairs. Brooke's image anticipates Auden's treatment of the skyscrapers as cathedrals in one of his first New York poems, *New Year Letter* (1940). But in Auden's case the same image has quite another significance. For him the skyscrapers are monasteries where the toilers of industrial society "vow / An economic abstinence," where the monastic rule of frugality and self-denial changes from a spiritual to a financial imperative. They are "secular cathedrals," planted on land which is commercially valuable not consecrated. Whereas Brooke can only consider the skyscrapers as cathedrals once they've purged themselves of their laboring inmates and their economic purpose, to Auden it is this economic purpose which makes them the cathedrals of the age of commerce. They testify to the noble delusion of commercial America, which believes in an economic immortality, and hopes to overcome human infirmity by accumulating treasure.

If the skyscrapers are cathedrals, advertising is their theology. Business has become a religion, Brooke says, and the writers of advertising copy are its mystagogues, childishly trusted by the American people. The existences of American consumers are ruled by images, which regulate their "most private and sacred wants," because advertising is a sinister, manipulative kind of art. The copy writers in department stores, as Brooke discovers, are all poets, painters, and literary men, who for instance adapt the style of Matisse to sell summer suits. In the age of faith, the believer is admonished by priestly images. In the age of commerce, the consumer is subliminally enticed by the images projected by advertisements. Though Brooke derides such credulity, he is intrigued by advertising because it is akin to his own poetic manner, which is also a hieratic, mystifying species of image worship. Cathedrals and department stores both demean images, forcing them to glorify the faith or to sell products. Brooke's claim is to have released the image from this dual servitude, to have respected its purposelessness. He allows it, as he says of the skyscrapers or of Niagara, a meaning and existence of its own. New York is to him an enchanting parody of art. In the streets the "unradiant glare" of artificial light robs people of their humanity (as the light of early morning or sunset rids the skyscrapers of their mean, commercial, human function) and turns them into identical images: faces disappear behind a mask, "hard, set, wolfish, terribly blue." The sky meanwhile is peopled with divinities. The ageless Queen of the Night, a sibyl who like Pater's Mona Lisa has endured through the ages by assuming successive identities as Isis, Ashtaroth, Venus, Cybele, and the Virgin Mary, recurs above New York, enigmatically winking as she recommends the purchase of pepsin chewing-gum. Her threefold wink, an image of her strange self-enclosed secrecy, parodies the ambiguous smile of Pater's Mona Lisa (who is present as well at Brooke's Niagara). Leonardo's necrophiliac woman is, Pater says, "older than the rocks among which she sits." Brooke's neon version of her is "older than the skyscrapers amongst which she sits." The smile of Pater's Mona Lisa corruptly hints at the arcane pleasures she has known. The wink of the chewing-gum lady is also a cryptic signal, semaphorically indifferent to human anguish: "the only answer to our cries . . . is that divine stare, the wink, once, twice, thrice." She is the poetic image, intermittent, inhuman, inane: "she has no name," Brooke remarks, just as Niagara has no meaning. But because, hovering above New York, she is the goddess of a mercenary civilization, she represents the image mechanized. Brooke notices that "one, certainly, of her eyelids is weary," but the reason for her weariness is not the orgiastic fatigue of Pater's Mona Lisa. Her trouble is an electrical fault.

The image purifies itself of human emotion. The wink is not a sexual invitation, like the Mona Lisa's smile, but merely an electronic twitch. And Brooke correspondingly is interested less in the human qualities of Americans than in their bland expressionlessness, which pained the Victorians but which for him draws them close to the saintly superficiality of the image. He insists on the eager, infantile nature of Americans, and says they are like kindly children anxious to impress with their grown-up antics. Wilde makes the same point, but in order to criticize the nonsensical inversion of a society which allows toddlers to rebuke their elders. For all his perversity, Wilde remains a moralist, who wants to correct the solecisms of American behavior, and this is why he is so disgusted by the liberty allowed to children. Brooke calls Americans children for a quite different reason. Children cannot presume to possess either character or manners, so the old Victorian concern for moral evaluation can conveniently lapse. He even finds in the heads of upperclass Americans a phrenological regression which justifies his indifference to mature character: they all have the faces "of an only child who has been brought up in the company of adults." Americans have the faces of angels or of images, smooth and vacuous. They are a race of Adams whose countenances never wrinkle, and the reason, Brooke suggests, is "the absence of a soul." Instead of souls, they have perfect bodies, and are kept in vital health (Brooke thinks) by exercise and by the habit of drinking water between meals.

Brooke's Americans resemble images in being bodies without souls. Wilde in the preface to *The Picture of Dorian Gray* praises the surface of the poetic image, and warns that those who fret to "go beneath the surface do so at their peril." Yet Brooke adds that Americans of both sexes are very often handsome but hardly ever beautiful. He doesn't explain what he means, and the comment trails off into a yearning trio of dots, but the implication seems to be that handsomeness is the privilege of rude health, whereas beauty is the more difficult acquisition, being the product of mental cultivation. Angels are handsome, because unreflecting. But beauty belongs to fallen nature, because it is the exterior sign of a complication within. Pater's Mona Lisa is witchily beautiful because her centuries of carnal experience and mental tribulation have "moulded the changing lineaments, and tinged the eyelids and the hands." Brooke's lissome Americans are merely handsome, performing feats of physical prestigidation without apparent mental motive. On Broadway he sees a young man doing double-jointed eurhythmics to demonstrate the suppleness of a brand of underwear. He never speaks to the onlookers, but instead displays a series of placards to vouch for the flexibility of his costume. He is an acrobat, making images from the arabesques of his body. Like Brooke's images, these contortions have neither meaning nor purpose, since the showman mimes motion rather than moving: he "smote imaginary balls, belaboured invisible opponents, ran with immense speed but no progress." His physical convolutions are a full-time job. Brooke remarks that "he did this, I discovered later, for many hours a day." Whitman's body electric has become Brooke's body elastic. Brooke doesn't dare, he says, to imagine the young man's state of mind—but why, given what Brooke has said about "the too wide and too smooth" faces of the New Yorkers, should he be assumed to have a mind at all?

The same retraction of mind into body occurs among the commercial travelers Brooke watches in a hotel off Broadway. They are frenetically active, giving dictation or making deals on the telephone, but between bouts on duty they "relapse into a curious trance" and sit supine, without the energy even to smoke or to chew. Like the acrobat in the underwear, they are bodies uninhabited by soul or mind: "the expressions of their faces never change. It is impossible to guess what, or if anything, is in their minds." The immobility of the salesmen like the restlessness of the acrobat is idyllically mindless. Americans remain, as Brooke sees it, in an otiose state of nature, as yet unperturbed by intelligence or unenlightened by souls.

The Victorians despaired of Americans because they could discover in them no private life, no interior resource; but for Brooke this is the charm of America. He derives a political moral from this physical relaxation. America is a free society because its men wear belts not braces, and are therefore sinuous and swinging in gait. Democracy is a matter of unbuttoned physique. Brooke's Americans are pastoral people, "unashamedly shirt-sleeved." If the Victorians were preoccupied with American manners, Brooke is preoccupied with American bodies.

Like Wilde, Brooke worries about what Americans wear on those bodies. But whereas Wilde had wanted to dress his Americans up, Brooke wants to undress them. Wilde turned the cowboys of the West into fops: their floppy hats, loose corduroys, knotted kerchiefs, and trousers tucked into their boots were the costume of cavaliers. Instead of dandified finery, Brooke favors an enticing dishevelment. Americans flaunt their liberty in their sartorial habits—the casualness with which they discard their coats, the willowy cut of their trousers. Matthew Arnold in 1888 in his *Civilization in the United States* had compared American institutions to "a suit of clothes" which fits the wearer without impeding his movements, able "to adapt itself naturally to the wearer's growth, and to admit of all enlargements as they successively arise." But in place of Arnold's well-tailored informality, Brooke finds a frank and arousing negligence. A sculptor carving the embodiment of America must, he says, represent a virile young man in his shirt sleeves, his coat slung over his arm. In Union Square, Brooke sights such a creature, a Greek god driving an open motor-car, his mane of red Swinburnean hair streaming in the wind. Like the baggy-trousered statue of America, this young man is also allegorical because physically exposed. He is a hulkingly muscular mechanic, clad "only in a suit of yellow overalls, so that his arms and shoulders and neck and chest were bare." The specificity of the description conveys the concentration of excitement: Brooke has to notice separately each uncovered area. A divinity of physical delight, the young man is an angel because he is so democratically typical. He is ennobled only by the machine he drives, and "in private life, no doubt, [is] a very ordinary youth, interested only in base-ball scores."

The sky over New York is a convocation of such deities. The galaxies have been replaced by neon signs. An igneous advertisement for underclothes lights up the night, and "a young man and a man-boy, flaming and immortal, clad in celestial underwear," box inconclusively and disappear. Their combat is enacted nightly over the city, and Brooke assigns a series of identities to them: they may be Thor and Odin, or perhaps Michael and Lucifer. In America, the gods are not naked, but wear underclothes. Latter-day Greeks, the Americans are obsessed not only with exercising and exhibiting the body, but have also undertaken to chemically redeem it, cleansing and disinfecting it so as to rescue it from coarse nature. Hence the aptness of another of Brooke's nocturnal visions: he watches "two vast fiery tooth-brushes" routing a carious devil in mid-air.

The homoerotic Hellenism which charms Brooke in America derives from Wilde, whose lectures had set out to transfer the aesthetic movement from dilapidated, debilitated Europe to nubile, juvenile America. "There is something Hellenic in your air," Wilde had said. In Chicago, he admired "the strong, healthy physique of your men and women" and, converting athleticism into aestheticism, was sure that this, together with the "wonderful climate" of the country, would suffice to produce a race of noble artists. At Harvard,

Wilde visited the gymnasium and proposed that a statue of a Greek athlete should be erected there, to symbolize this reunion between mental acuity and physical vigor. He even discovered the sculptor for the job, and from Newport wrote to Charles Eliot Norton praising the work of John Donoghue, who "could do any one of your young athletes." Setting a sculptor to work in the palestra would, Wilde argued, heal "the medieval discord between soul and body." He enclosed a photograph of a young Greek sculpted by Donoghue, adding that "the slight asceticism of it is to me very delightful."

This chastening asceticism has given way in Brooke to a riotous, abandoned hedonism. The marble poise of the athlete Wilde longed to place in the Harvard gym contrasts with the lithe, ecstatic energy of an athlete observed by Brooke at the baseball game against Yale, played during his visit to Harvard. He is entranced by the antics of a long-limbed pitcher, and just as the gum-chewing electric lady had been turned into Pater's androgynous goddess, so the sportsman with his tight hooligan's cap becomes a gambolling faun, specifically the limber sensual faun danced by Nijinsky to Debussy's music: the pitcher, combining "speed, mystery, and curve . . . gets into attitudes of a very novel and fantastic, but quite obvious, beauty. M. Nijinsky would find them repay study." Wilde had sought to ally art with the muscularity of sport; Brooke more decadently turns sport into ballet. And in the same month that Brooke started on his American tour, just such a ballet opened in Paris, with music by Debussy and choreography by Diaghilev for Nijinsky: *Jeux,* about a sexual triangle at a tennis game. Diaghilev called the piece "a plastic apologia for the man of 1913." Brooke's young men are also creatures of preternatural plasticity, in whom the body is not merely the soul's habitation, as Wilde assumed in the letter to Norton, but self-sufficient, abandoned to the elation of its own rhythmic coilings.

The Commencement march of Harvard graduates, some in sailor suits, some with "samples of their male children" in tow, seems to Brooke an Olympic celebration of physical power. The baseball players also participate in this reversion to an ancient world undisturbed by Christian condemnation of the body: they are attired, Brooke says, for gladiatorial combat. He is affronted because, in their knickerbockers and thick boots, they are overdressed, as if for football "rather than a summer game." The cheerleader at the game is another of Brooke's Dionysian dancers. The dancer makes images from his body; the cheerleader conducts a crowd with it, "passionate, possessed by a demon, bounding in the frenzy of his inspiration from side to side, contorted, rhythmic, ecstatic." But his hysteria is episodic and rationed, which makes it peculiarly American. Like those commercial travelers in the Broadway hotel, who alternate between spasms of activity and hours of stupor, or like the neon lady with her series of winks punctuated by darkness, the cheerleader is wild but intermittently so. Every five or ten minutes he goes through his dervish-like antics, but between bouts of triumph sits placidly on the sideline awaiting his next cue. Brooke considers this contradiction to be "wonderfully American" because Americans are both agitated and idle, and switch from one state to the other automatically, dispensing with intermediaries, rejoicing equally in the body's dynamism and its inertia, its paroxysms and (as if postcoitally) its repose.

Arnold Bennett had been to America the year before Brooke, and he also describes a baseball game, but he interprets the spectacle differently. Bennett the excluded provincial (his father was a draper and pawnbroker at the time of Arnold's birth, in what is now the charred and derelict city of Stoke-on-Trent) craves the privileges of inside knowledge. Bennett affected membership in a society in which he didn't belong by memorizing its habits and by coveting its luxuries—yachts, fast cars, opulent hotel suites. He adores his own celebrity because it is a reassurance of acceptance, and his account of his American visit, *Those United States* (ingratiatingly retitled for the American market *Your United States*), published in 1912, smugly records the fuss which his hosts made about him. Brooke, as James's preface regrets, prided himself on knowing no one in New York, because social exclusion confers on him the freedom to transform the place into imagery: his is a poet's New York, a place of gaudy dazzling surfaces, not the interior city of social relations which a novelist must know. Bennett, however, describing the baseball game in New York, takes care to make each detail a covert boast of the privileged status he enjoys as an honorary insider in a foreign city. It is of course a championship game; he is taken as the guest of rich friends; and is driven there at speed in an express automobile. From within his pampered fortress, he surveys the milling of the less fortunate mob. At the stadium he complacently notes "the excellent arrangements for dealing with feverish multitudes." During the game he preens himself on his knowing astuteness. The unintelligibility of its games is one of the final defenses of any society against aliens. The English remain unwilling to explain the procedures of cricket to bemused foreigners; but the Englishman abroad finds himself at a loss with baseball, which is a tribal rite he cannot comprehend. Brooke solves this problem by breezily simplifying it. He is in any case only interested in aesthetic admiration, not in understanding, and he says that "baseball is a good game to watch." If it must be understood, it is best approached on the analogy of a children's game: Brooke therefore calls it "merely glorified rounders." However, Bennett's desire is to participate, not to gaze from a wistful distance, and he declares himself instantly able to fathom the rules. He studies the proper repertory of barracking cries, and learns to pass informed judgment on the play. So determined is he to insert himself into this confraternity, to acquire an identity by behaving with impeccable conformity, that he remarks "I did what everybody else did and even attacked a morsel of chewing-gum."

Judging the players, Bennett emphasizes technique and its precision, not, like Brooke, callisthenic grace. Brooke's pitcher is a faun, Bennett's a technocrat. Bennett has been told that the players "follow the law and other liberal professions" out of season, which means they are not Brooke's children of nature but trained and business-like specialists, less athletes than engineers who have "carried the art of pitching a ball to a more wondrous degree of perfection than it has ever been carried in cricket." Bennett considers "the absolute certitude of the fielding and accuracy of the throwing . . . profoundly impressive to a connoisseur," managing to compliment the players while praising his own slick acumen. The players are praised by Bennett their fellow celebrity, who is gratified to learn that "in the matter of expenses they were treated more liberally than the ambassadors of the Republic." In contrast with the pitcher's lithe elongation of line which thrills Brooke, Bennett finds the game inelegant, and criticizes the dowdy unshaven ground on which it is played. Brooke formalizes sport into dance, but Bennett envenoms it into warfare: he is distressed by the brutality of college football, which is too ferociously competitive, as if intended as a training for the vicious acquisitive careers to which its players will graduate. It is no longer playful because it is too crassly determined to "get results."

Brooke's elegant athletes change in H. G. Wells into regressive brutes. In *The Work, Wealth and Happiness of Mankind*, Wells decries the sportsman for being obsessed with "the extreme exploitation of his neuro-muscular system" and neglecting the responsibilities of mind. Whereas Wilde thought the gymnasium the center of Harvard, the place where its sound minds exhibited their symmetrically sound bodies, Wells deplores the sporting infatuation of American universities. Claims for the educational value of sport are, he argues, no more than a cynical cover for academic treason. The scholars have given way to the demands of their richer and more clamorous pupils, and make good their loss by pretending that games are of some benefit to the mind. American universities, which ought to be laboratories experimentally shaping Wells's lucid, cerebral future, have at least in part converted themselves into "athletic training centres." The coach, often no more than a jumped-up masseur, is promoted to equality with the professor, and the stadium supplants the library. Intellectual life, Wells says, is "devastated." Brooke finds in his athletes a liberation of animal spirits which are lissome, feline, and harmless, but for Wells those same animal spirits are violent and latently criminal. Rich Americans play games; their social inferiors, also seeking to ventilate an excess of energy, begin as bully-boys and end as gangsters. The American Indians are for Wells a warning that sport leads to an evolutionary dead end: "the American Indian was so great a sportsman that he subordinated all the rest of his life to the exaltation of the warpath." For Brooke though, the Indians are a race of Roman nobles, complementing the Greek athletes who are his American young men. Greece is the classical land of youth, Rome of sober age, and on a Canadian reservation in the Rockies Brooke remarks that the older men "have wonderful dignity and beauty of face and body" and a superb physique, with "features shaped and lined by weather and experience into a Roman nobility that demands respect." The corruption of the race is signified, for Brooke, by their compromise with trousers. He is dismayed by "a Canadianised young Indian in trousers, who spat." To wear trousers (adjusting Mrs. Trollope's standards to aestheticism) is as off-putting as to spit. Brooke hopes that the Indians will not be overborne by "that ugliness of shops and trousers with which we enchain the earth."

As Brooke leaves the inhabited East of America and crosses the continent through the Canadian wilderness, he shifts from a sport like baseball, which is formal and social, as much governed by rules as is polite conduct, toward swimming, which is neither ceremonial nor competitive but simply projects the body into the element of water and relishes the sensations of immersion. He watches campers running toward the beaches of Lake Superior "in various deshabille," and later sums up the experience of the Canadian forests by recalling the pleasures of the swimmer. Brooke was an enthusiastic skinny-dipper, who identified naked bathing with "the free life." This freedom flirts with destruction—the swimmer has only his stroking limbs to keep him buoyant—and eventually embraces it. One of Brooke's 1914 sonnets, "Peace," describes the chivalric enthusiasm of recruits enlisting for the war by calling them "swimmers into cleanness leaping"; and his war poems are an anthem for the doomed youth which he sees sunning itself in America. Canada startles the body, Brooke says, like "the brisk touch of clear water as you dive," with a freshness which first shocks the nerves then braces them. As one whose body is a connoisseur of different waters, he contrasts this "unseizable virginity" with the languors of "bathing in a warm Southern sea" or the grateful refreshment of "a river in a hot climate," with the alienness of the ocean and the mere frigidity of icy water. The experience of the continent proves itself on the naked flesh. This sensation, "and none of sight and hearing," according to Brooke, is the token of Canada.

The tour reaches its sensuous destination in Samoa, where the intellect drowses while the body slithers free for "a life of swimming and climbing and resting after exertion." Floating in tepid lagoons, titillated by the tickling currents of water which support him, Brooke wishes that the white man could grow into equality with the "glorious golden-brown" natives by learning "to *be* his body (and so his true mind)." This reconciliation of mental division and social diversion has been transferred from exhausted, self-destructive Europe across frenetic America to the South Seas. Brooke's is a renunciatory journey, traveling through civilization to bid it farewell. Its shape therefore contrasts with those cautious, circular excursions of the Victorians, edging into the American vacancy but swiftly returning home. Brooke too returned to Europe, but only to die. Wilde's intentions had been similar to Brooke's: one of his projects was to travel on from America to Japan. However, Wilde's imaginary Japan was a different place from Brooke's Polynesia. The one is an intricate civilization in which feudalism enforces a code of rigorous courtly artifice, the other a tribal release from the evasions and constraints of civilization. Aestheticism, which in Wilde is an inverted evangelicism, hoping to civilize America by introducing into it the wickedness of art, in Brooke verges on a primitivistic rejection both of civility and of art. Brooke likes America because it is so paradisially pristine and, as he says of the Rockies, so "irrelevant to humanity."

From now on, America's emptiness and (for Kipling) even its unkempt crudity are the authentications of its unique freedom. Wyndham Lewis in 1949 called modern America a "wholly excellent vacuum," where the lonely ego can feel exhilaratingly unattached among anonymous crowds of uprooted strangers. In their different ways, Wilde and the Victorian novelists were trying to load America with accomplishments, to improve its manners and reform its institutions; Brooke's is the first modern imaginative appreciation of the country because it joyfully discerns in America not social accoutrement or complication of detail but irrelevance, irresponsibility, absence.

4

EPIC (AND CHIVALRIC) AMERICA
Rudyard Kipling
Robert Louis Stevenson

Ever since Homer's account of the fashioning of Achilles' weapons, epic has been an image of industrial process. It does not imitate the decorative surfaces of things, but dramatizes their manufacture. Novels describe the leisure of society: the refinements of private life and emotional association. Epic describes the work of society: the creation of wealth which subsidizes that novelistic leisure. This is why America is such a problem for the Victorian novelists, because its obsession with work censures idleness and with it the cultivation of mental privacy which makes the novel possible. Hence Henry James's coyness about the sources of that fairy gold which frees his characters for their lives of luxurious speculation and emotional intrigue: the article manufactured in the Massachusetts factory in *The Ambassadors* can never be named. Writing about the social season at Newport in 1870, James made it a rule that "a society that does nothing is decidedly more pictorial, more interesting to the eye of contemplation, than a society which is hard at work"; and an otiose society like Newport is for this reason suited to the leisurely introverted investigation of the novel. Wilde's aesthetic America is equally averse to work: in 1882, also writing from Newport, he called Rhode Island "this little island where idleness ranks among the virtues."

If the novel withdraws into indolence and superfluity, the epic pledges itself to industriousness and activism. This is why it acclimatizes itself in America, where epic changes from a martial to an industrial form. The whaling technology in *Moby-Dick* or the crafts and terminology of fishing in Kipling's *Captains Courageous* make epic from the economic spoliation of nature. The novel is feminine, the epic masculine. James at Newport says that women everywhere are "the animating element of 'society'," and they are therefore the benign genii of the novel. Epic excludes them. There are no women on Robinson Crusoe's island, on Ahab's whaler, or on the fishing boat in *Captains Courageous*. James described the American businessman as a democratic latter-day version of the epic hero, "seamed all over with the wounds of the market and the dangers of the field," and this description suits both the fisherman Disko Troop and the railway magnate Cheyne in *Captains Courageous*. But, alarmed by the belligerent commercial heroism of the male, James seeks the intervention of the female. She cannot exist in epic, but presides instead over the novel, and he chooses to emphasize "the unique relation" of the businessman to "his lawful, his immitigable womankind," because his wives and daughters are "his social substitutes and representatives." They redeem him by reclaiming him from the commercial affray, winning him back from rude epic to the domestic civility of the novel.

Despite James's misgivings, other critics at the end of the nineteenth century were pleased that the novel was returning from feminine passivity and inert subjectivity to the masculine values of strife, stress, and successful action. Conan Doyle called the boys' books of Robert Louis Stevenson examples of "the modern masculine novel, dealing almost exclusively with the rougher, more stirring side of life, with the objective rather than the subjective," and Joseph Conrad praised Captain Marryat for removing his characters from the insidious artifice of society and isolating them "between water and sky." The masculine epic work refuses the temptation of love, which Victorian novelists had employed to seduce their heroes from the public world into a cloistered emotional privacy. Conan

Doyle suggested that this kind of fiction was "a reaction against the abuse of love," and Kipling, when negotiating the sale of film rights to *Captains Courageous,* was careful to inquire if the work was to be supplied with a love interest. The film magnate said of course it would be, and Kipling at once reduced love from an emotional to a biological event, remarking that "a happily-married lady cod-fish lays about three million eggs at one confinement." The love which intrudes into the film of *Captains Courageous* is, however, aptly pederastic. Kipling's plot is distorted to make way for a fatal romance between Manuel (Spencer Tracy, improbably impersonating a Portuguese tar) and the adolescent Harvey Cheyne (played as a petulant Fauntleroy by Freddie Bartholemew). Harvey is jealously incensed when Manuel admits to liking girls, and forces him to make a retraction; after Manuel's death, he abandons himself to tearful despair, praying that he may be Manuel's dory-mate in heaven.

The original hero of industrial epic is Robinson Crusoe, who cannot be a novelistic character because on his island there is no society, but who sets about the epic task of constructing an economic order for himself. Crusoe naturally translated himself to the American frontier. Mrs. Trollope, visiting a forest farm outside Cincinnati, remarks on "the entire dependence of the inhabitants upon their own resources." They stitch their own clothes, manufacture their own soap and candles, and extract their own sugar from the trees. They need money only to exchange for coffee, tea, and whisky, and they earn it by bartering butter and chickens. "These people were indeed independent," Mrs. Trollope says, "Robinson Crusoe was hardly more so." But their self-reliance is to her a privation, since there is no society to contain or console them. She pities Crusoe as a miserable outlaw. Kipling, however, admires him. His father sent him a copy of the book while he was away at school, and he at once turned it (as he remembers in *Something of Myself*) into a manual for solitary employment. Like Crusoe, he seized on the random matter of the world in which he found himself and engineered it into shape: "my apparatus was a coconut shell strung on a red cord,

Spencer Tracy as Manuel and Freddie Bartholemew as Harvey in
Captains Courageous © 1937 Metro-Goldwyn-Mayer.
Reproduced by permission of Metro-Goldwyn-Mayer.
Courtesy of National Film Archive/Stills Library, London.

a tin trunk, and a piece of packing-case which kept off any other world. Thus fenced about, everything inside the fence was quite real." Crusoe's constructive arts are defensive, as Kipling realizes. The encampment or stockade keeps out an area of mystery or threat. The solitary child behaves like a settler in the American West inside a ring of wagons, barricaded off from an empty but hostile nature, or like the adult Kipling, building his house in Vermont. The Crusoesque construction of this house is described later in the memoir. Kipling has to measure dimensions, excavate a basement to keep out skunks, dynamite rocks to clear a drive to the road, dig a shaft through the granite as a water conduit, and install an atmospheric pump. He learns from the experience, like Defoe's character, a fondness for "playing with timber, stone, concrete and such delightful things."

As a writer, Kipling is also a laborer, a pen-pusher who depends on his tools and is grateful for their serviceable sturdiness. In *Something of Myself* he mentions his change from hand-dipped pens with Waverley nibs to a time-saving fountain pen as if it were a scriptorial version of the industrial revolution. He is strict about ink and paper because these are the ingredients of his books, and the books themselves are industrial products whose integrity he as their manufacturer guarantees: he vows that he uses only the blackest ink, never insipid blue-black, and custom-built blocks of paper "of large, off-white, blue sheets." It would be no surprise if he affixed to a book a label asserting it to be hand made. The content of epic is industrial and the process of its manufacture, as Kipling's comments on his implements imply, is just as virtuously laborious.

The epic hero has his opponents. H. G. Wells in *The Shape of Things To Come* (1933) derides Crusoe as economically implausible and socially irresponsible. He denies that a man alone can accomplish even the simplest of social operations. The food grower can't make his own tools or select the most fruitful seeds and plants, and "Defoe's queer story of Robinson Crusoe is an impossibly hopeful estimate of what a single man . . . could on a desert island contrive to do for his own comfort and security." Men, in Wells's reckoning, must depend on one another and submit to the division of their labors, and America alarmed him because its economic individualism impeded social collaboration. Economic stupidity such as Wells attacked in Crusoe goes with aesthetic slovenliness. Henry James, writing to Wells from Cambridge, Mass., in 1911, denied that *Robinson Crusoe* was a novel, because the autobiographical form is too indulgent toward "the loose, the improvised, the cheap and the easy." Crusoe's art, that is, is the slipshod and tacky equivalent of his bourgeois commercialism.

But whereas Wells believes that Crusoe inhibits social adhesion and mental maturity, for Kipling, Crusoe's value is his exclusion from society; and while Wells's polemical essays persuade Americans to limit their greedy individualism and become members of a compassionate, cooperative society, and greet Roosevelt's New Deal as an augury of this enlightened state, Kipling wants to unmake America, to fragment a novelistic society into an epic agglomerate of antagonistic self-dependent tribes. Kipling's first experience of America was in the summer of 1889 when, at the age of twenty-four, he traveled across the continent from west to east. He arrived from India, where he had been working as a journalist, with a commission to send travel essays back to the Allahabad *Pioneer*. These sketches, collected in *From Sea to Sea*, describe an unsettled, unlettered America, a place which because it is not yet a society can provide the setting for an epic. They conclude, appropriately, with a visit to Mark Twain, one of the writers of that masculine epic alternative to the novel suggested by the brutal conditions of the country.

The Americans Kipling encounters are all noisily patriotic, but their asseverations that "I am an American by birth—an American from way back" only serve to alert him to the fragility of their connection with the land. He remarks that "it must be an awful thing to live in a country where you have to explain that you really belong there." The American is not native but adoptive, a foundling; he doesn't inherit a patrial identity but has to earn it. America is a root less, emigrant tribe, and only by self-congratulatory bragging does it hold itself together. Kipling understands this defensiveness because he shares it. He writes not as an Englishman but as an ersatz Indian (he was born in Bombay, where his father was a crafts instructor at the Jeejeebhoy School of Art), having elected to assume an identity other than the one assigned to him by birth. Citizenship is a moral qualification, maintained by constant, denunciatory vigilance. At Yellowstone, a German Jew, anxious to establish his own claim to membership in America, reviles England, and when Kipling ignores these taunts accuses him of being no patriot. Later an American asks him if he intends to make expiation for his profiteering business activities in America by taking out naturalization papers. Kipling replies that in England a man can live unperturbed by inquiries about whether he is a British subject or a child of the devil. The jingoistic smugness which disgusts Kipling on the fourth of July is uneasy self-assurance. Americans are struggling to constitute a society by "patriotic exercises." The individual's nervous suspicion of his own unreality is connected with the society's shiftiness, so that people cleave to an identity by attaching themselves to a locality. Kipling is intrigued by the American habit of nicknaming individuals after the states they come from, which turns territorial jealousy into the self-defense of a rebarbative, insecure individuality.

There can be no community because there is no language to cement it. Societies have a language, but tribes have only dialects, which are mutually unintelligible. "A Frenchman is French," Kipling says, "because he speaks his own language; but the American has no language. He is dialect, slang, provincialism, accent, and so forth." Even this tribal integrity has been outraged. Kipling identifies a black waiter as "a Yoruba man," but he is a Yoruba who wears trousers and does "his thinking in English." As the American has no language, so "he has no meals. He stuffs for ten minutes thrice a day." The earlier Victorians had found Americans unmannerly because inelegant; Kipling finds them savage. Their drunkenness has a similar significance. It is an offense against society, because the

American respects no proper drinking hours or drinking occasions but swills regardless; and in its instant stimulation of joviality or aggressiveness, it is a substitute for society and its relationships. The drinker sedates or ignites himself alcoholically, and thus conducts his emotional life without needing to enlist human companionship.

Since Americans submit to no social rule, they can't discriminate between public matters and the sequestered private existence. A Baptist commercial traveler, whose merchandise is biscuits, tells Kipling how religion has consoled him on the death of his wife, speaking "with the artless freedom than an American generally exhibits when he is talking about his most sacred private affairs." Kipling's Victorian predecessors had made this same objection, but with a different purpose. They were offended by an institutional irregularity: American homes are not private enough, and American cities are not public enough. Kipling's concern is anthropological, not bureaucratic: America hasn't assumed a social form, so it cannot distribute tasks and characters to the human beings it contains, who in consequence don't know the difference between private emotion and public interest. America has undergone no rite of socialization. The same failure to adjudicate between separate activities prompts false claims for American versatility. Kipling mentions a notoriety-hunting preacher who performed a marriage in a balloon. The ambidextrous versatility of the American is to Kipling an anarchic, spendthrift dissipation of resources. Instead of learning "the inwardness of an employ" by apprenticing himself to a single craft, the American wantonly experiments with a variety, which means that all his work is makeshift. He lays railway lines carelessly, and causes fatal accidents. The complexity of social relations which their country lacks Americans have hoped to supply by extending themselves, each one performing a repertory of different roles. Kipling wants to imprison them tribally in single specialisms, to limit their dangerous flexibility, to deprive them of a social freedom they are tentatively creating for themselves. He reproves the "unlimited exercise of private judgment," which he identifies with the slovenly restlessness of

American deportment: this same cocksure carelessness, he says, makes the American "crawl all over the furniture when he is talking to you."

To Henry James, America fits itself for treatment by the novel because of its decadent economics. Money exists not as a token of work or even as a means of exchange but as a sinecure of leisure. James welcomes the idleness of Newport because it signifies "the somewhat alien presence of leisure." Money creates society by furnishing time and enjoyment, and the virtue of Newport for the novelist is that "nowhere else . . . does business seem so remote, so vague, and unreal," even though it is business which sustains this idyll of affluence. In Kipling's America, on the contrary, economics is regressive. Money doesn't stabilize society, but disorders it. Economic uncertainties and the fluctuations of capitalistic fortune recreate for Americans the buoyant fatalism which primitive societies learn from their exposure to the elements. The rich admit the possibility that they may lose their wealth overnight. San Francisco captivates Kipling because of its general awareness of "possible disaster," which excites recklessness. Economic chance prohibits people from settling into society and accustoming themselves to their position, because it "delights in making the miner or the lumberman a quadruplicate millionaire, and in 'busting' the railroad king." This fickleness of fortune warns of the savage beneath the business suit, the swamp beneath the city. Watching the crowds on Kearney Street, Kipling sees them as barbarians, despite their fine feathers, and the moneyed clubmen of the city atavistically enjoy reminiscing about the recent savage past when "the water came up to the foot of Market Street" and no man was suspect until "he had committed at least one unprovoked murder."

Since there is no social motive, communities have to be wired together technologically, held in place by invisible, ingenious machines. Kipling emphasizes the temporariness of San Francisco's planting in its landscape, pitched down on sand bunkers and reclaimed land. The "ragged unthrifty sand-hills" are "pegged down by houses." This geological infirmity is an image of the flimsiness of social impositions on the earth's unsteady and untrustworthy surface. Fastened by the houses, these unreliable hills are wired internally by the cable cars. Society is a lie, because it depends on machines whose workings are tactfully concealed. The cable cars seem to scale their altitudes by magic, because the secret of their operations is guarded from view. Occasionally you "pass a five-storey building, humming with machinery that winds up an everlasting wire-cable, and the initiated will tell you that here is the mechanism." Kipling interprets the efficiency of the cars as a mechanical admission of social defeat. Society has failed to combat the natural obstacles which confront it, and invents a machine to circumvent them. "From an English point of view," he says, "there has not been the least attempt at grading those hills. . . . The cable-cars have for all practical purposes made San Francisco a dead level." A cheap, evasive, technical miracle has eased the natural, invigorating antagonism between man and his surroundings.

The novel is about man's enmeshment in society, the lyric about his incorporation in nature. Neither form is possible in Kipling's America. Society is nonexistent, a mere mechanical pretense, and nature is inimical. But Kipling does discover a literary form appropriate to the place: epic, which is made from man's battle against the inflictions of nature.

The impossibility of a lyrical trust in nature is first asserted by the subsiding sand hills of San Francisco and confirmed by the appalling emptiness of the prairies, which defy men to feel anything for them but an unremitting tedium which sickens into fear. In Kipling's West, men are driven mad by the dazing vacancy of space. At Pasco Junction, he reflects that a sailor sleeping with a thin plank between him and a watery death is secure in comparison with those unaccommodated settlers who have only a "frail scantling, almost as thin as a blanket, to shut out the immeasurable loneliness of the sage." The plains are a featureless ocean; and in Vermont, Kipling's own house rode on its hillside like a boat "on the flank of a far wave," its lights a meager comfort to remote householders. Kipling finds in Vermont the same unbearable solitude which twists into insanity. The farmers on their sterile, denuded land are both cheated of a rational social existence and driven back into themselves by a harsh and grudging nature, so that "what might have become characters, powers and attributes perverted themselves" and twined into religious mania. "Strange faiths and cruelties" flourish there "like lichen on sick bark." Kipling describes his neighbors in *Something of Myself* as a race of exiguous Crusoes, protecting themselves from the derangement of their solitude by organizing boredom into a domestic routine. Crusoe in desperation made himself industrious in order to pass the time; the stranded householders in Vermont solace an "immense and unacknowledged boredom" by erecting defenses against empty space, putting up fly screens or unfreezing their water pipes, busily acquiring material possessions but failing to find contentment in them.

Because Kipling is unmaking America, reducing society to a precarious encampment, and regressing from the furnished, domesticated territory of the novel to the outdoor exposure of epic, it is appropriate that he should, on this first visit to America in 1889, have crossed the continent from west to east. In doing so he was reversing what H. G. Wells saw as the progressive logic of history. Wellsian technology thrusts across America from east to west: the railways and the telegraph made possible the westward expansion of civilization, as Wells argues in his *History of the World,* pressing toward the Pacific coast and subduing the bleak infinity of Kipling's open spaces into a scientific unity. Cheyne the railway magnate in *Captains Courageous* makes the continental crossing from west to east in his private train; in 1907 Kipling and his wife made the journey in the opposite direction, following the Wellsian arc of progress. After he collected an honorary degree from McGill University, they made a triumphal tour overland to Vancouver, in a private car (like Cheyne) provided by the Canadian Pacific Railroad. By 1907 Kipling had become the laureate of empire, and on that journey he was faithful to the impetus of empire, which moves from east to west. The philosopher Berkeley, who lived in Rhode Island from 1728 to 1731 planning to found a college in the New World, and who gives his name to a university city at the far limit of the continent, had declared this to be the direction of history in "Verses on the Prospect of Planting Arts and Learning in America" (1726): "Westward the course of empire takes its way." Wells's railways are the advance guard of technological empire, and Kipling in 1907 traveled in imperial style on the railway, pausing to address groups of loyalists in each major city. But the journey of 1889 is savagely regressive, not triumphal. Rather than proceeding from the settled East to the western outposts, it begins on the brawling, temporary frontier—begins indeed subterraneanly, as Kipling witnesses a murder in a den of fiends "deep down under the earth" in the Chinese quarter of San Francisco—and suffers across the emptiness of the plains toward the edge of society in Chicago.

Chicago ought to be a destination, since it marks the perimeter of society. Actually Kipling finds it to be a pestilential abattoir, even more primitive than the frontier on which he began, a settlement of scavenging butchers. He appraises it like a visiting missionary, assessing the numbers of inhabitants to be salvaged for the faith or consigned to perdition: Chicago "holds rather more than a million people with bodies, and stands on the same sort of soil as Calcutta." The Chicagoans are equipped with bodies but do not aspire to the dignity of souls. A style of ill-tempered reduction refuses to accredit Chicago as a society and traduces it as a foul tribal wilderness: it "stands on the same sort of soil as Calcutta. . . . It is inhabited by savages. Its water is the water of the Hughli, and its air is dirt." A deliberate obliquity, possible because Kipling is addressing the letters not to England but to India, allows him to treat American manners as heathen fetishes and American localities as blasted deserts. He proceeds by omission, sanitarily refusing to inspect detail (as when he is shown canals filled inspecifically "with untold abominations"). The result is to deny the society complexity. He simply states, with murderous brusqueness, "then I went out into the streets, which are long and flat and without end." Because the style censors close observation, it works as a vicious means of dissociation. Kipling says, for instance, "they told me to go to Palmer House, which is a gilded and mirrored rabbit-warren." People spit in its tessellated marble hall. He prefers not to avail himself of the benefit of a common language, and watches the hustle and babble uninquisitively. He ensures a double alienation from America by writing not as an Englishman but as an ersatz Indian, whose hygenic tribal habits make him recoil from the unclean horror of Chicago. India, he claims, has taught him to "distrust the orthodoxies of every right-thinking white man." He even refuses to admit a racial connection between himself and the vile throng of Americans, and remarks "I had never seen so many white people together," as if he were not one of them himself.

Crowds are reduced, as in his initial summary of Chicago, to bodies or to pigment; buildings (also by the suppression of detail) to grotesque piles or infested burrows: a cab driver conceives that "it was a good thing to huddle men together in fifteen layers, one atop of the other, and to dig holes in the ground for offices." The American regression is infantile as well as savage, for savagery is the race's infancy. Kipling therefore says that the American habit of boastful quantification, the numbering of assets and mass-produced articles, reminds him either of a child babbling of its hoard of shells or else of an idiot enumerating buttons. The inventive commercial American is no further advanced ethnologically than Adam, because he is a slave to his need to scratch for food. All evolution has done is to equip the American with the delusion, by which his hirsute forebears weren't embarrassed, that "palm-trees lead straight to the skies": he pitiably imagines that the scramble for provender is a drama of spiritual growth, not a low biological necessity.

Epic in Kipling is technological, and devotes itself either to maintaining defenses against nature (as with the do-it-yourself ingenuity of the Vermont householders among whom Kipling lived, digging wells, thawing pipes, screening out insects) or else to pillaging and despoiling nature (as with the fishermen of *Captains Courageous*). Therefore the only institution which interests him in Chicago is the stockyards, and these he considers to be a more coherent society than the human settlement: he calls the yards "a township of cattle-pens." Here is enacted a bestial and industrial parody of epic warfare. This city of savagery is given over to the carnage of the animal population: into one of the chambers are crowded "very nearly all the pigs ever bred in Wisconsin." The comportment and morale of the victims are differentiated according to the bellicose values of epic. The pigs are shamefully agitated and squeal pusillanimously; the cattle queue up with ruminant stoicism to die. A Texan steer officiates as epic chieftain, establishing discipline and exemplifying fortitude.

Kipling's is a deathly technology, declaring the victory of the sleek, unforgiving machine over panicky mortality. The western railways are described in earlier letters as instruments of slaughter. The train carrying Kipling nonchalantly kills bulls, cows, and horses in its way, and constantly risks sacrificing its passengers. Kipling suggests that the railway lines are allowed to cut across the main street of Omaha, Nebraska, because the abundance of accidents must benefit the local undertakers. The pigs in Chicago are dispatched on a thanatological railway, "an overhead arrangement of greased rail, wheel, and pulley," and Kipling himself is almost shunted along by this unpausing, undiscriminating belt. The pigs are the meek servants of the infernal machine which kills them. Their throats cut, swamped in boiling water, they wallow "in obedience to some unseen machinery," just as in San Francisco the cable cars had trundled up sheer hills in obedience to the uncoiling wires of their unseen machinery. Dismemberment is entrusted to a production line of twelve men, each of whom lops off "a certain amount of [the pig's] individuality." Cattle are disposed of with record-breaking efficiency. Five are slain in a minute, and each one is transformed from a steer to two halves of beef, decapitated, and carried off along an overhead rail, in half a minute. Technology refines slaughter into benign surgery: Kipling calls the abattoir an "operating-room." Nature has been improvingly obliterated by the machine. Dissected, unindividualized, the animals have been transformed into food but also into a ghastly kind of art, "very beautiful to behold."

Instead of looking, as Wells does, to a rational future in which this violence and rapacity will be brought under the tutelage of a state supervising the general welfare, Kipling confidently expects America to get worse. Rather than coalescing into a society, America will, he predicts, further fragment as disgruntled factions compete for shares of its diminishing natural resources. America will remain an epic archipelago of warring tribes because the future will foment trouble between those tribes. Kipling predicts the emergence of a society convulsed by internecine strife. When the land no longer crops like Eden and needs expensive stimulants, the farmers will protest against the profiteering of the manufacturers of fertilizer. Agriculture by then will no longer be plentiful enough to justify the cost of protection against imports. Americans will soon be unable to continue casually looting nature, and the government will have to establish a Woods and Forest Department which, Kipling foresees, the manglers and burners of timber will resist. Other challenges, further decomposing society, can be expected from the blacks, the industrialists, and the railway interests. The energy of this antisocial atavism is eternal delight to Kipling. Against it the only recourse is the vindictiveness of machines, insidiously organizing (as the cable cars do) or randomly annihilating (as at the stockyards) the boisterous muddle of human discontent.

Kipling's journey in 1889 reveals America to be an epic society, hard pressed by the challenges of nature, not a novelistic society able to afford refinements of manners and morals. The destination of that journey is therefore a meeting with one of the writers of American epic, Samuel Clemens (Mark Twain), and this interview is itself presented by Kipling as a cross-country epic pursuit. He tracks Clemens from Buffalo to Elmira, New York, then asks after relatives who are not to be found, and hires a cab to drive to the outlying home of Clemens's in-laws only to discover that he has just left. He bounds down the hill in pursuit of him, and their eventual encounter anticipates one of Harvey Cheyne's proud catches on the fishing boat in *Captains Courageous*: "that was a moment to be remembered; the landing of a twelve-pound salmon was nothing to it. I had hooked Mark Twain." The skill which Harvey learns aboard the boat is his qualification for membership in the epic fraternity of fishermen. Kipling here deploys that skill in advance, and against a writer who gruffly and ungovernably embodies the epic.

He approaches Clemens with the ceremoniousness due to a monarch. The unacknowledged legislator of mankind is not a politician or a poet but a novelist and, rightly in this epic version of America, a novelist who disdains the novel. Clemens doesn't care, he tells Kipling, for "fiction or storybooks. What I like to read about are facts and statistics of any kind." The epic of America is statistical, a prodigal numerosity. Clemens's preference marks the rough primitivism of the country: "Get your facts first, and then you can distort 'em as you please." Epic is about the aboriginal facts, the harsh first principles of subduing nature in order to make a country habitable. The novel comes later, at the same time as the fanciful distortions, and embroiders social comforts which don't yet exist in epic. Clemens, praising facts, refuses to recognize imagination, because America is too young and vital to need it. He has the child's consuming interest in factual and technical detail which underlies Kipling's interpretation of Crusoe and the epic house-building in Vermont described in *Something of Myself*.

Clemens describes his own early career to Kipling, and in doing so he exhibits an epic dexterity of craftsmanship. Like Crusoe, he has a multiplicity of skills. His artistic training has been the experience of working in a variety of jobs. The writer of epic, like the hero of epic, must undertake an apprenticeship—Crusoe on his island, Melville's Ishmael on the whaler, Harvey Cheyne on the fishing boat. Kipling prepared himself for *Captains Courageous* by learning, just as his hero has to do, how to make surgical incisions in cod fish, by helping on tugboats which hauled schooners around the harbor in Boston, by studying the implements of navigation, even by consuming "queer meals in sailors' eating-houses." Prescribing for himself the same arduous initiation to which he submits his hero, Kipling ventures "out on a pollock-fisher, which is ten times fouler than any cod-schooner," and is "immortally sick." Clemens likewise has worked at a series of jobs, scattered across the continental expanse of America, so that his polymathic epic training is also an epic exploration of the country: "He has been journeyman-printer (in those days he wandered from the banks of the Missouri even to Philadelphia), pilot-cub and full-blown pilot, soldier of the South . . . private secretary to a Lieutenant-Governor of Nevada . . . special correspondent in the Sandwich Islands, and the Lord only knows what else." Coleridge thought that the poet preparing himself for the composition of an epic should equip himself with a universal education in the arts and sciences, philosophy and religion: he must settle down to an encyclopedic acquisition of knowledge, and Clemens indeed when Kipling arrives had been reading an encyclopedia entry on mathematics. Kipling changes the induction from scholarship to labor: the writer of epic limbers up by doing everything except literary work.

Because America industrializes epic, creation is now conceived as manufacture. Clemens's conversation is therefore concerned with the relations between literary creativity and the economic creation of wealth. He discusses the issue of international copyright, which treats a writer's books as his goods, and he even identifies literary property with real estate. Tom Sawyer is his invention, a commercial novelty which he has patented and in which he owns all rights. This makes him reluctant to talk about the possibility of a sequel, because that is a private matter of craft. Kipling at first declares that Tom Sawyer "belongs to us," as if Clemens had willed the character to his readers, but learns to respect the inventor's exclusivity about his product as Clemens expands "on the rights of a man to do what he liked with his own creations, which being a matter of purely professional interest, I will mercifully omit." The professional colloquy isn't protected because it is a precious confabulation of aesthetes. Rather it is a tribal rite, the final stage in Kipling's regressive journey back through American history, for it converts him at last into an honorary savage: he smokes two cigars with Clemens, as if at an Indian ceremony of pipe passing, and he covets his colleague's cob pipe, understanding "why certain savage tribes ardently desired the liver of brave men slain in combat." In Kipling's personal epic, even a professional chat becomes surrogate warfare.

At the beginning of this chapter, Conan Doyle's commendation of Robert Louis Stevenson was mentioned. Stevenson, like Kipling, had converted the novel into an epic form, transferring it from feminine subjectivity to a masculine relish for "the rougher, more stirring side of life." Stevenson's experience of America belongs with Kipling's in an account of this change. He was there a decade before Kipling, in 1879, traveling in love-sick pursuit of a married woman, Fanny Osbourne. They had met in 1876 in an artists' colony at Grez, in the Barbizon region of France. He had escaped from the practice of law in Edinburgh, she had escaped from a scapegrace, shiftless husband, who remained behind in San Francisco. They fell in love, and stayed together until Fanny's husband withdrew his financial support and forced her to return to California. In August 1879, a year after they had parted, she cabled for Stevenson to come to her. He left at once, and traveled from Scotland to Monterey in California, where Fanny was recuperating from an illness, ruining his own health in his haste to reach her. Eventually in 1880 she relieved herself of Osbourne and married Stevenson. After the wedding they left for Silverado, an abandoned silver mine in the mountains north of San Francisco. Here, in a derelict cabin, they spent their honeymoon, and late in the summer, when Stevenson's health seemed to have been restored, they returned to Scotland. The torments of his journey to California on an emigrant ship and a congested, fetid emigrant train Stevenson recorded in *The Amateur Emigrant*; the honeymoon in the ghost town is described in a second essay, *The Silverado Squatters.*

If the test of epic is its misogyny, its exclusion of women (who represent the enfeebling comforts of society and the leisure of introspection), Stevenson's knight-errantry in the service of Fanny belongs to a quite different literary world from Kipling's. Kipling's journey across America has the shape of epic, Stevenson's of romance. Kipling is an epic activist, apprenticing himself to the hardships of nature, Stevenson a chivalric quester chasing a fancy. Kipling's epic characters are persecuted by nature, and they struggle to survive against its opposition. Stevenson belongs not in embattled epic but in vagrant, self-indulgent, digressive romance. His journey is as gratuitously idealistic as Kipling's is urgent and atavistic. Stevenson's titles admit the element of chivalric imposture: as an emigrant he is an amateur, and at Silverado he fatuously squats in a landscape of desolation which is not the picturesque ruin he expected.

Stevenson calls the emigration of the impoverished European masses to America a "great epic of self-help," but he uses the word to flatter a less pleasing reality. Everywhere in Stevenson's America, images come to the aid of a truth which, without their cozening, would be unbearable, and this is so with his invocation of epic. The term derives an aesthetic consolation from social defeat. The emigrants are the victims of privation, but the reference to epic turns their ignominious retreat from Europe into an optimistic advance. The pretense is a frail one. Stevenson concedes that epic is a title for the mass which is hardly deserved by individual emigrants, whom he finds to be grumbling and boorish; and as he edges further into America, virile epic falters into wistful romance. America expands itself not, as in Kipling, by desperate exertion but by effortless magic: "vast cities . . . grow up as by enchantment," and, having flourished, molder into abject decay, like Silverado. Stevenson's fellow passengers on the emigrant train are all hastening toward a fabled El Dorado. For Kipling, the ghost towns of the West symbolize the theoretical bravura of pioneer planning, making abstract choices of location wherever railway lines intersect and abandoning the site when economic trends change. They are free of the sentiment of place, and the bleak refusal of the settlers to be intimidated by their surroundings makes these towns heroic. But for Stevenson the ghost towns are solacing evidence that social and economic change is inexplicable and agreeably motiveless. San Francisco itself is the product of a shaky illusory miracle, not of vigorous prosperity, and is best described by a reference to romance: "what enchantment of the Arabian Nights can have equalled this evocation of a roaring city, in a few years of a man's life, from the marshes and the blowing sands." San Francisco is not built but evoked, conjured up.

During his crossing of the continent Stevenson often refers to the competition between epic and romance. The western railways are an "epical turmoil," and the engineers exhibit a heroism rivaling that of "Troytown," but Stevenson makes epic dwindle into whimsical romance when he recalls that the railways after all are run not by energetic paramilitary tycoons like Cheyne in *Captains Courageous* but by "gentlemen in frock-coats" accumulating riches with the effete intention of affording a visit to Paris. A Homer is necessary, Stevenson says, to describe the West, but that Homer will turn out to be a writer of mellifluous romance not belligerent epic. Stevenson is ravished by the "sweet and romantic vocables" of western place-names and, repeating them to himself, reflects that the new Homer will find waiting for him a continent in which even geography is lyrical: "his verse will be enriched, his pages sing spontaneously, with the names of states and cities that would strike the fancy in a business circular." Places are resolved into the weirdly melodious names they've been given. Whereas Kipling decomposes society and language into a chaos of slangs, dialects, and specialized technical vocabularies, Stevenson, commenting on place names, finds their polyglot confusion "rich, poetical, humorous, and picturesque," like the piquant incongruity which places Pekin in the same state as

Euclid or makes Chelsea a suburb of Memphis. Even when place names suggest a linguistic atavism, Stevenson turns the buried stratum of meaning into something decoratively antique, as in his commentary on the Indian word Manhattan: "old, red Manhattan lies, like an Indian arrowhead under a steam factory, below Anglified New York."

Crusoe, who for Kipling is an honorary American because of his epic hardihood and his improvisatory industrial skills, changes in Stevenson to a romantic recluse. Crossing Ohio, he disbelieves "the anxiety of Robinson Crusoe and others to escape from uninhabited islands," and adds, "just you put me on an uninhabited island . . . and then we'll see!" Americans share the condition of Crusoe or of Adam, since on the frontier each of them can seem the first and only man in the world, but rather than setting to work (as Kipling prescribes) to fabricate shelters and subdue nature they linger over their poetic prerogative of inventing delicious names for things. Stevenson says that "as when Adam with divine fitness names the creatures, so this word Susquehanna was at once accepted by the fancy." The empty spaces of America, for Kipling a deranging horror, are for Stevenson merely decor, "wall-paper with a vengeance—one quarter of the universe laid bare in all its gauntness," as he says of the Nebraska plains. In Kipling the settlers run mad in the vacancy, but in Stevenson they suffer a debility of vision which derives from aesthetic revulsion. There is, he notes, "a sickness of vision peculiar to these plains," because the eye is offended by having nothing to look at.

America generally abets the fond hopes of imagination. Its sunrises, Stevenson discovers, are not clear gold as in Europe but livid and effulgent like sunsets, belonging to "some subsequential, evening epoch of the world, as though America were in fact, and not merely in fancy, farther from the orient of Aurora and the springs of day." Where America affronts the imagination, it is saved from itself by being complicated and distorted. Stevenson considers "the simplicity of a decimal coinage . . . revolting to the human mind," so he sympathizes with the ingenious circumlocution whereby sums are calculated in terms of a coin which no longer exists, the bit or Mexican real. Thus mental arithmetic can become an imaginative game, juggling with values which are merely presumptive.

But if prosaic America proves too obdurate, the imagination won't scruple to destroy it in order to make it lovable. Stevenson declares that "a place does not clearly exist for the imagination, till we have moved elsewhere." Nor, his literary practice suggests, does the imagination approve it until it has been ruined. Hence his response to the destructive instability of Californian nature. Discussing the San Francisco earthquake, Kipling sees it as a summons to human resilience, which instantly rebuilds the shattered town. But Stevenson treats it as a benign Providence, and wishes on the city a picturesque dereliction, predicting that "such swiftness of increase" as it has shown in accelerating its own growth "suggests a corresponding swiftness of destruction." Stevenson is interested not in the drab commercial present of California but in the chimerical promises of its past during the gold rush and the disillusioned wreckage of its likely future—in what precedes or what follows human habitation. In San Francisco he is conscious of the proximity of that past as well as the imminence of that future, and hears the citizens recollecting the days when they waded in sand and scrub on the sites of their present houses. The ghost towns which so fascinated him—a Christian Seaside Resort near Monterey, the roofless mission at Carmel, the forsaken settlement of South Vallejo, or Silverado, an exhausted remnant of the mercenary romantic illusion which made the West an El Dorado—are images of society's reversion to a tumbledown despair. The drearily continuous streets of San Francisco act out the same process, bumping into the air and tapering off to founder in the sands. Kipling derives an epic moral from San Francisco's drift to dissipation, because it must be mechanically resisted: hence the cable cars which internally knit the powdery hills. But Stevenson, writing not epic but romance, assists that dissipation. California's career, for him, is the passage from the bewitching allure of a golden image to the wrecked aftermath of that image: "California has been a land of promise in its time, like Palestine; but if the woods continue so swiftly to perish, it may become, like Palestine, a land of desolation." He helps to speed up this tragic degeneration of the image by setting fire to one of the Californian forests. Wanting to know whether the moss, "that quaint funereal ornament" of the trees, is inflammable, he lights one of the tassels, instead of carrying off a specimen for safe experiment elsewhere. At once the tree flares up and Stevenson decamps, lucky to escape the ire of a lynch mob.

The extravagance of Stevenson's style suits his chivalric dilettantism. His improbable, ideal quest for his elusive lady-love is also a quest for an imaginary America, which no longer exists and therefore has to be evoked and sustained by his style. Images are America's redemption. On board the ship a proletarian emigrant tells Stevenson that "in America you get pies and puddings." Stevenson interprets this remark so as to promote the man's physical craving to equality with his own more abstract and ideal aspirations. America is the place where dreams come true, in which both physical and mental hungers are satisfied. In his way the starving worker is as ardent a fantasist as Stevenson, for he expects America to yield not rude nourishment but delicacies to tickle the appetite. Stevenson justifies both his own gratuitous devotion to Fanny and his companion's lowlier expectations in saying that "a man lives in and for the delicacies, adornments, and accidental attributes of life, such as pudding to eat and pleasant books and theatres to occupy his leisure."

Stevenson's exotic images are his delicacies, because they are prettifications of America. As the emigrant yearns for puddings, so Stevenson expects gustatory wonders in America, and identifies the imagination with the satisfactions of appetite. He urges California to exchange the mining of gold for the planting of greenery in vineyards, to relapse from labor into a bibulous hedonism which joins art and enjoyment, for "wine is bottled poetry." California will become a home fit for the imagination to inhabit only when it forgets about gold and worships wine and art instead. Stevenson and his bride point the way by taking the detritus of social and economic calamity at Silverado and converting it into an imaginative dwelling. They burrow into the wreckage of the mine "like mites in the ruins of a cheese." Wine and cheese are both made from decay; so (in Stevenson's estimation) is art. He and Fanny domesticate the decrepitude of Silverado, turning the broken-down assayer's office into their alfresco living-room and the miners' dormitory into their bedroom. By elaborate pretense, they make economic distress into imaginative delight.

Kipling's America belongs to the canny professional, equipped with that special technical know-how which is the criterion of epic. Stevenson, however, is always the chivalric amateur, masquerading in the grubby practical roles of emigrant on board the ship and miner at Silverado. He derides professionalism. His destitute companions on the ship are genuine emigrants, but Stevenson is traveling to America in the pursuit of an illusion. He resembles the Devonian stowaway in Glasgow, who secretes himself on board "not from any desire to see America," but merely to obtain food and shelter. Stevenson is a poseur, but so is America, since it is a vacuity onto which each emigrant projects his own fantasy, and the images into which the fantasy is refracted range from the paradisial to the infernal—as the ship approaches New York, for instance, grisly tales about the city circulate as if it were a cannibal island. At Silverado, Stevenson impersonates a squatter, just as earlier he had impersonated an emigrant. He neurasthenically mimics the pioneer's rugged health: actually he took to the mountains not because Silverado was to be an epic outpost but because he hoped the benign climate would soothe his ague-stricken body. When he is caught acting the part, Stevenson is discomfited. Ronalds the mine owner appears and (like a Kipling character) flaunts an expertise which shames the amateur.

Calling himself the lord of Silverado, monarch of all the worthless but picturesque realm he surveys, Stevenson claims for himself an ineffectual, imaginative sovereignty. Kipling's epic exercises in endurance have slackened into a spurious idyll from the different literary world of romance. Crusoe, for Kipling the first industrialist, has become a trifling romantic solitary.

Stevenson returned to Scotland in 1880 an invalid and remained sickly until 1887. After this long recuperation he sailed again to the Pacific, settling at Vailima in Samoa, where he died in 1894. Kipling meanwhile had returned to live in his epic America. Reaching London after the journey across the country described in *From Sea to Sea,* he befriended a young American journalist, Woolcott Balestier, and they collaborated on a romance, *The Naulahka.* Its action is divided between western America and India: Balestier contributed the American opening, and Kipling assumed control when the characters, coveting a temple necklace, reach India. In 1891, with the work completed, Kipling returned to India and Balestier left for Dresden where, suddenly, he died, the victim of typhoid. Kipling sped back from Lahore and, in the confusion of his grief, married his dead friend's sister Caroline. They departed for a honeymoon in Japan, but the failure of a bank cut off their funds and forced them to retreat to Brattleboro, Vermont, where the Balestiers were farmers. They bought land from Caroline's brother Beatty, and built a house which they named "Naulahka," in memory of Woolcott. Here they remained from 1892 to 1896.

Epic is about the sturdy human response to a punitive nature. In Kipling's San Francisco, that nature is treacherously unsteady; in his Vermont, it is cruelly icy. In California, the enemy is the slippery soil and the volcanic turbulence of the earth; in New England, the enemy is not geological but climatic. Kipling's epic experience of Vermont concentrates on the human battle against the weather. Climate is a challenge, a dare issued by nature to frail mankind. In New York (as Kipling reports in the essay about his first impressions of Vermont, "In Sight of Monadnock") he is urged to test himself against a climate more taxing than the muggy heat of the city: "Go north," he is told, "if you want weather—weather that *is* weather. Go to New England."

Epic societies are generally straitened by military necessity. Men are conscripted as warriors, and denied the chivalric leisure for the pursuit of private fantasy which Stevenson enjoys in America: they are denied indeed any right to an individual existence for as long as the emergency lasts. In Kipling's Vermont, however, the necessity which cramps individuals and prohibits both privacy and society is not military but meteorological. The weather reduces human individuals to miserable freezing animals, and reduces society to a mean struggle for survival. Kipling dislikes cities because they have weakly evaded the challenge of nature by manufacturing their own mild weather indoors. In the American north, weather regulates human activities and confines work to the summer months of thaw. But cities abolish nature by making work possible all the year round. For the same reason Kipling disapproved of the Great Lakes which (as he says in the essay on "Cities and Space") have no right to act like an ocean so far inland. Like cities, they are an infraction of natural rules. Lake Superior is to Kipling merely a rampaging waste of fresh water on which the epic combat with nature cannot take place because the weather is lethal but not serious. It's only pretending to be a land-locked ocean, so that mastery of it is no achievement: "some people go sailing on it for pleasure, and it has produced a breed of sailors who bear the same relation to the salt-water variety" (the heroes of *Captains Courageous*) "as a snake-charmer does to a lion-tamer." The final ignominy is to call the lake "a useful piece of water," because it is so conveniently and slavishly close to the Canadian Pacific Railroad tracks.

In the older, military epic, men recoil inside their armor, and take on a steely impersonality like that of the protective exoskeleton they wear. In Kipling's climatic epic, men recoil inside an armory of pelts. On the way to Vermont, as the cold bites and the thermometer registers a numbing "thirty below freezing," Kipling and his party transfer from their train to a sleigh and protect themselves inside borrowed furs, goatskin and buffalo hide, until "we looked like walruses." The rigors of nature force men to retract into a fur they have had to pillage from the animals, who are more rationally equipped for survival. Nature's impositions drive evolution into reverse, and men learn to mimic their animal inferiors. When Kipling leaves the train and, stepping out into the snow, wraps himself in furs, modern urban man changes as we watch into a hirsute savage.

Snow obliterates society, as it suppresses the landscape. Kipling likens it to a tyrannously tidy mother fussily tucking nature under its white counterpane. Only the tall spruces and hemlocks poke out their heads and won't be pacified into a deathly sleep. The snow becomes an active force, choking the earth. But nature resists this suffocation, and the landscape is animated in a contest of wills. Nature suffers and endures. Like a beleaguered epic character, the Connecticut River under the torture of packed ice "kept up its heart"; the heart of a frozen tree breaks "in him with a groan." This is not the pathetic fallacy, which makes landscape sycophantically sympathize with human emotion, but rather an epic fallacy, which attributes power and contentious will to landscape, and sees natural processes as an organic warfare. Kipling can therefore interpret seasonal change in Vermont as a record of the fierce emotional impulses which quicken the landscape. A snowy hillside moves, dreaming of spring, and creates a landslide. The turning of the leaves is "the insurrection of the tree-people against the waning year."

Heroic streams or rebellious trees withstand the assault of weather. Humans invent machines to batter and bruise an adversary nature. In Vermont, men "kill, for one reason or other, everything that moves," bears, hawks, eagles, foxes, even trifling birds which have the misfortune to be pretty. The railway in Kipling's view is a machine which victoriously slices through or tramples on an obstreperous landscape. Short of exterminating nature, Kipling's Americans can survive in it by cunning attention to technical expertise—by becoming, that is, crafty versions of the epic hero Crusoe. In *The Naulahka* a callow young Englishman out West undergoes a Crusoesque induction. He learns by humiliating experience that "ridingcrops were not used in punching cattle" and applies this wisdom in the profession of cowboy. New Englanders, in coping with the alternately arctic and tropical excesses of nature, acquire skills which not only keep them alive but are the epic poet's literary credentials, because he too must know how to do things, not merely how to describe them. Craftsmanship is required of both the epic poet and his hero. Therefore Kipling is scornful of those who cannot tell a sleigh for riding from a hauling sledge, or who think that oxen can be driven "by scientific twisting of the tail." He provides information about maneuvering snowshoes and mastering the wolf-step, and warns of the lunge into crevasses of snow which awaits if you cannot manage it; he learns, like a self-improving Crusoe, how to distinguish the snowtracks of foxes from those of dogs, and how to ensnare deer. The epic poet, like Homer deciphering the shield of Achilles, must know about manufacture and use, not only about appearance, and Kipling warns that sleigh bells are "not, as a Southern visitor once hinted, ostentation, but safeguards." The penalty for technical incompetence is ostracism from the epic confraternity: "the man who drives without them is not loved."

Climate determines a minimal human character. Kipling argues that the snow and its dumbfounding silences invent the New England conscience, since activity is halted and the solitary is left to brood in a wilderness of purity. Weather also enforces the economic self-sufficiency of epic, in which characters must wrest a living from their surroundings rather than (as in a novel) relying indolently on the labor of others. Kipling points out that the Vermont woods are a source of fuel and even of nourishment, for the maples yield sap for syrup.

As well as defining character and constructing an economy, landscape dictates the kind of art which can be made from America. Because there is no society on which it can batten, there can be no novel, but in its stead is elemental epic. Kipling calls the thrust of Canadian settlement into the icy wastes "a spectacle . . . out of some tremendous Norse legend," and the form which suits his America is classical epic or its northern equivalent, the saga. In contrast with the eventful, intricate form of the novel, epic is ponderous and laggard, because it describes a society in which nothing except the perpetual dogged effort to wrest a livelihood from nature ever happens. We even colloquially call a dreary, prolix story a saga. But Kipling discovers in this monotony a principle of uncomplaining heroic resolution which is the temper of New England and the mood of epic. "New England stories," he says, "are cramped and narrow," because they concern an iron-bound life without the elegant diversifications after which the novel hankers. The bleak unvarying landscape has the rhythmic uniformity of epic. The Canadian landscape is flat and featureless like a tale told by an idiot, a saga of disconnected uneventfulness. Towns occur "for no obvious reason" and then disappear as "the wilderness took up the tale." But the tedium of its narrative is an index of epic's refusal to be hurried, because it is dealing in epochal expanses of time or in the recurrent cycles of seasonal work, in time which unfolds with steady ceremonious regularity not the time of urban men or of characters in novels, which is mechanically apportioned by clocks and crammed with engagements. Monotony is an education in patience and endurance, the virtues of the epic hero. On the prairies, Kipling says, a man loses his urban restlessness and, rather than being harassed by a mechanical time-scheme which keeps him constantly on the go, returns his watch to "where it should be—in his stomach." Another symptom of the elongation of time in epic is "the long, unhurried drawl of Vermont." Speech slows down and expands into the empty spaces and aeons of unoccupied time which it has to fill. Drawling becomes a kind of arch, premeditated epic declamation. An aged itinerant quack selling boluses is an epic narrator because the longueurs of his story match the blank spaces across which he plods: "he told a long tale in which the deeding away of a farm to one of his family was mixed up with pride at the distances he still could cover daily."

Because life in Vermont is so predictable, the occasional unexpected event swells into ominous significance. In epic, the slightest alteration of routine announces an emergency. Kipling describes such a case in his 1895 winter notebook, unraveling an anecdotal saga from the casual observation that a neighbor has changed his path to market; and it was his own fate to be the victim of a petty temperamental friction which in a city (or in a novel) would have passed unobserved but which in the emptiness of Vermont distended into an epic feud and drove Kipling from the country. People in Kipling's Vermont live tribally, not exploring social possibilities and expanding into multiple relationships as in a novel, but locked together in an epic encampment with nothing outside the ramparts but a snowy waste. Kipling marvels that the settlers "live (and without slaying each other) on terms of terrifying intimacy." Vermont terrifyingly combines claustrophobia with vast vacancy, so that a trivial disagreement can detonate epic warfare. In Kipling's case the provocation was a family tiff. The alcoholic, irresponsible Beatty, ranklingly dependent on the charity of the Kiplings, petitioned in March 1896 to be declared bankrupt and two months later threatened to kill Kipling, who had him arraigned before the Brattleboro court. The trial shamed Kipling and antagonized the local people, who resented what they saw as his lordly persecution of the genial scapegrace Beatty. In August, Kipling and his wife left for England.

But he was already at work on his story of the Massachusetts fishing boats, *Captains Courageous,* which was published the following year. It is his most magnificently inclusive account of his epic America, and it begins appropriately by disjoining epic from novel. The pampered Harvey Cheyne is doubly detached from a cosseting, effeminate society. First, he has been removed from landed luxury, dispatched on a liner to complete his education in Europe. Then he is removed even from the liner, and in a rough sea lunges providentially overboard onto a fishing boat. He spends the season with the fishermen, who chasten the pert, spoiled child into an honest and industrious young man. Harvey's removal from the protection of his mother to the rough masculinity of the fishing boat, and from leisure to work, is a passage from novel to epic. At the same time it is a regression from society to a tribe. On the fishing boat, there are Irish,

Scandinavian, Portuguese, and black Americans. But Harvey's fatuous inexperience leads him to brag, "I'm an American. . . . I'll show 'em that when I strike Europe," because he is foolish enough to imagine that a national identity means something.

Hurled overboard and parabolically drowned, Harvey soon has another miniature death when he's struck down for his sauciness by the fisherman Troop. After this comes resurrection and his arduous initiation into the tribe. Once he is inside the tribe, narrative and its emotional complications, which suit the land-locked society of the novel, are replaced by the different structural devices of epic: custom, ritualized work (the fish cleaning), and folk songs. Harvey's initiation follows the same course as Kipling's preparation for the composition of the epic, since both have to learn how the work of the boat is organized. The epic poet must certify himself as a competent technician: hence the chapters devoted to the technology of whaling in *Moby-Dick*, and hence too Kipling's exactitude about the craft of fishing. Epic turns art from lazy fantasy into exertion, and the epic poet's techniques are the same as those of the workers or businessmen he describes. Enumeration, for instance, is a poetic device (in Homer's catalogue of ships, or in Kipling's statistical details about the economic interests of Harvey's father) but also a skill required by the characters of epic. Uncle Salters is ridiculed when he cannot count the fish he has caught. Epic replaces the developing sequences of novelistic narrative with the recurrent task of enumeration. Each day the catch has to be counted; each day Harvey has to calculate the latitude with a quadrant; each day Disko Troop enters these sums and meteorological notes in his log book.

Epic language is not blandly descriptive but purposeful and energetic. Kipling describes the moon walking on the sea, and when Harvey tilts overboard the sea actively takes possession of him, assuming the function of his mother, who is languishing in her cabin: "a low, grey mother-wave swung out of the fog, tucked Harvey under one arm, so to speak, and pulled him off and away to leeward." In a furious sea, the fishing boat protests vocally ("every square inch of the schooner singing its own tune") or mimics in turn a drunk addressing a lamp post, a kitten pouncing, a puppy chasing a string, a decapitated hen, or a cow stung by a hornet. The sea itself is "unresting, clamorous." Epic attributes animate force to the objects it represents. It even enlivens clichés by noting their reference to the work which sustains the epic world: thus when Long Jack is drilling Harvey in the schooner's gear and tackle, "Tom Platt, of course, could not keep his oar out of the business," and contributes expansive accounts of the sails on the *Ohio*, the first U.S. Navy ship to round the Horn.

As the epic poet employs a specialized jargon, a language exclusive to the occupation he is describing, so his characters employ dialect (as members of racial or national tribes) and argot (as members of a professional clique). The black cook hardly ever talks, but when he does uses a "home-made Scotch" from Cape Breton, where Negroes fled during the war and learned to speak in imitation of the local farmers. However, even this miscegenated dialect is suspect, and the Pennsylvanian says it is not Scotch but Gaelic. Though ignorant of French, Uncle Salters learns a curse in that language to enrage the Miquelon boats.

Dialect is the linguistic form of tribal warfare. Insults are ceremonially exchanged between the *We're Here* and the *Carrie Pitnam*, and "to call a Gloucester man a Nova Scotian is not well received." When Dan is defamed as a Gloucester shrimp and a Novy (meaning Nova Scotian), he retaliates with "Novy yourself, ye Scrabbletowners! Ye Chatham wreckers!" Abuse, like dialect, is territorial, acting out the fragmentation of society. Men acquire identities by adhering to places, and superstitiously revere their chosen patches of land even when adrift in the ocean. The fleet is a watery impromptu town where each crew member finds a temporary social attachment: "Manuel's countrymen jabbered at him in their own language; and even the silent cook was seen . . . shouting Gaelic to a friend as black as himself." In this liquid Babel, Harvey is mocked for his rowing in "every dialect from Labrador to Long Island, with Portuguese, Neapolitan, Lingua Franca, French and Gaelic."

The *We're Here* is not a United Nations, a floating world-state such as Wells might have made it, but a fractious ark containing single representatives of each of the world's disparate tribes. During a storm it takes on as refugees a Swede and men from Chatham, Hancock in Maine, Provincetown, and Duxbury. The flotilla is an offshore version of the assortment of contiguous, incompatible nationalities which fill up the American continent, and rather than wanting to organize these into a union, Disko longs to escape into a solitude of his own: his son Dan fights with Otto simply because he is a Dutchy and hasn't (in the uproar of competing dialects) "a Christian tongue in his head," and Disko similarly is adept at slipping away from the other boats. Like Huck Finn lighting out for the unsettled territory, he distrusts society: "he objected to the mixed gatherings of a fleet of all nations," a motley of boats from Gloucester, Provincetown, Harwich, Chatham, and the Maine ports, with crews assembled "from goodness knows where." He is at ease only with a tribe of his own choosing.

Combining the slang of his characters with their occupational jargon, Kipling invents an epic diction which is the dialect of a tribe not the language of a society. The characters have a rough, proverbial lyricism (Dan says that Manuel's dory with a full catch is "low ez a lily-pad in still water") because poetry is the primitive rhythmic song which precedes the literate, social complications of prose. The epic condition of speech is exemplified by Tom Platt, who was on the *Ohio* when it rounded the Horn and "never talks much else, 'cept when he sings." The epic character, like the epic poet, never talks, only sings. This is why fishermen suit Kipling's purpose, because they sing at their labor, while hauling in their catch. Tom Platt bellows melodiously as he rows in, and his colleagues can assess his catch from his choice of repertory: "If he gives us 'O Captain' it's toppin' full." Later, Disko sings a ballad about the transatlantic passage of the *Dreadnought,* and his singing not only describes work but, as an epic should, embodies it: "There were scores of verses, for he worked the *Dreadnought* every mile of the way between Liverpool and New York as conscientiously as though he were on her deck."

Epic reverses the history of language, just as it reverses the evolution of society. It retreats from the analytical sophistication of prose to the mnemonic primitivism and rhythmic encouragements of verse, and from the leisure of a novelistic society which lives off the work of others to the struggle of a tribe to subsist on its own labors. The economy of the *We're Here* is a model of self-sufficiency, which wastes nothing: the blood-ends collected after the catch is cleaned at night are cooked up for breakfast the next morning. The same regression is prescribed for Harvey, snatched from his affluent, indulgent parents and set down in a cruel, demanding, toilsome tribe. Because the epic society is constrained by military emergency or (in Kipling) by the elements, its characters do not invent self-exploratory courses of action as they would in a novel. Instead they obey orders and this, the epic morality insists, is good for them. Harvey learns this after attempting to issue his own order to be returned to New York: "like many other unfortunate young people, Harvey had never in his life received a direct order."

The action of epic consists in obeying orders and learning skills. Harvey's moral education is a technical apprenticeship. When he rows, he finds his childish experience on Adirondack ponds irrelevant. Technical ignorance teaches him humility. When the anchor fouls, he doesn't understand the problem: "this was a new world, where he could not lay down the law to his elders" (like the obnoxious American infants of Wilde) "but had to ask questions humbly." Epic is a world of monitory objects which the initiate must learn to identify and manipulate, and Harvey's apprenticeship proceeds through bruising physical exposure. Long Jack instructs him in the difference between fore and aft by rubbing his nose along the boom, and makes him remember "the lead of each rope" by thwacking him with "the end of the rope itself." The characters of novels foment intrigues; the characters of epic patiently graduate from one rite to the next. Harvey is first baptismally immersed in the ocean, then blooded: Dan slashes him with a razor when he has a rash of gurry-sores, boils caused by the abrasion of his wet jersey and oilskins, which are "the mark of the caste that claimed him."

In Chapter IX of *Captains Courageous,* Kipling sets two versions of the American epic into exhilarating counterpoint. One is tribal, the other technological, and they thrust in opposite directions toward a point of convergence. As the fishing boat defies storms to make its way westward home to Gloucester, at the eastern edge of the continent, a railway carriage containing Harvey's parents shuttles frantically across the continent from west to east, San Diego to Boston. The superimposition of actions connects the physical heroism of the fishermen with the mechanical heroism of the railway magnate, Harvey's father. Because of America's telescoped history, the antique epic battle with the elements takes place at the same time as the modern scientific conquest of the elements, and *Captains Courageous* dramatizes this simultaneity. Disko Troop rules his unstable watery empire by instinctive cunning; Harvey Cheyne senior rules his landed empire by gestures of will which machines transmit: the telegraph projects his impulses across astonishing distances. The fisherman and the tycoon share a heroism which derives from technical ingenuity. Disko knows the trends of currents and the habits of cod as intimately as Cheyne knows the railway timetables. Both are genii of restless motion. Disko is at sea for half the year; Cheyne the railway pioneer first goes east in June to collect his anguished wife after the loss of their son, then crosses to Boston again at terrifying speed in the autumn to meet Harvey.

Kipling proposes an analogy between life aboard ship and life on a train in *Letters of Travel,* during a journey across Canada. The passenger, he says, after a week on wheels becomes "a part of the machine," just as young Harvey learns to become part of the boat, and develops an instinct like the machine's own for watering stops or the sound of air brakes or the differences between signals. Harvey's father is a triumphant machine: his success story is "like watching a locomotive storming across country in the dark." Older epic heroes want to become as stern and unflinching as the weapons with which they fight; the newer kind want to become as rapid and dauntless as the machines in which they travel. Cheyne is the new technological epic hero, who doesn't perform feats of physical endurance as the fishermen do, but presides over the machines which perform superhuman feats on his behalf. Kipling's account of Cheyne is not only a tribute but also an incentive to heroism. He asked a railway magnate to supply him with a complete schedule specifying "watering halts, changes of engine, mileage, track conditions and climates," and because art is a bracing physical challenge to life, another magnate set out in his private car to beat Kipling's imaginary timetable, and succeeded. *Captains Courageous* doesn't merely describe epic deeds but stimulates them.

Cheyne's business dealings filament the continent, making him, by way of his typist and telegraphist, a presence superintending operations in every corner of the land mass. He has Chinese junks in the bay at San Diego, palaces there and in Colorado; he thinks of taking his wife to recuperate in Washington or the South Carolina islands. His retainers are a polyglot collection of vagrants from scattered tribes: Suzanne the French maid, the telegraphist Miss Kinzey from Milwaukee, a doctor who has been lured from New York to the west coast. His commercial realm stretches the length of the coast: he is dealing simultaneously with a war of rates between the four western railroads in which he has an interest, a strike in his lumber camps in Oregon, and a refractory legislature in Sacramento. He and Troop divide the oceans imperially between them. Troop fishes the Atlantic, Cheyne colonizes the Pacific, with a line of tea clippers plying between San Francisco and Yokohama. As Cheyne is economically omnipresent, so Troop is biologically ubiquitous: he has distributed his kin around the oceans, and boasts that "we Troops, livin' an' dead, are all araound the earth an' the seas thereof."

But as Chapter IX begins, Cheyne is listless, becalmed in depression. His torpor enables Kipling to sharply differentiate the values of epic and novel. Trollope complained that American men were so relentlessly industrious that they had no private lives, and therefore couldn't be characters in a novel. Kipling's complaint about Cheyne is the opposite. He has neglected his epic duty of activism to lapse into an irrelevant, despairing privacy, from which the first sentence of the chapter rouses him: "Whatever his private sorrows may be, a multi-millionaire, like any other working man, should keep abreast of his business." The telegram from Harvey startles Cheyne into an assertion of geographical will which technologically forces the quarrelsome inchoate continent into a unity as he speeds across it. Studying roller maps of America, he prepares a military assault on distance. But he vanquishes by deploying technological intermediaries not armies. "As a general brings brigades into action," he signals Miss Kinzey's adept fingers to call up the continent, arranging for his private railway car to be fetched from Los Angeles and planning for it to reach Chicago in 60 hours and to connect there with the New York train via Buffalo and Albany to Boston. Technology abolishes space and contracts time: the crossing to Chicago is actually made in 57 hours and 54 minutes. Technology even resolves tribal disaffection. As Cheyne mobilizes himself, his competitors assume he is declaring commercial war, and hasten to capitulate, sending in messages from Los Angeles, Chicago, and Topeka. But his announcement that his errand is a sentimental reunion not an economic assault prompts an accord between opposed interests. The continent is pacified over the wires.

The journey passes in a blizzard of numbers, as if a quantifying Crusoe were recording it. A private car 70 feet long has to be expedited over 2,350 miles, taking precedence over 177 other trains, which all must be warned. The operation requires 16 locomotives, 16 engineers, and 16 firemen; 2½ minutes are allocated for changing engines, 3 minutes for watering, 2 minutes for taking on coal. The anticipated speed is 40 miles an hour, and the representatives of $63 million worth of railroad interests cooperate in the enterprise. The narrative is so intent on numerical precision that Kipling even calculates the height of the engine driver (which is 6 feet), as if that were part of the equation. Cheyne marks the progress of the car by periodically advancing his watch as they cross into a new time corridor. The trip is completed in 87 hours and 35 minutes or alternatively (because Kipling has to present as many statistics as possible) in 3 days and 15½ hours. Harvey is meanwhile acquiring a comparable skill in measurement: his job is tally-boy, and at the sale he declares the total of $3,665¼. He prides himself on the techniques he has learned and tells his father how he can handle a dory, bait up a trawl, and pitch fish.

Reunited with his son, Cheyne in Chapter X reminisces about his early years. His narrative recapitulates and reverses the journey of the previous chapter. That rushed from west to east, and in its velocity is a model of the technological subjugation of the continent. Cheyne's memories follow the opposite course, beginning in Texas and moving west, for he is describing the opening of frontiers not (as on his railway journey) celebrating their obsolescence, their surrender to omnipotent machines. Cheyne's early career extends across the whole of the West, traversing states as effortlessly as it encompasses professions. He is so ubiquitous and so multifariously talented that he ceases to be a man and is dispersed as an embodiment of America. The diversity of this apprenticeship matches Mark Twain's recollection of his own epic training in the interview with Kipling in *From Sea to Sea*. Cheyne has been "deck-hand, train-hand, contractor, boarding-house keeper, journalist, engineer, drummer, real-estate agent, politician, dead-beat, rum-seller, mine-owner, speculator, cattleman, or tramp." Each of these careers constitutes a separate existence. Like Whitman, because he is an American he can contain multitudes, rather than being confined to a single identity; or as Mae West raunchily puts it, he has been things and seen places. The old epic hero's monster-slaying physical prowess is here diversified as an adaptable variety of skills. Cheyne becomes an epic figure because his self-interest is a patriotic virtue. Amassing wealth, he is seeking his own ends and so, he says, "the glory and advancement of his country." Old epic heroes used to exalt their tribe by going to war for it; the new epic hero honors it by making money for it. Cheyne's career also modernizes that of the romance hero, whose weird perils and mysterious encounters turn in the democratic age of prose into economic opportunities: "chances of gigantic wealth flung before eyes that could not see, or missed by the merest accident of time and travel."

Cheyne's memories make the new West seem as elementally unfixed (cities evanesce into waste, waste suddenly rears up into a city) and as responsive to bold initiative as the sea off the Grand Banks. This suggests a further analogy between the two geographical trajectories of the work, offshore and cross-country. The young Cheyne revived by these reminiscences is a partner for Troop at sea. Cheyne crawls "round, through, or under mountains and ravines, dragging a string-and-hoop-iron railroad after him," as Troop negotiates fickle tides. The Cheyne of Chapter IX, vanquishing distance in his luxurious private car, is a different creature, an imperial epic hero, manipulating economic destinies through the mediation of the wires. Troop graduates to this status at the end of his voyage. Returning ahead of the fleet with his catch to Gloucester, he waits smugly in port until the merchants are ready to meet the price he demands, knowing (like Cheyne affrighting his competitors by remote control) that he has the monopoly of advantage because he is first home.

Cheyne the technological warrior spans the gap between Kipling and the next writer in this succession, H. G. Wells. Likened by his son to a talking locomotive, he answers to Wells's scornful description of Kipling's deity as "a Mohammedan God, a modernized Allah with a taste for engineering." But his transformation of cupidity from a private vice to a public benefit makes him an honorary Wells character. Discussing the extension of the railways across America in *The Work, Wealth and Happiness of Mankind,* Wells justifies the inordinate riches accumulated by buccaneers like J. D. Rockefeller, Cornelius Vanderbilt, and Jay Gould, men who are historical equivalents to Cheyne. Balzac had declared that behind every fortune lay a crime. For Wells, behind each of these great American fortunes lies a technological innovation, which the millionaires have exploited for the good of humanity. With Vanderbilt and Gould it is an innovation in transport—steamboats and railways, respectively; in Rockefeller's case it is oil production. The hero of the American industrial epic begins in Kipling as a primitive self-subsistent Crusoe and ends in Wells as a tycoon turning scientific discovery into commerical gain. *Captains Courageous* demonstrates the change from one style of industrial heroism to the other by implicitly pairing Troop and Cheyne, and by setting Cheyne's youthful adventures against his later achievement. Pirates like Rockefeller are the protagonists of Wells's history because they adapt newly available substances and sources of power to harness an antagonistic nature. Their rapacity is blameless because they are history's emissaries, charged with the task of remodeling Kipling's tribal America as a rational world-state. Kipling's America is an atavistic rabble, Wells's the laboratory in which the future is experimentally concocted.

5

FUTURISTIC AMERICA
H. G. Wells

The Victorians were disconcerted by America because it lacked a past, which condemned it to unreality. Time had not validated social arrangements or tamed an untidy, meaningless landscape. America affronts the Victorian novelist because it has not yet become the kind of upholstered bourgeois society which can sustain complicated personal relationships. But this imaginative liability is for the next generation America's enviable freedom. Kipling and Wells find there something both less and more than the European idea of a society. For Kipling, America is an exposed and exiguous preliminary to society; for Wells, it is a futuristic epilogue to society. Its destiny, he thinks, is to evolve beyond the social inequity and economic greed of the nineteenth century, creating a new charitable order in society and an intelligent reconstruction of the economy. Whereas the Victorians miss in America any attachment to locality which might make the society an organism, for Wells this very absence is promise of the country's angelic future. Not being an organism, it can the more easily become a machine.

While the Victorians long for America to become a society the novelist can inhabit and analyze, Kipling and Wells find in it alternatives to the novel. Kipling's America exists in a condition of elemental strife more appropriate to battlemented epic than to the leisured, introspective novel. Wells's America has renounced the helpless eccentric privacy of character and the picturesque inequalities which deface nineteenth-century society and disfigure its novels. Turning itself into a technological millennium, it can be comprehended only by the novel's logical successor, science fiction. For Kipling America predates, for Wells outgrows, the novel.

Wells shared its ambition to actualize the future. His parents were domestic servants who had self-improvingly opened a china shop in the London suburbs, and here their son was born in 1866. He rescued himself from their class by studying science and espousing Fabian socialism. Social mobility resembles the time machine he described in one of his first scientific romances in 1895: the ambitious individual speeds up evolution, thrusting himself into a future unknown to the previous generation. Having planned his own life, Wells set about planning the world. His own success is discovering the future he made a formula for an ailing world, mired in an outworn past. The schemes he devised for global recovery always depended on America, which dedicates itself to individual self-betterment and to the reformation of the world; and at the same time America suggested to Wells the kind of art most suitable to the technical utopia it prefigures.

He traveled to America for the first time in 1906, not, he explained, to see what it was, but to divine what it might become. The account of this tour is therefore called *The Future in America*. His quarrel with the squalid, disorganized American present is also a quarrel with the antiquated form of the novel. Wells's is an aspiring America, restlessly stretching into the future. The skyscrapers in New York spring toward "some needed terminal," sending off "jets of steam" as if to proclaim that they are "still . . . in a process of eruption." The Statue of Liberty strains on its pedestal, daring competition with the "fierce commercial altitudes" of lower Manhattan. Even the air of the city is lucid, an image of unclouded intelligence. Henry James—who had returned home in 1904 after an exile of twenty years and published his impressions in *The American Scene,* the year after Wells's tour—lamented the grimly bright absence of pictorial atmosphere in New York, but for Wells this deficiency is an encouraging sign of scientific purity. Atmosphere is pollution: Wells admires "the clear emphasis of detail" from which James sensitively flinches, and commends "the freedom from smoke and atmospheric mystery that New York gains from burning anthracite" and "the jetting white steam clouds that emphasise that freedom."

America's scientific responsibility is the transformation of past into future, a quarrelsome chaos of individuals into a planned and ordered society. The image of this process is the policy which "turned a waste of rubbish dump and swamp and cabbage garden into Central Park, New York," dispersing the ugly rubble of the nineteenth century and clearing a diagrammatic empty space worthy of the prescient twentieth century. (Wells's contempt for cabbages reverses Trollope's praise for the kitchen gardens of England, and his revulsion from the bareness of Central Park.) Henry James was skeptical about this Wellsian manufacture of the future, and quizzed the skyscrapers along Fifth Avenue, archly demanding of them, "since you've had no past . . . what are you going to make your future *of?*" For James the future is only tolerable if it is a hesitant growth from the past; for Wells it is an obliteration of that past. This is a future, consequently, without room for the novel. The novel stubbornly adheres to the minutiae of social detail and emotional nuance which the scientific future will have outgrown. Hence Wells stalks James around America, undoing his colleague's efforts to endow this coarse and ill-mannered society with the psychological refinement on which the novel relies. Arriving in Washington, Wells finds that James in the previous year had dubbed it "the City of Conversation," to the evident gratification of the locals. Wells sourly spoils the compliment, in order to insult the novelistic imagination which proffered it. He finds the title only too trivially apt, for conversation in Washington is all small talk, gossipily inimical to the theoretical debate about the future Wells wished to inaugurate.

Wells's America is futuristic, James's (as the title of his book declares) is scenic, which means that it concentrates on the past, since its picturesque impressions take time to compose. James admitted that he saw no profit in scanning the future, since it was incalculable. His own intention was to retrieve the country's brief but vanishing past, which coincided with a search for his own youth: his quest had been for "the America of my old knowledge." He and Wells exchanged presentation copies of their American books, with barbed civilities. Wells, after reading *The American Scene,* noted that James had novelistically confined himself to "life and manners" and the evaluation of "an ineffectual civilization." The innuendo is that James has wished his own ineffectualness on America, decoratively describing the social fancies not the social and economic substance of the country. James, after reading *The Future in America,* protested mildly against Wells's stridency, but blamed this raucousness of tone on shrill America. This demur is a covert accusation. Wells has, for James, taken on himself the squalling vices of his subject. James thinks Wells "too *loud,* as if the country shouted at you," but with murderous condescension understands that "the only way to utter many things you are delivered of *is* to yell them." With a grimace of mock deference, he compares his own discreet semitones with Wells's "splendid clashing of the cymbals." He deftly manages to blame the country as a cover for blaming Wells. The fault is that of America, with its vulgar din; but this uproar is convenient for Wells, who has after all only brawling, cacophonous things to say.

Yet their disagreement is more a matter of character and style than a feud about the significance of America. James deplores Wells as a pushful, cheeky cockney, Wells derides James as a precious, prevaricating dotard. About America, they are near to agreement, for both Wells's criticism of its social and economic mess, and his project for its future, invoke the terms and standards of James's criticism of the novel. Wells criticizes America for resembling the kind of garrulous, congested Victorian novel James disliked; and Wells's prescription for America's future resembles James's prescription for the future of the novel. The social policies Wells commends echo the aesthetic policies James adopted in the prefaces (written after his return to England from the tour described in *The American Scene*) to the New York edition of his novels. James there proposes that the novel should purge itself of the promiscuous Victorian interest in ramshackle intrigues and mobs of characters. Characters are refined into disembodied intelligencies, inquisitorial points of view; plots are refined into scrupulous elaborations of psychological conundrums. The novel's future lies in scientific self-consciousness about its own techniques; and for Wells, America's future points in the same direction. James mocks Victorian novels by associating them with the greasy richness of English cooking, calling them indigestible fluid puddings. Wells even adopts the gastronomic slight. In *Boon* he calls America a spectacle of mental and racial confusion, "like a burst haggis," and in *The Future in America* he contrasts Boston's planned growth with the disorderly sprawl of London, which is "like a bowl of viscid human fluid" boiling over sloppily.

In Chicago, Wells surveys the undisciplined litter left by "the progress of the Victorian time." He is offended by the rapacious individualism of Victorian social enterprise, as James is by the omnivorousness and obesity of Victorian fictional form. Wells wants to bring this commercial affray under the rational control of the state, James to submit the self-indulgent novelistic muddle to the abstinent control of art. Wells's call for "order, prevision, a common and universal plan" in economic organization duplicates James's demand for structural prevision in art. The "unsanitary aggregation" Wells dislikes in American cities is the same overpopulated clutter which James criticizes in Victorian novels. The duty of America is to chasten the brawling present and make a regulated future. Wells watches this transformation at work on immigrants arriving at Ellis Island, and praises the same rationalization which distresses Dickens in his account of the Mormons embarking in London. The "gravid liners" disgorge troops of Europeans, "crude Americans" who earn their membership in the new country by renouncing divisive national individuality. Ellis Island synthesizes them, assembling a human chaos into a methodical card-index.

James proposes for the novel, as Well does for the anarchic filth of Chicago, "the coming of new conceptions, of foresight, of large collective plans and discipline to achieve them." American institutions are based, Wells complains, on "the liberty of property and the subordination of the state to business," just as the novels of Dickens are, in James's estimation, corrupt because based on the liberty of character and the subordination of form to content. The slighted idea of the nation is, like the slighted theory of the novel for James, in Wells's terms "a comprehensive abstraction . . . the ultimate reality." Wells contradicts the American enthusiasm for unrestricted immigration by invoking the criterion of assimilation, which might be a term from James's aesthetics. "By 'assimilate,' " he explains, "I mean make intelligently co-operative citizens of these people," which is what James intends to do with the supernumerary crowds of Victorian fictional characters. American "state-blindness" is like the absent-minded multitudinousness, engrossed in detail and neglectful of the whole, which James attacks in the older novelists. The American, Wells alleges, sees the world as if it were a bad Victorian novel: he perceives it "in fragments; it is to him a multitudinous collection of individual 'stories,' as the newspapers put it."

When the future arrives, this novelistic pandering to private affairs will no longer be permitted. Fiction will turn into science fiction. The novel instead of prattling about the present or sighing for the past will invent the future. Science fiction acclimatizes itself naturally to America, because that country is the laboratory in which the world's future is devised. In an early scientific romance, *When the Sleeper Wakes,* written before his first visit to America, Wells points out that the future is "essentially an exaggeration of contemporary tendencies. . . . Everything was bigger, quicker, more crowded. . . . It was the contemporary world in a state of highly inflamed distension." It was, that is, America—for America is contemporaneity exaggerated or inflamed; it is not (like Europe) the

present fretting to extricate itself from the past, but the present hastening into the future.

The War in the Air chides humanity for failing to adapt to the
mechanical future, and warns that global disaster will be the result
of this lazy conservatism. Wells himself is not guilty of this inertia.
His book exonerates him: in later years he prided himself on having
described air warfare in advance of the fact, since in 1908 no "prac-
ticable flying had occurred," as if the projections of science fiction
could actually invent the future instead of merely fantasizing about
it. Infesting the sky with machines, Wells revises a myth. When, in
the modern world, gods and devils descend from the sky, machines
heavier than air but all the same navigable in the air take their
place, and Milton's war in heaven is replaced by Wells's aeronautical
combat. Defiance of technological law is now as fatal as, in the older
mythology, defiance of theological edict. Wells accounts for the air
war by saying that science had outstripped local social and political
divisions but, instead of accepting the need for amalgamation, nations
had intensified divisive loyalties and protected their obsolete frontiers by accumulating weaponry. To disobey the machine is as impious as to flout the god. In *The War in the Air* Wells blames "the
lamentable incidents that followed the surrender of New York" on
the incompatibility between technology and obsolete patriotic emotion. The city has been conquered by science, by the technically
superior German air squadron, and this enrages the rebellious, sentimental pride of the New Yorkers. But their local loyalty can express
itself only in destruction, so they rampage through the city wrecking
public buildings in an ecstasy of humiliation.

When war becomes air-borne, history transfers itself from the
earth to the upper atmosphere. His balloon trip to Germany grants
a perilous elevation to the vulgar earthbound Bert Smallways, and
Wells contrives a similar levitation for his own narrative in aerial
perspectives of New York. Because New York is a vertical city, it
can only be destroyed from above (unlike the California of Stevenson, Huxley, and Isherwood, destroyed from below by subsidence or

slippage, ruined by its insecure foundation in the earth), and can also best be described from above. New York seems to have been built in the expectation of being admired from the air, "disposed to display the tall effects of buildings, the complex immensities of bridges and monorails and feats of engineering." Because its scale diminishes individuals, events in the city are matters of mass response, and the movements of crowds can only be seen from above: if you are in the crowd you can't discern its size or direction. Hence, in *The War in the Air* Wells adopts an angle of omniscient surveillance, gazing down at crowds assembling in Madison Square to listen to patriotic harrangues, at naval exercises in the East River, or at children flying air balloons in Central Park. The crowd which riots through the city is possessed by a collective emotion, and is therefore overheard from above: to Bert, in one of the airships at an altitude of five hundred feet, "it seemed that the city was now humming like a hive of bees."

The aerial perspective has political and scientific implications for Wells's imagined future. The high angle lifts the head into the sky while leaving the body in helpless inertness on the earth, and this is precisely the separation of faculties which Wells proposes for the human race. The futuristic mutants of Wells's science fiction are intelligences unimpeded by embodiment. The Martians in *The War of the Worlds* are "practically mere brains, wearing different bodies according to their needs," the lunar Selenites in *The First Men on the Moon* are "big heads" with expanded brain cases. The prostrate New York of *The War in the Air* is a sprawling body which the Germans have decapitated by destroying its administrative center. Once the head is off, the undirected nervous system runs amok: they "struck at the head . . . only to release the body from its rule. New York had become a headless monster, no longer capable of collective submission," truculently arming itself and raising flags. The German air armada is a sapient head punishing the spread-eagled body beneath it. The head is punitively severed from the comical, treacherous body during the Atlantic crossing, when one of the

Germans is executed for carrying matches aboard the airship. The culprit is swung in mid-air on a long rope, but "his head came right off, and down the body went spinning to the sea, feeble, grotesque, fantastic, with the head racing in its tail." The war likewise is the lucid head's self-separation from the slovenly, obtuse body: its cause is the failure of "intellectual and social organization" to keep up with the velocity of "mechanical invention."

America often seemed to Wells a deranged body without a head. On one occasion he sums up the intellectual confusion of its leaders by saying that "the Race . . . has lost its head," and on another he refers to the "picturesque headlessness" of America, which erects facsimiles of decrepit ivy-strangled European universities rather than planning a rational and modern system of higher education. Aviators, in contrast, are heads serenely disjoined from the terrestrial body, and in *The Shape of Things To Come* (1933) Wells installs in his imagined future an elite of those professionals, the Air Dictatorship. Their occupation implies a detachment from physical necessity, and they enforce a harsh carnal hygiene, "ruthlessly eliminating sexual incitation." Wells's faith in the caste of airmen was, however, mistaken. Lindbergh, instead of discerning from his en-skied vantage point a world without envious national boundaries, became a propagandist for American isolationism, against which Wells was campaigning, and recommended that Britain should negotiate a peace with Germany during the war.

Nevertheless, Wells continues to see the problem of the American future as the acquisition of a head. Hence his interest in the institution of the Presidency. He even optimistically salutes Theodore Roosevelt—the bearish apostle of strenuousness, whose political style merely exchanged the big gun he carried on his safaris for the big stick with which he belligerently conducted diplomacy—as a universal mind. The Roosevelt described by Kipling is a gruff brute, and it is apt that many of their conversations should have taken place among the ethnological exhibits of the Smithsonian Museum. In Washington in 1895 they visited the Zoo together, and Roosevelt "talked about grizzlies that he had met." Wells, however, meeting Roosevelt at the White House in 1906, sees him not as a predatory body but as a self-conscious mind which "assimilates contemporary thought, delocalizes and reverberates it." For Kipling, Roosevelt's policies are acts of atavistic tribal aggression. In a letter to Kipling at the time of his seizure of the Panama Canal, Roosevelt derided the Panamanian President as a "Pithecanthropoid," an ape-man. For Wells, capture of the Canal was not physical bullying but mental ingenuity, a rationalization of world communications and therefore not evidence of tribal greed.

Wells later hailed the New Deal as a national nervous system of welfare and social superintendence, with Franklin Roosevelt as the coordinating intelligence at its head. Just as Wells had overlooked the first Roosevelt's bull-moose brashness, so he overlooked the second Roosevelt's lubricity, and made F.D.R.'s confinement to a wheelchair symbolic of his detachment of mind from body: "his peculiar health makes him float rather above the level of everyday temptations," like one of the futuristic aviators in *The Shape of Things To Come*. Like an aviator, F.D.R. ruled by controlling the air waves, employing the radio to educate his subjects. To Wells he is less a man than a radio station for receiving signals and transmitting initiatives of action, "a responsive and synthesizing intelligence." The politician on television is at the mercy of his own image, and is tempted to confession and maudlin self-exposure like Lyndon Johnson in his speech of renunciation or Nixon in his blubbering farewell to the White House staff. Roosevelt on the radio was invulnerable because invisible. The invisibility of the speaker on radio turns him into an abstracted intelligence, thinking aloud: he becomes an avatar of that early Wells hero, the albino Griffin in *The Invisible Man*, who discovers, as F.D.R. did, that "an Invisible Man is a man of power."

The world state which Wells envisaged, and of which he declared the United States to be the prototype, was a global brain. He devotes the final section of his *Experiment in Autobiography* (1934) to the issues of international order and social planning because his memoir is, as he says, the biography of a cortex, not a novelistic narrative about the vicissitudes of the body in which that brain is entrapped, and the world state is his own psychological destination. His career extends triumphally from the grimy physical imprisonment of the London suburbs to the mental freedom of the world, "from a backyard to Cosmopolis; from Atlas House" (the miserable impecunious china shop in Bromley kept by his father) "to the burthen of Atlas." Wells sees the construction of the world state as a reintegration of the brain. During the 1930s he busied himself in shuttling between Moscow and Washington as the unelected diplomatic conscience of the world, hoping to negotiate an accord between two cerebral hemispheres, the two lobes of the global brain which had become futilely antagonistic. F.D.R. and Stalin represented different brain types, the one supple and scientific, the other posturing and dogmatic. Wells dialectically volunteers his own "very ordinary brain" as an intermediary between them.

In a letter sent to Woodrow Wilson in 1917, Wells nominated America as the instigator of a rational world-order, first because it is aloof from the sectarian squabbles of Europe, and second because it has a head, and can therefore talk. The British constitution condemns that country to acephalous inarticulacy: "monarchy substitutes a figure-head for a head," a totem pole for an intelligence, and leaves the political system untenacious and invertebrate, suffering the random fragmentation of its territory rather than pressing toward unification. The Presidency institutionally performs a benign decapitation, turning the incumbent into a talking head. Wells describes the crippled F.D.R. as a head which has no effective body and which doesn't need one because its "mental arms are long." In his autobiography Wells concedes that perhaps F.D.R. is "humanly, not quite all that I am saying of him," but that hardly matters, because F.D.R.'s attributes of character are subsumed in the symbolism of office. He is no longer a character but an idea. In Wells's own literary career, conversion to the principle of the world state entails a renunciation of the novel and its concern for the vestigial individualism of character. The cause of world peace, to which he turned when he decided to write an outline of history, convinced him that he could not continue as a novelist. His duty, he explains in the autobiography, was to write planetary history, not to fondly chronicle the trivial doings of idle unpolitical individuals. The novel is at best a relic, at worst a disease: like the haphazard nineteenth-century cities he decries in *The Future in America,* it represents a cancerous "growth without form," too attached to personal fates to abide the planned and logical future.

Because America has a franchise on the future, it is the model for science fiction, the form which to Wells supplants the gossipy European novel, and America's technical ingenuity equips the writer with the means of representing the future it is unfolding. Steenhold in Wells's *The Holy Terror* (1939) claims that America has been directing world history for a century, thanks to a series of mechanical innovations: ironclads, airplanes, machine guns, big business, and mass production. The benefits of these mechanical inventions are transferred to the writer. The airplane, for instance, makes possible the world-conscious omniscient vistas of Wells's science fiction. Another American machine which the futuristic Wells exploits is the kinetograph. Like the airplane, it is an invention which belongs symbolically to America. Technology has been the guardian angel of American history. The railway, telegraph, and printing press first made possible the expansion of settlement to the Pacific, Wells argues, and then prevented the disintegration of the Union during the Civil War. The airplane and the cinema stand for different magical facets of this angelic technology: the one its conquest of distance and its freedom to take the world-minded overview which Wells declared to be the aviator's mental privilege; the other its conquest of matter, the obdurate physical substance of the world. Wilkins in *Boon* hails the cinema as an inspiration of "the real Mind of Humanity," the mind's discovery of an organ by which to express itself. Whereas the aviator merely soars above nature, the cinematographer transforms nature, for, as Wells points out in *The Work, Wealth and Happiness of Mankind,* film is a miracle of scientific mutation. Cellulose is a technological victory over nature, because it is compounded from vegetable cell-walls. It is infinitely versatile, whereas unresourceful nature only imagined a single purpose for it: it can be made into artificial fiber or glossy varnish, and when treated with camphor yields celluloid, the material of film.

Wells instantly connects the cinema with aviation. Film, as he says in 1929 in his preface to *The King Who Was a King* (a futuristic fable written as the script for a film which was never made), is a form of surveillance or mental omniscience, a release from the personal point of view. Its field is sublimity, the aerial perspective, "the bird's-eye view of a mountain chain, or a great city." Describing his millennial hopes for the medium, he remembers that he once "had a joy-ride in an aeroplane over the Medway and prophesied Lindbergh. This is the same sort of thing." The film's ease in shifting place, transferring time, scanning vast areas, makes it a model of technological grace and adapts it to Wells's global ambitions, which the novel couldn't contain: he wants to write "a film dealing with a theme of world-wide importance." In harmoniously aggregating the various arts—music, drama, and spectacle—the film is also formally an emblem and an anticipation of the cooperative world-state which it alone will be capable of representing. The novel's destiny is to turn into science fiction and subsequently into film. Art, Wells says, is becoming cinematically spectacular as it evolves beyond particular personal crises to an account of general human fates. Although a single individual may still be employed as a hero, he is merely the concentration of a mass, a group-man synthesized from "hundreds of committees, thousands of leaders and millions of mute followers," and is therefore "highly generalized." This generality is both very cinematic and very American. The cinema is an American form because only it can comprehend the vast extent of the land, and its heroes are essentially American characters because the cinema is restricted to physical exteriors and the average American is idyllically healthy, a perfect specimen such as Wells requires, "good-looking, able-bodied . . . not so much the average man as the quintessential man," or what in America would be called the all-American man.

Auden objected to this cinematic reduction of character to physique. He preferred the unregenerate European form of opera, arguing that the grotesque corseted corpulence of the singers at least acknowledges that love is the spirit's transformation of matter: from these elephantine bodies issue seraphic voices. The movies, on the contrary, "make love seem a natural effect caused by animal beauty." Wells has no such reservations, and encourages the camera to ignore the internal subtlety which creates novelistic character. The cinematic heroine, he says, must also be "simplified beyond any vividness of characterization," a bland physical nonpareil. Since character has been reduced to body, the actors in Wells's script for *The King Who Was a King*, unlike characters in a novel, can dispense with names, and are minimally differentiated as A., B., C., and D. Personal individuality has been forfeited in the cause of amalgamation: this reduction of persons to initials corresponds to the plan for the reunion of national entities (for instance the reincorporation of Britain and the United States) which *The King Who Was a King* discusses.

The film adopts the cosmic view, beginning with a fable of evolution, followed by an image of the world rotating. This glimpse of the earth from god's eyrie in space dissolves into a view of New York from an airplane, and that narrows into another image in which the camera is the omniscient trespasser, requisitioning secret intelligence: through a window frame it spies on "the intimate conference room of a great business organization" in lower Manhattan. From a view of the world, the camera has contracted to a map of the world: a map which is "a bold revision of all known geography" is being pinned up inside the conference room. From the map, the camera proceeds to a global enumeration of the flags which stud that map: from the conspectus of the world, that is, to the badges of single nations. The American and British flags flutter across the screen as issues of national policy are discussed. American resistance to amalgamation with Britain is signalled by an associative montage of American history, dreamily superimposed on the argument between C. the isolationist and the internationalist D. The cinema evokes the blur of patriotic memory in images of Concord, Lexington, and Valley Forge, moving down the length of national history as effortlessly as from one continent to another (later it recounts in a series of silent images the flight of the Zelinka family from Europe to America).

Christopher Isherwood, whose fascination with the cinema will be discussed in a later chapter, is attracted to Robert Flaherty's definition of film as the longest distance between two points. The paradox is apt, because to Isherwood a film is a meditation on images, and must therefore be prolix and mystically repetitious. One of its virtues is the dissolution of the impatient, consecutive time to which the chore of narrative condemns the novelist. For Wells film is not a mystical deceleration of narrative but a technological acceleration of it. Like all technology, it saves time. Wells might have called it the shortest distance between two points: the artistic equivalent of air travel.

America not only invents the machines which science fiction converts into artistic techniques, but remains the irresistible subject of science fiction. In *The War in the Air,* New York is destroyed. In a later scientific romance, *The Shape of Things To Come,* towering, tumescent New York has simply been superseded. Wells now revises the future, and declares that after the air war New York need not be rebuilt. It is now a victim not of catastrophe but of the serene process of modernization which Wells calls "the ultimate revolution." Sending back dispatches from the year 2106, Wells reports that during the twentieth century New York was abandoned and dangerous, its "huge unoccupied skyscrapers" teetering unstably, its bridges trodden only by packhorses and mules. Until recently, Manhattan "has been the most old-fashioned city in the world, unique in its gloomy antiquity," but now in 2106 the Empire State Building is at last being demolished. On Wells's first visit to America, the

" AS THE AIRSHIPS SAILED ALONG THEY SMASHED UP THE CITY AS A CHILD WILL SHATTER ITS
CITIES OF BRICK AND CARD."

New York destroyed: an illustration from *The War in the Air* by
A. C. Michael.

provisional jumble and straining verticality of Wall Street seemed
to yearn for a future of "free, high circumstance, and space and
leisure, light and free living." Now Wells fabricates that future. The
new world envisaged in *The Shape of Things To Come* was built
for the film of the work, *Things To Come* (1936). Wells wrote the
script, and in his introduction to the published version he discredits
the robotized future conjured up by Fritz Lang's film *Metropolis*.
Lang's city, a labyrinth of bizarrerie in which airplanes buzz like
moths above elevated highways, and skyscrapers flaunt horned pro-
trusions and fantasticated caps, is an alternative version of New
York: it derived from the Manhattan skyline, which he had first seen
from a ship docked at a westside pier in 1924. Wells corrects his
prediction and amends his image of New York. Lang's error, he
argues in a memorandum circulated to the designers of *Things To
Come*, was to believe the future would be brutally mechanized and

inhumanly disproportionate. The signs of his error are his prepos-
terously exotic skyscrapers, flattered by searchlights. Wells's future
is to be leisured and harmonious, and will be subterranean not
stratospheric. In 2055, he specifies, there will be no skyscrapers:
cities will be excavated, dug into hills. Wells's future gives up the
hyperbolic ambition to rival nature which erects the man-made
mountains of Manhattan, because, as Passworthy remarks in the
film, "we have got the better of nature." A little girl, learning history from a televiewer, is amused by the vertical bombast of ancient
Manhattan and remarks, "What a funny place New York was—all
sticking up and full of windows." Her sage grandfather, who in this
millennial future has lived to be 110 years old, explains that this is
evidence of a pathetic dependence on nature which has since been
overcome: there was no light inside those antedeluvian cities, so
"they had to stick the houses up into the daylight—what there was
of it."

The cinema adapts itself to Wells's prognostication of a world
fragmenting and reassembling itself because it specializes in swift
alternations which elide time. Montages foreshorten history. At the
beginning of Wells's scenario, Brooklyn Bridge appears in a series
of images which survey the teeming cities of the unreconstructed
world. Crowds hurry across it, the river below is littered with traffic.
Then, after the global war, it is seen again as wreckage and refuse:
"The tangle of cables in the water. Shipping sunk in the harbour.
New York, ruined, in the background." Montage also compresses
geography: the script suggests supplementary images of Palm Beach
or Coney Island devastated. The cinema by making aerial summaries
of events can photograph the movements of history. Hence Wells
sets it "to bridge, as rapidly and vigorously as possible, the transition
from the year 1970 to the year 2054," when industrial recovery
began. As a medium of global surveillance and global simultaneity,
the cinema is hailed in the film itself as the art work of the future. By
a technical miracle it can represent "the enormous range . . . of
thought and discussion in the new world," allowing a single person,

New York rendered obsolete: the history lesson from *Things To Come*,
1936. The little girl says, "What a funny place New York was—all
sticking up and full of windows." Reproduced by permission of
London Films.

the demagogue Theotocopulos, to speak to the whole world and
elicit an immediate reaction from every corner of the earth.

Wells's dual technological trust in the future and in the cinema
which was to transcribe it dismayed Graham Greene, who reviewed
Things To Come in the *Spectator* of February 28, 1936. He mocks
its transformation of technology into religion, its postulation of a
heaven made from labor-saving devices and shiny dynamos, but admits that Wells's dream suits the cinema, precisely because it is base-
less and unorganized. The medium, as Greene sees it, is a harmless

147

lie-machine, manufacturing a sedative unreality, a cheap parody of religious consolation. Film itself is, he says (commenting on the precarious moments of joy in a Sacha Guitry film at the end of the same review), "the nearest to a Utopia poor mankind is ever likely to get." Whereas Wells considered the cinema to be the actualization of Utopia, Greene can only think it a poignant, vulgar, and absurd substitute.

But Wells's conviction of the cinema's redemptive power persisted. Early in 1936 he made a trip to Hollywood to publicize *Things To Come,* and was interviewed on his way home by the *New York Times.* He assured the reporter that Europe would subside into war again in 1940, but spoke of his own allegiance to the cinema as if it indemnified him against the approaching disaster: "I have entered the motion-picture field and leave things to come, pestilence and famine, to others." Prediction is his protection. Because he has foreseen and foresuffered the future in *Things To Come,* he has earned a personal immunity to the gruesome things which are coming. In this interview, published on January 12, Wells also transfers to the cinema his diplomatic hope for the supercession of national divisions and the constitution of a world state. Wells had promoted himself as a world-minded go-between, and hoped to consolidate international union by disregarding frontiers and convening meetings between Roosevelt and Stalin; in Hollywood, he claims to have engineered a comparable diplomatic coup by arranging the first encounter between Charlie Chaplin and Walt Disney. Though both were working in Hollywood, they had never met, and Wells uses this anomaly to point to the obtuse introversion of the film studios, which are as self-immersed and as jealous of their own interests as the nation states whose boundaries he hoped to break down. Furthermore, Chaplin and Disney are, like Roosevelt and Stalin in Wells's estimation, both latent internationalists. He praises them for doing the only "film work today that remains international." Chaplin is international because his comedy is silent, and communicates without the intercession of language; Disney is international because his comedy is mechanical, a scientific application of animation techniques, and Wells praises his "most marvellous machinery" and "most interesting experiments."

Like the airplane and the cinema, American architecture has a symbolic virtue for Wells, freeing man from shaming, lowering nature and endowing him with the mental freedom of the skies. Skyscrapers like aviators exist in defiance of gravity, but the altitudinous excitements of both are made possible by technology. In *The Work, Wealth and Happiness of Mankind,* Wells describes the development of structural steel as an incident in the scientific conquest of nature. The steel framework freed building from the need to grow by accumulating weight, which confirmed architecture's enslavement to gravity. Steel buildings cast off this pile-like ponderousness and could be light and graceful as well as hubristically tall. Building used to be wet, grubby, and primeval: "Up to the present the mud hut has been clearly traceable in modern building. Cement, mortar, the dried brick are all mud at one remove." Technology dries building out, makes it cleanly mechanical not soilingly organic. Once the American building industry had developed techniques for riveting or welding steel frameworks, the wet dabbling in mud could give way to "the 'dry' putting together of fully fabricated parts." Steel-frame construction isn't messy like stone or brick but elegantly hollow, so that the rooms inside it resemble vacuum flasks which can be maintained at a constant temperature, or soundproofed, or even made of glass. The antique house was a mere ziggurat of "masonry boxes," but "the modern building becomes more and more like an engine, with tubes for air, hot and iced water, sanitary apparatus of all sorts, wires for heating and lighting, telephones, speaking-tubes and the like." The Englishman's home is a cave, the American's apartment a machine.

Because steel-frame construction is quick, it encourages constant rebuilding, and inaugurates a systematic remaking of the world, already evident in New York. Wells calculates that "England is being rebuilt at the rate of a complete new world in a hundred years," but in New York architectural generations are briefer and therefore the historical turnover is faster: the economic life of a skyscraper is assumed to be no more than thirty years. Architecture is a Wellsian time machine, working (like the cinema) to accelerate the draggingly regular pace of human history.

Having renounced the novel to campaign for the world state, Wells set himself to write the world's history in order to speed up that history, hastening the establishment of international order by demonstrating its necessity. America appears in this world history like a modern, secular incarnation. The *Short History of the World* (1922) calls the United States "an altogether new thing in history" or "a new kind of occurrence." Christ's occurrence in history marked the entry of eternity into time, the descent of grace into nature; the incarnation of America signifies the machine's conquest of nature and human history. The discovery of America is a technological achievement, made possible (as Wells says in *The Shape of Things To Come*) by "the keeled sailing ship, the science of navigation, and the mariner's compass," not by the determination of individual explorers. Technology also presides over the process of continental expansion: the railways rather than adventurous backwoodsmen press toward the Pacific and compose "the vast territory of the United States into one indissoluble mental and material unity—the greatest real community . . . in the world." The uniformity which depressed the Victorians is for Wells a technological virtue. The railways and the telegraph prevent the regressive fragmentation threatened by the Civil War, and cancel out the estrangements of distance. This capacity for assimilation is the source of America's historical novelty and of its admonition to the world: "the United States in scale and possibility is half-way between a European state and a United States of all the world." It is the model for the actual constitutional future, as well as for the magical futures of Wells's science fiction.

In Wells's encyclopedic *Outline of History* (1920), the historical apparition of America in 1492 and the subsequent acts of self-definition by the United States in 1776 (when it declares its independence of Europe) and 1918 (when it emerges from that independence to rescue Europe from itself) are the most significant events.

By an ethnological quirk, just as in the modern world America's mission is to release other nations from the impasse of their history, so in the ancient world it has no prehistory to hamper it. The *Outline* notes that there is no evidence of man in America before the end of the Pleistocene age. All human remains are Amer-Indian, so there can have been no "preceding race of sub-men." Human life begins on this favored continent in a dazzling instantaneous incarnation, not as the result of a prolonged evolutionary preparation: "Man was fully man when he entered America. The old world was the nursery of the sub-races of mankind."

As man was fully man when he entered America, so Wells's America was fully America when (in another of these secular incarnations) it entered history. The chapter on its discovery is interestingly entitled "America Comes into History." America doesn't passively await Columbus, but chooses to enter history, as if possessing a will of its own. By attributing the initiative to America itself, which decides to emerge at this point into history as Christ had earlier bewilderingly materialized in nature, Wells diminishes the heroic undertaking of the navigators. Columbus's notion of a westerly trip across the Atlantic, though it stretched the fifteenth-century imagination, is discounted as "to us a very obvious and natural enterprise." His venture reveals not the dizzying reach of his speculation but his mental narrowness and misinformation. He knew the world was spherical, "but he underestimated its size," and complacently believed that the wealth of Japan lay temptingly to hand somewhere near Mexico. He died unaware "that he had discovered a new continent," convinced "that he had sailed round the world to Asia." Credit is displaced from Columbus to America itself, which has chosen to awake from the slumber of its nonentity but is ignominiously denied the discoverers and explorers it deserves. The ambitions of those who opened it up were mercenary not scientific. The Spaniards were too incurious and rapacious to make "intelligent observations" of native culture. Later in the *Outline,* America is seen as history's legacy to an overcrowded and impoverished Europe. But Europe proves itself unworthy of the benefaction by squabbling greedily over territory. Nor are the inhabitants of the original thirteen colonies worthy of the idea of America they invoke to justify their desire for independence from Britain. Their revolt, Wells says, is provoked by a short-sighted resentment of taxation, and only later do they interpret independence as a moral immunity, and repudiate what Washington called the "entangling alliances" of the European Great Power system. Even then they are in error, for in the pursuit of independence they sentence themselves to isolation. Wells's America comes of age, attains self-consciousness, only in 1917, when by declaring war on Germany it incarnationally re-emerges into history and international politics after a century of isolationism, exchanging passivity for the evangelistic propagation of a "new spirit" in human affairs.

Having entered history to become the prey of European rapacity, Wells's America first defensively acquires an idea of itself with the Declaration of Independence, which brought "a new sort of community into the world" and created a political state appropriate to the new continent. In 1776 America claimed a dispensation from the sordid accumulation of guilt which is European history. Its new political models were therefore a return to the innocent "bare and stripped fundamentals of human association." The preamble to the state constitution of Massachusetts relieves the citizen of his burden of obedience to the state and declares that he can freely elect to participate in its society and government. History is muddlingly and messingly organic. America prefers the sleek pristine cleanliness of the machine, which makes things happen rather than suffering them to grow. As Wells says, while modern European states haphazardly evolved, "the United States were planned and made" by those rational, historically guiltless gestures commemorated in the constitutional preamble. In 1492, America was merely discovered. In 1776, it was invented—or rather, it imagined itself for the first time. Invention is a mechanical initiative, interrupting and accelerating the sluggish drift of history. The initial act of invention in the Declaration of Independence therefore generates other inventions which speed American development and save it from the natural torpor of history: among those Wells enumerates are the railway, the steamboat, the electric telegraph, new agricultural technology, and the flying-machine of the Wright brothers. Even American social organizations are technical novelties: the communistic projects of Robert Owen at New Harmony, Indiana, or the paternalistic factories of Henry Ford.

In 1776, Wells's America declares itself to be a new kind of state. In 1918, it emerges from a century of aloofness to declare a new order in world politics, with Woodrow Wilson's mediation at the Versailles peace conference. Wilson's Fourteen Points are for Wells another secular incarnation. Like divinity descending into nature, like eternity punctuating human time, Wilson stated "the essential differences of the American State from the Great Powers of the Old World. He unfolded a conception of international relationships that came like a gospel, like the hope of a better world, to the whole western hemisphere." Taken together, the actions of 1776 and 1918 make America the tutelary god of Wells's world history. 1776 arrogates to America a moral superiority which is at first guarded in lofty solitude. In 1918 America sets out to remake the entire world in its image. The passage from one to the other resembles that from the retributive justice of the Old Testament to the redemptive compassion of the New. 1918 exchanges the Old Law of arrogant rectitude for a New Law of evangelizing internationalism. America is now the world's better self. Wilson's criticism of secret agreements and military aggression, his demand for free seaways and national self-determination, were "the commonplaces of American thought," but also "the secret desires of every sane man." In articulating the desires of sane men everywhere, Wilson universalized the idea of America. The League of Nations which he proposed was a United States of the world.

But the god fails. Wells's world history ends in calamity. Woodrow Wilson suffers the automatic fate of an angel venturing into the ingeniously evil world. His American innocence is unequal to the guile of European experience. He sets out for Versailles as a symbolic conscience, but he ends by being trapped inside a nineteenth-century novel. Wilson's failure, as Wells presents it, is specifically a capitulation to the novel, which world history should have made obsolete. In the *Outline,* Wells calls the novel a "pseudo-real account of ways of living, of going about in the world," suiting periods of mannered luxury like the decadence of the Roman Empire or the eighteenth century, when history has lost its urgency and people are engrossed in the busy diverting detail of the world. For Wells, the novel is too easily contented with social gossip about ways of behaving in the world. He wants instead to change the world, and the novel conspires to frustrate him, because it is happy with the world as presently constituted. Woodrow Wilson's apostasy is to turn Versailles into a social outing, an incident from a novel. Wellsian world history ends as a novel by Henry James: the "immense inexperience" of Wilson is baffled and betrayed by the "seasoned and bitter and intricate experience" of Europe, as in James's story of Daisy Miller. The history of mankind peters out in a series of chatty pleasure trips. Wells objects that "a social quality, nay, almost a tourist quality, was introduced into the world settlement" by the wives of the American representatives, who had come along for a treat and organized scenic excursions which interrupted the political negotiations. Kipling's epic alternative to the novel prides itself on its exclusion of women, since its concern is the work not the leisure of society; now women are blamed for a reversion to the novel with its lazy deambulations.

As history lapses into an idle, vagrant novel, so Wilson—who ought to be an institution, a disembodied head like Wells's F.D.R. or a mere abstract initial, like the disputants in *The King Who Was a King*—lapses into a character. He condescends to be a man when he might have remained an absent, omniscient god, like F.D.R. invisibly manipulating his constituents over the air. Wilson's mistake, Wells says, was to have appeared at Versailles: "he should have remained in America, in the role of America, speaking occasionally, as if a nation spoke." Wilson squandered his intellectual and institutional superiority to become a mere "character," one of those inept, anarchic individualists whose presence Wells found offensive in the Victorian novel. Martin Chuzzlewit and Mark Tapley hate America because it wants to make institutions of them, which means depriving them of their unruly English freedom to be characters, and this it does by bringing them close to death. For Wells the disaster is the opposite one. The Presidency ought to have freed Wilson from the "narrow egotism" which is the fatal charm of the novel. He ought to have generalized himself into an institution; when instead he chose to be a character he had to cede control to a character more treacherously limited and more skillful at deception and self-dramatization than his own, that of Clemenceau. Wilson wanted to make the world safe for democracy. Clemenceau objected to his messianic ranting: his own desire, Wells says, was to make the world safe for Paris. He is a recrudesence of the selfish wit and scheming allure which is the dubious attraction of characters in nineteenth-century novels, and his devious humanity mocks the austere and priggish allegory of America.

The novel wins. 1918 is both America's second incarnation, and its possibly fortunate fall from innocence into the experience of history. The incarnation is itself now a betrayal, for an immaterial idea has been diminished to meager, meretricious human form: "Wilson, the Hope of Mankind, had vanished, and . . . all the illustrated fashion papers contained pictures of a delighted tourist and his wife, grouped smilingly with crowned heads and such-like enviable company."

Historically, Wells's prophecy about America doesn't fulfill itself. But in restitution he makes new prophecies, which prove equally fragile. After Wilson's failure, Wells nominated a new god, only to watch him fail as well. In 1934 he saluted Franklin Roosevelt as the world's savior, but a year later, in *The New America: The New World,* he acknowledged that control of the air waves had passed from Roosevelt to his demagogic opponents. Though in 1906, writing *The Future in America,* Wells had looked forward to a New Deal which would organize the mess of America, when that New Deal was enforced by Roosevelt Wells found he didn't like it. America's problem in 1906 was a riotous excess of energy, but in 1935 Roosevelt simply suppressed that energy rather than canalizing it. The government, Wells complained, had devitalized the economy, and paid farmers not to produce crops. *The Future in America* is about boom and the embarrassments of plenty. *The New America* of 1935 is about the neurotic atonement for this affluence, as society lunges toward restriction and purgative under-living. Like a medieval chiliast, constantly revising the chronology of his prophecies as time catches up with him and disproves his predictions, projecting his dream state into ever remoter futures as if to protect it from actually coming to pass, Wells needs the science fiction of *Things To Come* as a time machine to carry his prognostications into a future so distant that he'll never reach it and so won't have to suffer disappointment.

America forces Wells and his successors to make art not from recollection of the past but from anticipation of the future. But prediction is a perilous business, as Wells's disappointments reveal. We trust the future to make things better, though we suspect it may make them worse. "Things to come" is both a promise and a threat. And whatever the outcome, we naturally resent the future because it won't include us. Our predictions will come true only when we're no longer there to enjoy the credit or the benefit.

Thus Wells falters between a millennial and an apocalyptic America. But an extra problem, which hasn't yet occurred to Wells, is that in America the two conditions, millennium and apocalypse, might not even be alternatives. Science fiction makes maps on which heaven and hell are interchangeable. Huxley's hellish brave new world, for instance, is a Wellsian heaven of social engineering. This is why Huxley's novel so irritated Wells, who considered it a libel on the technological revolution he was promoting. In *The Shape of Things To Come* he reproaches Huxley for impeding understanding of the future by being so alarmist. Wells doesn't see that the heaven of science fiction would be to most of us a hell. The states of perfection and perdition are alike alien to complacent earthlings, who would rather not be translated to either of them. America regenerates the world, but it does so by speeding up history. The faster it actualizes the future, the closer it brings the end: hence the bombed New York of *The War in the Air,* or the bombed Los Angeles of Huxley's *Ape and Essence.* Science fiction graduates with terrifying alacrity from rectifying the world to ruining it, for science's ultimate conquest of nature is the discovery that it can destroy nature. The career of America follows a similar course, for it simultaneously shows how the world began ("in the beginning," Locke said, "all the world was America") and how it will end.

The best Wells's successors can say about America is that there at least one's bad dreams can be relied on to come true. Isherwood neatly inverts Wells's millennial hopes for America and turns Wells's disappointment into gratification by saying that America's tendency to error is its virtue: "this is where the mistakes are being made—and made first; so that we're going to get the answers first." For D. H. Lawrence too, the only future in America was death and putrefaction, but he accepts this morbid degeneration as the necessary preliminary to rebirth. And Huxley, having delineated hell in *Brave New World,* moved to Los Angeles to live in that hell and dream there of heaven. The value of America, he explained, lay in its being the Great Wrong Place, a garish hell which prompted one to postulate the existence, somewhere else, of a compensatory heaven. The optimism of the Wellsian social engineer, melioristically hastening the "ultimate revolution," is first warped into the despairing rage of the satirist, impatient instead for Armageddon; but when

Huxley went to live in America he found satire undergoing a further change into mysticism. Thus the progress circles back to where it began in Wells, for Huxley's mysticism is a mutation of Wells's engineering—it employs not social technology but the psychological, vision-inducing technology of drugs; it creates not a new world but a new chemical heaven.

The novelist is trained to imitate the unsatisfactory world which exists already. In America he must concentrate on the heaven and hell which don't exist, inventing worlds and destroying them. The European societies in which the novel is at home seem to be everlasting. America lacks their self-satisfied stasis and provokes in an acute form the problems of the beginning and the end. European societies began so long ago that they encourage us to believe they will never end, but America began yesterday, and may therefore end tomorrow, or this afternoon. It is at once an innocent new beginning and a corrupt, exhausted ending, both a mystical liberation from history and a satiric termination of history. It paradisially predates society as European literature knows it and yet also—millennially or apocalyptically—outlasts it. At the same time it is Kipling's epic past and Wells's technocratic future.

6

PRIMITIVE AMERICA

D. H. Lawrence
in New Mexico

Once America has mechanically organized itself for the future, Wells permits no ethnic objections to its unity. For Kipling the American blacks are a troublesome throwback, but Wells cites them as a case of that "self-suppression," whereby unruly individuals submit to the common good, which is the moral of his global history. American Negroes, Wells argues, disprove the philological rule (which lies behind Kipling's decomposition of America into warring tribes, each with its own dialect) that linguistic groups are racial groups. The fact that the blacks speak English is for Wells evidence of ecumenism not—as it would be for Kipling—of miscegenation: "a common language" bespeaks "a common intercourse . . . and the possibility of intermixture; and if it does not point to a common origin, it points at least to a common future." That common future is the destiny of America and the destination of Wellsian history.

Wells dedicates Europe to the past, America to the future. But he is at once contradicted by D. H. Lawrence, who reverses the relationship. For Lawrence, the Victorian snobbery about America's lack of a history ignores the primeval antiquity of the country. The America of the white man is a superficial mercenary imposition on a continent much older than Europe, with a more primitive and savage racial memory. Lawrence dismisses Europe, as the Victorians dismissed America, because it is infantile and ignorant: it has forgotten its ancestral past, while in America that subterranean past slumbers just below the skyscrapers. Exploration of America must proceed vertically not horizontally. Rather than admiring the up-to-date, mechanized surface of the United States, the world erected by the newcomers, the explorer must excavate the visceral, autochthonous America supplanted by the Europeans.

This exploration is time-travel in the opposite direction to Wells's. Seeking out America's mythological past, Lawrence derided Wells's version of its technological future. His poem "Wellsian Futures" jeers at the glib hope of a humanity redeemed by science, breeding bodiless globules in bottles. Lawrence's own America is not a laboratory of sterilized, asexual rebirth, but a cemetery, "the open tomb of my race" as he says in the poem "The Evening Land," published in 1922, the year of his first journey to America. Lawrence here recoils from America as a place of death which promises only a grim Wellsian afterlife in a "social heaven": a "more-than-European idealism" will resurrect the human being as a machine. That uprisen self ("your single resurrection / Into machine-made perfect man") is an automaton: Wells's ideal, Lawrence's horror. Lawrence fears and loathes this be-aureoled, bleached, skeletal, futuristic America, in which, he imagines, the customs officers are Wellsian robots asking "machine-cut questions," and human contact is signalized by an "iron click" or the tintinnabullation of a cash register. But despite himself he is drawn there by his anticipation of another America under the metallic surface. Between 1922 and 1925 he wandered the world in search of an alternative to the industrial society he hated, visiting Sicily, Ceylon, and Australia, and the goal of this pilgrimage was America.

Lawrence hesitates between two Americas. One of them, Wells's, is petrified in mechanical death, the other is struggling to be born. Lawrence's own mission there, he decides, will be to bring that "unissued" America to birth. Another jibe at Wells is inserted into *Mornings in Mexico,* the account of Lawrence's time in the American Southwest. Here he mocks the pomposity of books with titles like *The Future of America:* Wells, it will be remembered, had written one called *The Future in America.* Lawrence's own America in this travel essay is not a product of scientific experiment like Wells's, but merely one of a series of combustible "Worlds successively created and destroyed" as the sun periodically convulses, for this is the explanation of history offered by Aztec myth.

Though Lawrence was impatient to transfer his quest for the buried pre-industrial past to America, circumstances between 1915 and 1922 frustrated him. During the war years, he couldn't obtain a passport, and later he was detained in England by the prosecution of his novel *The Rainbow.* Waiting, he came to dread America as much as he longed for it. But his fear is a psychological tribute to America, which he saw as a land of painful death and appalling resurrection, not a facile refuge. He despised the helplessness of the Latins, among whom he was living in Sicily before his American trip: they muddle on until disaster overtakes them, he said, and then emigrate to America. For him America is not a dream of wealth and leisure but the ultimate and most daunting test of his strength, from which his will shrinks in fear. "I daren't go there," he confesses in a letter in December 1916. His terror was fixed on forbidding, authoritarian New York, the citadel of that futuristic America which terrified him. New York is the brutal death beyond which lies resurrection. To Lawrence the Statue of Liberty radiated not hope but Plutonic despair: a letter in 1923 refers to Liberty clenching her fist in the harbor. The New York customs officials guard the entrance to the underworld: they had persecuted Lawrence even before his appearance in the country by confiscating copies of his allegedly seditious and obscene novels, and they would, he feared, destroy his paintings. The immigration officials used to inquire politely if it was the visitor's intention to subvert the Constitution of the United States. Lawrence couldn't have given them a truthful answer, for he was a symbolic saboteur, imaginatively pledged to the destruction of the mechanical United States and the liberation of primal America. Hence his anxiety to enter or leave by back doors, as if to evade inquisition. He was a smuggler whose contraband was his inflammatory ideas.

Avoiding New York also guaranteed that he was arriving in mythic America, not in the crass, mercantile conquered province of Uncle Samdom, as he called it. To make this symbolic gesture of repudiation, he organized circumlocutory itineraries and created preposterous difficulties for himself. In 1915, offered the use of an estate in Florida, he wanted to sail directly there, "without going to that cursed New York," and investigated the schedules of trading ships to Jacksonville, Susquehanna, or Fort Myers. This trip didn't occur, because he was detained by the trial of *The Rainbow*. In 1921 Mabel Dodge Luhan offered him an adobe in Taos, New Mexico, and again he laid plans to evade "that awful New York," considering merchant ships to New Orleans or Galveston, or even entry at Los Angeles. Exit was to be as circuitous and fugitive as entry. In December 1922, from the ranch at Questa, New Mexico, he planned to sail to England by way of Mexico City and Vera Cruz, because he detested New York and Boston. New York is the capital of the unnatural United States, and Lawrence therefore sets it against his own savage, native America. He told his publisher, B. F. Huebsch, that New York worried him more than "a savage jungle: not because it is savage, but because of the overweening mechanical civilisation."

Lawrence concedes in 1915 that "America is bad, but at least it has a future." That future, however, is to be made from a violent destruction of the present and a restoration of the past. Though Lawrence himself flinched from America, he sent his books on ahead of him as revolutionary catalysts. They would make the American future on his behalf. Denied a passport because he was liable to conscription during the 1914-18 war, he wrote a series of essays on American literature and dispatched them as his subversive deputies. The essays on classic American literature, first published in the *En-*

glish Review in 1918-19 and collected in 1923, denounce American literature as a record of Uncle Sam's apostasy. Hawthorne attaching the scarlet letter of shame to the sensual Hester and Melville pursuing and exterminating the white whale are writing about the persecution and eventual mechanization of mythical, vital America. Hester is branded and cast out, Ahab's whales are killed and cut up. Criticism for Lawrence is geographical exploration by proxy. He is interested always in the literature of territorial extremes. He calls the Sicilian novelist Verga one of the "genuine emotional extremes of European literature: just as Selma Lagerlöf or Knut Hamsen may be the other extreme northwards," and American literature is correspondingly the extreme, stretched extension of European culture, in which consciousness is tautened by guilt and sensual self-hatred and then snapped into derangement. Lawrence identified these essays—which celebrate the decomposition of consciousness into mania in Hawthorne, Melville, and Poe—with the unmaking of the world. He doubted if they could be published "while this world stands," and predicted that they would cause a convulsion in America. They were prescriptions for the millennium, written "for the world that will come after this poor, weak-stomached show," so dangerous that (as Lawrence reports in a letter of July 1918) even the typist transcribing them collapses, as if after exposure to their contagion.

The *Studies in Classic American Literature* interprets America through its literature as a place of extinction. Lawrence planned his journey to America in 1922 as a world-encircling, world-renouncing tour, a last circuit of the dying earth. He accepted Mabel Dodge Luhan's invitation to Taos but, rather than crossing directly to ghastly New York, he insisted on approaching America "from the West, over the Pacific." From Taormina in Sicily he traveled to Ceylon (where his friend Earl Brewster was studying Buddhism) and Australia, arriving in San Francisco on September 11, which was his thirty-seventh birthday. The roundabout itinerary is allegorized as a pilgrimage. Writing to Brewster in October 1921, Lawrence apportions the globe into categories of spirit: "the East seems to me the world to meditate in, Europe the world to *feel* in, America the world to act in." The route chosen is thus a spiritual progress. Leaving Europe signifies a retreat from the wasting pressures of personal emotion, from mere feeling. The East is a way-station for meditative purification. But to remain there is to fail, because the dialectic must be followed through. From the East, you return not to insipid, inspissated European feeling but to American action. A letter to Brewster from New Mexico in July 1924 rejects the lassitude of the East in favor of American vigor: "here one *must* act, or wither: and in Asia, it seems to me, one *must* meditate."

Before setting out, Lawrence deplored the strain of this world-losing, world-regaining circumnavigation, but recognized its symbolic necessity. The East is "the *source*," America "the extreme periphery," and "must one go to the extreme limit, then to come back?" But the East's attraction is a listless peace which Lawrence mistrusts because it abandons struggle. He is condemning in advance the mysticism of Isherwood and the drugged introversion of Huxley, who settle in California because it is America's approximation to this otiose East. For Lawrence, Brewster's reclusion in his Kandy monastery is an intermediary stage, not a goal: a death which has not yet turned into a resurrection. A letter to Catherine Carswell announces that he is going to Ceylon, though he shrinks as yet from the United States, because he wants "to withdraw from the world, away towards the inner realities that *are* real: and return, maybe, to the world later." He criticizes "Buddhistic inaction" but agrees that "the Buddhistic peace is the point to start from." Wondering whether, having traveled so far, he ought to reverse direction by returning from Ceylon to Australia, he asks "what is the good after all of going where everything is just *unlearnt* and confused to the utmost"—that is, America; "perhaps it is true, Buddhism is the true realism, *things as they are*. And America is utterly *things as they are not*." Calling America "things as they are not" suggests Auden's later description of it, with which Huxley concurred, as "the Great Wrong Place," the opposite extreme from the amenable idyllic "Great Good Place" of Henry James's story. But there is a disparity. Auden lives in hell in order to punish himself and in the hope of graduating, when purged, to heaven; Huxley lives in hell to dream druggily of heaven. The awfulness of America is for Auden a stimulus to self-improving self-reproach, for Huxley a stimulus to self-detachment. Both are using America in a way Lawrence would have called Buddhistic, as an aid to meditation. Lawrence acclaims its awfulness for a different reason, because America is to him the field of polemical action: like Marx and Lenin, or Engels in the filth of industrial Manchester, he is touring the world auditioning locations for revolution, which is likeliest to occur where the disease and decadence are the most putrescent.

Lawrence's symbolic western entry into America is anticipated by Kipling and replicated by Huxley, Auden, and Isherwood, but in each case the significance varies. Kipling in 1889 arrived in San Francisco from India and traveled across the country on his way to England. The western entry marks his reorientation of imperial geography. He claims to be an ersatz Indian not an Englishman, and for him the imperial outpost has become the center. He therefore crosses America not on the voyage out, but on the voyage back, and uses it as a gradual training in disillusionment, a stage between his withdrawal from India and his capitulation to the small mean world of England. Hence his dismissive comparison of Chicago and Calcutta. Kipling's imperial retreat is ironically echoed by Auden and Isherwood, who in 1938 toured the empire as photographically bland memorialists of its collapse. They returned from the war in China by way of Japan and made their American landfall at Vancouver, crossing Canada by train and descending into the United States at Portal, North Dakota. History for them has gone into reverse: they are forced by the absurd circularity of geography to go back to the point from which they set out, London, even though they no longer consider it home. They return to observe Europe's disintegration during the Munich crisis that summer, and leave again almost immediately, in the opposite direction. In January 1939 they traveled back to New York, this time as immigrants, refugees from European history not the wry spectators of historical calamity who had been sent to China the year before.

The itinerary closest to Lawrence's is Huxley's. In the journey recounted in *Jesting Pilate,* Huxley left Genoa in September 1925 and traveled through India, Burma, Malaya, Singapore, and Java, changing ships in Manila and visiting Hong Kong and Japan on the way to San Francisco, where he arrived on May 5, 1926. From San Francisco he made his way to Los Angeles, Chicago, and New York, then back to London. *Jesting Pilate* was published later in the year. Huxley's conclusions resemble Lawrence's. They met in Lincolnshire in August 1926, and Lawrence was gratified that Huxley had also "simply hated India," because (he suspected) of its philosophical defeatism, its resignation from the life struggle. But Huxley's is a satiric journey, Lawrence's a mythic one. Huxley is glibly scornful about a world in disrepair: hence his presentation of himself as a flippant, indifferent Pilate, asking what truth is but not waiting for an answer. He finds in the East only an anticipatory parody of America. The natives in Batavia gape at Hollywood films which depict America as an internment camp of inane criminality, inhabited exclusively by crooks, half-wits, sharpers, and voluptuaries. Huxley's America, on this first trip, is a travesty of revelation. Commerce there is piously evangelical while evangelism (this was the period of Aimée Semple McPherson's soul-saving vaudeville) is brazenly commercial. The satiric western itinerary, which sees America as the final stage in a process of dissolution originating in the Far East, recurs in Huxley's *Ape and Essence,* which is set in Los Angeles in the year 2108. Now, after a third world war, scientists set out from New Zealand, which has survived the radioactive holocaust, to rediscover America from the west coast. America is no longer an adjunct of Europe, as entry from the east coast presumes it to be, because there is no Europe: the Africans are reported to have taken it over.

"To travel," for Huxley, "is to discover that everyone is wrong."

In *Jesting Pilate* he therefore ends where he began, sadder but no wiser. Lawrence travels in the urgent hope of identifying the wrong and redeeming it. His is a thanatological voyage, solemnizing the "death-happening" of a moribund Europe and the resurrection of a new America. He often likened himself to Columbus, and his novels to acts of exploration. He called *The Rainbow* a "voyage of discovery . . . like Columbus," and in Cornwall in 1916 announced that he felt like Columbus confronting "a shadowy America" which is not merely territory to be annexed and despoiled but "a new continent of the soul." However, the realm opened up by Columbus turns out to be the country from which no traveler returns. The last book Lawrence read on his deathbed was a biography of Columbus, as if in preparation for the reconnaissance which lay ahead. This apocalyptic sense of America explains why Lawrence must approach it from the East, which initiatically prepares him for the rite of entry, and why he must so scrupulously dissever America from the United States. America is the Great Good Place, the United States the Great Wrong Place. America, approached from the Pacific, is the Eastern hope, the macabre destination of those who have traveled around the world to abandon the world. The United States, approached from the Atlantic, is the Western decay, a monument to the cupidinous dreams of Europeans hustling to enrich themselves. The United States offers a sleek affluent new life: Auden and Isherwood in 1938 were ravished by the luxury of New York, dizzied by their own celebrity, teased by the availability of athletic sexual partners, and sustained in a state of euphoria by daily doses of Benzedrine and Seconal; no wonder they hastened back in 1939 for more of the same. America, on the contrary, promises death and a rending but salutary resurrection. The first versions of Lawrence's critical essays treat the American death as a passage into futurity. American literature, he says, re-enacts the history of the race from its first fall (in Hawthorne's parable of sexual guilt, *The Scarlet Letter*) to its post-mortem decomposition in Poe, a psychotic monster in whom "the after-effects of life" are vampirishly evident. America guarantees rebirth to its converts, while the United States attempts to abolish death. Lawrence's undead Poe is a warning of even more ghoulish phenomena to come: the scientific immortalization of the body in Huxley's Californian novel *After Many a Summer,* or the cosmetic transformation of corpses into grinning, rubicund dolls in the funeral parlors of Evelyn Waugh's *The Loved One.*

Lawrence's initial distinction between primal America and the mechanical empire of Uncle Samdom is the source of the other contrasts which cleave the critical essays. For instance, the study of Richard Henry Dana's *Two Years Before the Mast* sets the homeland of the blood against the sterile homeland of the spirit: the former is aboriginal America, the latter the automatized United States. White Americans, Lawrence says, refuse to acknowledge their country as a blood homeland but treasure a supposed spiritual affinity with Europe. Imaginatively, Americans prefer the sea to the land, because "earth is too specific," whereas the ocean is the medium of bloodless universality and can therefore be idealized. Love of the sea—in Dana, Melville, even perhaps (though this lies outside Lawrence's terms of reference) in *Captains Courageous*—means hatred of the soil. Elsewhere in the essays, the west coast stands for sensual America, the east coast for the intellectualizing United States. Dana flees from one to the other—"the Pacific is his glamour-world: the eastern States his world of actuality, scientific, materially real." Melville too renounces Typee and the idyll of the Pacific to return to the deathly idealism and industrialism of the United States. Lawrence's own experience of the country conforms to the same dismaying dualism. He had been invited, he thought, to western America, a homeland of the blood. But when he got there in 1922 he found that Mabel Dodge Luhan had re-created at Taos the psychological hell of the east coast. She had made the place an outpost of the tyrannous United States, a prison of mechanical lusts and domineering will. The essays discover in America a fiendish "lust of control": the conquistadors lust sensually for the suppression of spirit, the Anglo-Saxon colonists lust spiritually for the suppression of sense. Mabel,

an ogre of jealous pique and sexual rapacity, turns out to be the embodiment of that authoritarian lust, not a patron but an evil genius.
Repelled by her mad possessiveness, Lawrence left Taos and rented
a ranch in the hills at Del Monte, just as he had earlier described
Melville escaping from Typee.

In Mabel's own memoir, *Lorenzo in Taos*, she seems to be
one of Lawrence's inventions, a vindictive demon to whom sex is
the gruesome satisfaction of the will. Lawrence hoped that she
would meet him and his wife Frieda in India or Ceylon and conduct him back to America, shielding him from the inquisitions of
the customs officers and the nervous strain of that brawling country.
Her memoir gloats that she had no intention of meeting him half-
way. She was determined to will him to Taos, not to coax him there
in person, and to do so she used the egotistic telepathy Lawrence so
abhorred: "I'd sit there and draw him until he came." Her womb,
she says, roused her to reach out and take him, to incorporate him
into her pueblo. She justifies her impersonal lust as humanitarian
service: "My need to bring Lawrence and the Indians together was
like an impulse of the evolutionary will, apart from me, using me
for its own purpose." She must possess Lawrence, and the thrill of
possession must be made more piquant by the knowledge that she
has stolen him from someone else. Her biological mission, as she sees
it, is to remove him from his dependence on Frieda. This is also a
racial imperative: she and the red-bearded Lawrence are "Latin together, subtle, perceptive, infinitely nimble," while Frieda (born to
the Richthoffen family) is an obtuse Goth, insensitive and robust.
"I *would* save him!" Mabel vows, and inaugurates a psychic struggle
with Frieda. The two are competing mothers, bartering for Lawrence, and their dismemberment of him continues posthumously.
After his death Frieda acquired a ranch on Mabel's estate in exchange for the manuscript of *Sons and Lovers*. If property is an extension of the body, then Lawrence's manuscript is the last frail appendage of that body to be cannibalized by the survivors.

Mabel insists, like one of the castratingly idealistic women of

Lawrence's novels, that she didn't covet his body but wished "to seduce his spirit" and will him to formulate her experience at Taos
"into a magnificent creation." Because hers is a mesmeric lust, a
form of spiritual remote-control which can will him to her from Ceylon, it can also vengefully pursue him when he breaks free. After he
had moved away from Taos she retained the power to hurt him in
absentia. Lawrence's first escape was to Lobo Ranch, where he and
Frieda invited two Danish painters, Knud Merrild and Kai Götzsche,
to winter with them. Mabel spoiled the plan by sending a message
refusing them the use of more than one cabin, so they were forced
to move farther off, to Del Monte. Even here they weren't safe, for
Mabel elaborately snubbed Lawrence by not inviting him back as
her guest for Christmas. The very form of her memoir is a model of
her sorcery, for it transmits her oppressive lust in the direction of a
new victim. It is addressed to Robinson Jeffers, whose name invades
virtually every paragraph, as if Mabel is making to him a gift of her
past (inside which Lawrence is sealed), but using that gift at the
same time to capture him: "You can imagine, Jeffers, how Lawrence loved this hot spring," and so on.

Lawrence left for England in September 1923 and returned to
Taos the following March. This time he and Frieda brought with
them a painter friend, Dorothy Brett, who became their ally in the
psychic tussle with Mabel. Together they settled down to damaging
and defaming their hostess. Brett, trimming Mabel's hair one night,
sheared off the end of her ear. Painting the lavatory in an outhouse
with a scene of Eden, Lawrence and Brett cast Mabel as Eve, "the
dirty little bitch," thus symbolically blaming her for the befouling
of a paradise pitched in the place of excrement. Lawrence's reaction
to New Mexico was, as here, a symbolic rage. He made symbols of
objects and incidents in order to defile them. Symbol-making became a substitute for killing, as if he were shaping wax models of his
enemies and then parabolically impaling them. Lawrence rated killing highly as a mode of knowledge: you couldn't understand something, he said, unless you'd slaughtered it. Thus he turned the copy

he had made of Piero di Cosimo's painting of the death of Procris into a symbolic instrument of revenge against Mabel. Procris has a hole gouged in her throat. Lawrence was intent on killing Mabel, but disdained the use of guns, which he saw as a cowardly industrialization of the vital energies which should thrill through the act of murder. He planned instead to cut her throat, and did so by proxy in the painting of Procris.

He vented the same symbolic frenzy on his dog Pips because it had the temerity to copulate. For him the dog symbolized, like Mabel, the impersonal mechanical lust of America, and he railed at it as a democratic dirt-eating Whitmanesque bitch. The fury in this case didn't remain harmlessly symbolic: he chased the animal and kicked it into obedience. On another occasion he remonstrated with his cow Susan for wandering off—for possessing, that is, a contrary will of its own. He preached sermons against the slaughter of rabbits but himself shot a porcupine and at once miserably repined. His symbolic indignation extended from animals to machines. Merrild and Götzsche owned a temperamental Tin Lizzie which boiled over on the grades when in the mountains, needed cranking, and regularly had to have its coils blown on and its plugs cleaned in midjourney. Lawrence hated it for being, like Pips, unintelligent and unreliable, and he jeered at it as an image of mechanical fallibility, evidence of the error in American values. Even the gasoline stove of the Danes received its share of contumely. Lawrence refused to countenance its use on camping trips, and instead labored to entice a smoky fire from sagebrush.

The critical essays written in 1917 and 1918 now also become a symbolic scourge. Lawrence revised them during his first season in New Mexico, and they were published as *Studies in Classic American Literature* in 1923. The revision debauches the essays, but with good reason. They had unwittingly foretold Lawrence's future, since they predicted the traumatic psychological prison to which he consigned himself at Taos. He therefore adapted them to the destructive, hysterical America they prefigured. The essays turn into an as-

Lawrence milking his cow Susan. D. H. Lawrence Collection,
Humanities Research Center Library,
The University of Texas at Austin, Austin, Texas.

sault on Taos. The shrieking hen-eagle from the American crest, which screeches "We are the masterless" in the first of the 1923 essays, is the emasculating Mabel. Melville's reluctance to stay with the Typees becomes a graceless rejection of Mabel's hospitality. Lawrence now argues that only life haters "glorify the savages in America": Mabel at the time had an Indian lover. The expository style of the first version is brutalized and enfevered. The rhetoric now bastinades its subject much as Lawrence had hoped to kick his dog or abuse Mabel into acquiescence. Lawrence torments the language to make a weapon of it, to raise it off the page into a pugilistic third dimension. Hence his recourse to capitals: America is "the land of THOU SHALT NOT"; Hawthorne's Hester wants "revenge. Revenge! REVENGE!" Capitalization typographically apes the inflated idealism of the Americans themselves: "LOVE is never LOVE until it has a pin pushed through it and becomes an IDEAL." Even this violent headlining isn't enough. Heckling Crèvecœur, Lawrence scoffs at his translation of his emotional life into a sedate affection for nature, and can't find a typeface strident enough to match his contempt:

> NATURE.
> I wish I could write it larger than that.
> # NATURE.

This stylistic belligerence is merely the adjustment of form to content. In corrupting his own language Lawrence was supplying America with a style appropriate to its overbearing crassness. Melville's lurid, pompous journalistic style is, he says, "natural to the great Americans." Clumsy verbosity is a reflex of their savage "desire to go to extremes." His own manner of expletive detonation uses America's hyperbolic language against America itself. At the same time, the critical direction of the essays is reversed. The first version found in America a salutary decomposition of stale, sterile Europe. Now the essays rouse Europe to a purgative, vindictive dissolution of

America. The essay on Benjamin Franklin ends with a battle cry: "while clever America lies on her muck-heaps of gold . . . let Hell loose, and get your own back, Europe!" In Europe, he uses America against Europe; in America, he invokes Europe in denunciation of America.

The new world of sensual freedom and totemic knowledge Lawrence hoped to find in America contracts into a diseased and distraught state of mind. America becomes the name of a neurosis. Its various regions are differentiated according to the specific nervous irritations they excite. Primal America, Lawrence declares, gives off shocks of electric force from its mysterious, willful landscape. The United States, the mechanical superimposition on this primitive culture, provokes its own kind of disturbance, a tension of the solar plexus which Lawrence describes in the essay "Au Revoir, USA." The land is a substratum of violence. In Mexico, this makes human behavior eruptive and temperamental; in the United States, where a natural subliminal cruelty cannot be admitted and everyone affects meekness and amiability, energies which have been denied expression revenge themselves by turning sour and sick, making behavior tautly, seethingly nervous. Even the task of world management which Wells assigned to Americans exacerbates the mental strain. They're worried by their responsibility for the race. As Auden put it in a poem written during the trip to China in 1938, their foreign policy is anxious unrequited love:

America addressed
Mankind: *Do you love me as I love you?*

Lawrence argues in the essay "Europe Versus America" that Americans are overwrought because they're sure that if they slacken the world will collapse. They are self-strangled "in a grip of care," while Europeans, blithely indifferent, can enjoy the world because they've long since ceased to care about it.

Americans lend themselves to Lawrence's invective because they are so preoccupied with the stresses of personal identity and the collective unease of national identity, and so fond of seeing themselves in symbolic terms. They have the habit of abstractness. Rather than simply and unself-consciously living, they are critical spectators of their own lives. Hence their obsession with mental and physical hygiene, with self-helping psychiatric manuals and underarm deodorants. One of Eleanor Roosevelt's volumes of homiletic instruction is called *You Learn by Living*, which implies that living is not a natural talent like breathing but a skill to be patiently acquired, like reading. The presumption reveals much about the American character, which is apt to symbolize life and thus (in Lawrence's terms) to mechanize it. For the American life is not what one has but what one might with effort obtain. Lambert Strether in James's *The Ambassadors* stirringly urges little Bilham to "live." Issuing from a character of another nationality, the advice would seem absurdly trite: isn't little Bilham alive already? Delivered by an American, it is positively messianic. Life is not a fact but a value.

This, for Lawrence, makes Americans predators on life rather than living creatures. Life for them is a symbolic spectacle which they observe but in which they don't participate. Hence their lust for entertainment. Lawrence detested the indigenous American art of the cinema because its gigantic mechanical replicas of life exempt the audience from the duty of living. Axel in the symbolist play, disdainfully committing suicide, says that, as for living, he leaves that to his servants. Americans have left living to the celluloid phantoms of the cinema. Living is something they pay others to do on their behalf. Lawrence observes a pair of American tourists in Mexico whose relationship is a compact of cinematic fantasies. The woman loves the man because she has conflated him with her passion for Valentino, who makes love to her at second-hand on the screen. Now she wants to see Mexico because the new hero of her erotic daydreams is Ramon Novarro. The same parasitism explains the eagerness of the Americans to attend the Mexican bullfight in *The Plumed Serpent* (1926). Lawrence's angry capitals again point to the deathly

American resurrection of life into an abstract ideal: Owen at the stadium is "convinced that this was life. He was seeing LIFE, and what can an American do more!" The Mexican prophet Ramón in this novel taunts the socialists for fitting out the peons in American suits and making them look "like life in the newspapers." Innocent observation of the life of others, like Owen's at the bullfight, graduates to covetous exploitation of that life. The Irish widow Kate Leslie in the same novel reviles "these Americans, picking over the garbage of sensations, and gobbling it up like carrion birds!"

Battening on the sensations provided by others, Americans even corrupt a rite into a show. At the Hopi snake dance in Arizona, described by Lawrence in *Mornings in Mexico* (1927), a girl with bobbed hair cries, "I never did see a rattle-snake and I'm crazy to see one!" Owen likewise says he doesn't approve of bullfights "but we've never seen one, so we shall *have* to go," and in this voyeuristic eagerness Kate hears the essential "American logic." The Indians, who have been turned into a troupe of shabby performers by their white conquerors, have no notion of entertainment, because they're not guilty of the American metaphysical crime, which is to separate spirit from matter. "The American-Indian sees no division into Spirit and Matter, God and Not-God," Lawrence explains; "Everything is alive, though not personally so." American puritanism, however, insists on the duality, and the idea of entertainment is a symptom of this wounding division between matter and spirit. The cinema is for Lawrence a model of the white consciousness alienated from itself. We gaze upwards from our cocooned darkness at the spectral giants cavorting on the screen. It is ourselves we are watching and patronizing. The audience is the detached mind or spirit, amused by the antics of the body which struts and frets on the stage or flickers on the screen. But we have neutered that body in settling back to admire it from a mental or spiritual distance. The cinematic actors to whom we have signed over our physical existences are not even alive: they are ghosts, and their deathly industrial mechanization of life makes them characteristic of Lawrence's United States.

Repudiating the white United States, Lawrence allies himself with primal America, and even tries to qualify as an honorary redskin. But he can do so only by mimicking the costume of the Indians, which turns empathy into travesty. Unable to shed his own identity, he has to content himself with dressing up as if he were someone else. Already in 1916, while still living in Cornwall, he accepted a counterpane Ottoline Morrell had sent him as a contribution to his New Mexican wardrobe. Thanking her for the gift, he said he intended to wrap it round himself "like a Red Indian." Costume is always an imaginative challenge for Lawrence. Desperate to insert himself into the existences of others, wanting to feel with them subjectively rather than objectively observing them, he tries to describe not how their clothes look on them but what it's like to be inside them. His anxious self-identification with the Indians is equally a matter of changing clothes, not changing character. Visiting an Apache encampment in New Mexico, he masquerades as a redskin, enveloping himself in a red serape as he'd swathed himself in Ottoline Morrell's counterpane and trying to convince himself that this is how it feels to be an Indian: "it is good to be wrapped to the eyes in a good Navajo blanket. Then you feel warm inside yourself, and as good as invisible, and the dark air thick with enemies." But those who wear such garments habitually don't thrill to a sense of existential alteration as they don them: they take them for granted. In his affectation of Indian costume Lawrence is guilty of the same fault he reproves in white Americans. They demean the Indians by treating them as a spectacle, by trivializing their rites into side-shows, but Lawrence demeans them even further by stealing their clothes and wheedling his way into their performance.

Though Lawrence despises tourists, crass collectors of trinkets who instead of experiencing the places they visit negligently plunder them, his own attitude to the Indians resembles theirs. Tourism markets cultures by reducing them to styles. Souvenirs are fragments of a style put on sale. Touristically, New Mexico is an emporium of bead braids, moccasins, and blankets. Lawrence at Taos sees the Indians as models for the merchandise, dancing "in their sheets and their best blankets, and in their ear-rings and brilliant scarlet trousers, or emerald trousers, or purple trousers, trimmed with beads." If imperialism is the highest stage of capitalism, tourism is its last expiring extension. First the white man takes away the property of the natives, then he returns to expropriate their art. Lawrence's time in New Mexico coincides with the colonization of American Indian culture by the Art Deco style. Indian totems, deconsecrated, are carried off as artifacts. The cactus, for instance, is a sacramental plant. Lawrence venerates it as a phallic emblem, its bud thrusting through a prepuce of tarnished flesh and exuding "sperm-like juice for the pulque." Huxley's hallucinatory drugs are synthesized from it. The cactus is not only the source of visionary experience but a subject of visionary art: Huxley admired the close-ups of its blossoms in Walt Disney's *The Living Desert,* because the magnified flowers were an example of psychedelic art achieved scientifically. When the tourists arrive, the sacred plant is secularized in fashionable living-rooms, and instead of yielding Lawrence's sperm or Huxley's hallucinatory chemicals is sterilized into an ornament. Lady Klein's house in Isherwood's *The Memorial* (1932) boasts "modernized lamps with petal-like bran shades, possibly designed to represent Mexican desert plants." Maxwell Armfield's *An Artist in America* (1924), the illustrated narrative of a tour, reveals the process of stylistic colonization at work on the Indians. He sees them as extravagant self-decorators, particularly admiring the Navajo "passion for scarlet," which is woven into their blankets, and flatters them as untutored abstract artists, whose squares and zigzags are a calligraphy encoding natural phenomena. One of his own designs for his book borrows the Indian manner of decorative abstraction. Instead of trying to make a realistic replica of the Grand Canyon, he translates its cubic volumes into the likeness of a Navajo blanket, sketching the colored cleavages of rock in grids of variegated cross-hatching. Lawrence too, covetously describing the silver earrings, turquoise necklaces and ochre-dyed rugs of the tribe at Taos, identifies culture with style, and equates the Indians with the clothes they wear and sell.

Lawrence was at Taos intermittently between 1922 and 1925. He died at Vence in 1930; in 1935 his body was cremated and its ashes transferred to a chapel at Taos. Frieda had acquired their ranch from Mabel, and in February 1938 Huxley was her guest there on his way across the country from Rhinebeck, New York, to Hollywood, where a script of his had been accepted by one of the movie studios. Later Huxley experimented with living in the desert. In 1942 he moved inland from the ocean, leaving Pacific Palisades in Santa Monica for Llano del Rio, in an oasis of the Mojave Desert. For the next five years he alternated between Llano and an apartment in Beverly Hills. But his experience of the desert ended as ignominiously as Lawrence's. Hoping to enact the dissolution of society in the desert, Lawrence found at Taos a society even more competitive and rebarbative than the one he had left behind. Nor could his health withstand the tropics. He fell ill with malaria at Oaxaca in Mexico in February 1925, and as well suffered an attack of dysentery, the proverbial affliction of the Englishman abroad; the next month in Mexico City his doctor diagnosed terminal tuberculosis. Huxley too was physically unequal to the desert, and retreated to Los Angeles after developing a rabid allergy to a species of ragweed growing under his window at Llano.

Both Huxley and Lawrence identify the primitive Southwest as their chosen American landscape, but they have very different designs on it. The nonchalant vacancy of America tolerates both. Huxley's desert is cerebral, Lawrence's sensual. Their remarks about cacti demonstrate the gap between them. The one values the cactus for its chemical secrecy, the other for its erectile potency. For Huxley the tops are crushed into peyote, which provokes visions; for Lawrence the fermented sap makes pulque, which intoxicates.

Their difference over the American desert derives from a fundamental disagreement about nature. Huxley's nature is classical, Lawrence's romantic. The classical assumption is that man is a brute who can only be rescued from the atavistic vileness of his biological nature by self-discipline and membership in society, and from the inflictions and inconveniences of physical nature by science, which harnesses the rebellious elements to human use. The romantic assumption is that man is an angel who can only be rescued from the decadent vileness of society by self-liberation and a return to the physical nature which science has abused and enchained. Lawrence leaves the cactus to bloom erotically in the desert, but Huxley carries it off to a laboratory to be analyzed and decomposed. Romantic art trusts nature, and seeks to marry the emotional nature inside man to the physical nature around him. Classical art fears nature, and enlists science and satire as weapons against it. Satire mocks nature into abasement, while science subjects it to the laws of engineering. The romantic conviction of nature's beneficence belongs to temperate Europe, and cannot, according to Huxley, be transferred to America. In England, nature is at worst neutral. It may be forever sulkily drizzling, but won't ever erupt in catastrophe. Hence Wordsworth could address nature as a mild-mannered garden goddess, the deity of suburban allotments and chaste, clipped greenery. But in America, nature is inimical and vindictive, pledged to the extermination of human life. Placid mediocre English weather becomes in America an alternation of extremes—drought and deluge, heatwave and blizzard. Nature sends plagues to vex its human victims—earthquakes and tornadoes, forest fires, mud slides, insect swarms. Americans live in nature as in a combat zone, screening their doors and windows defensively, snubbing nature by creating optional technological climates indoors.

American literature, as Lawrence's essays reveal, is a means of retaliation. From Fenimore Cooper's deerslayers to Melville's whalers, it is about the human extinction of nature. This is why, extending the title of Lawrence's *Studies,* it is not only a literature of classic status but also a classical literature: a literature, that is, which hunts and scourges nature rather than, like English literature, romantically blessing it.

Lawrence interprets Mexico romantically, as a sanctuary of the "oldest religion" which worships the life force pulsing through nature. Huxley interprets it classically, as a wilderness of natural iniquity unreclaimed by science, impervious to pantheistic sentiment, censoring "the mental and the spiritual . . . all that is not day-to-day animal living." Romanticism to Huxley is a luxurious hypocrisy, for it depends on the engineering it affects to despise. The connoisseurship of landscape, he reflects in Antigua during his South American journey in 1933, is "a product of good communications," which tame a sinister and obstructive nature and make it safely lovable. To the romantic, crevasses are sublime. To classical man they are grotesque, "not . . . evidences of God's handiwork, but . . . booby-traps put in your way by some insufferably waggish devil." Central America, Huxley remarks, makes one "understand the classical attitude to nature."

Two commentaries by Huxley define the opposition between his imaginative America and Lawrence's. The first is a discussion of *The Plumed Serpent* in the travel book *Beyond the Mexique Bay* (1934), the second a preface contributed to Knud Merrild's memoir of his time with Lawrence in New Mexico, *A Poet and Two Painters* (1938). During the tour described in *Beyond the Mexique Bay*, Huxley visits Miahuatlan, in the state of Oaxaca, where Lawrence had wintered in 1925. Lawrence's enthusiasm for the place has since then been shamed by one of those calamities which are the whimsical revenges of classical nature: an earthquake has shattered the town, and Huxley find the Indians (Lawrence's vibrant sensual dancers) foraging squalidly in the ruins. Huxley proceeds to discredit Lawrence's primitivism, pointing out that he made his desert retirement bearable by sneaking into it representatives of the mind and spirit he pretended to eschew: he needed books and civilized companions, and therefore acknowledged the impossibility of a primitive renunciation.

The tour Huxley describes in *Jesting Pilate* ends satirically. Travel persuades him that everyone is wrong. Pilate circumnavigates the world asking what is truth, and returns home without having heard a plausible answer. *Beyond the Mexique Bay*, however, ends ironically. Confronted by the ugliness and misery of Mexico, Huxley is less glibly cynical, more inclined to congratulate himself on his civilized safety. His conclusion in this case is not a satiric jibe but an ironic equivocation. *Jesting Pilate* expires in a gesture of dismissal, having disproved all certainties on its way around the world. *Beyond the Mexique Bay* expires in a gesture of acquiescence, as Huxley hastens back from barbarous Mexico to a society which values mind and spirit rather than submerging them in blood. His gratitude is grudging and ironic, for he admits that civilization is a state of servitude, but he prefers this bondage to the savage visceral freedom of Mexico. This ironic capitulation to civilization and its inevitable repressions makes it apt that Huxley should be rereading *The Plumed Serpent* on the ship back from Guatemala to New York in May 1933. Lawrence's novel counsels surrender to the sensual violence of Mexico, not retreat. In reading it on the return journey Huxley is disputing its conclusion. Lawrence himself abandoned Mexico, but left his heroine Kate Leslie behind him, resigning herself to inundation by "the grand sea of the living blood." Huxley seeks to revoke her sentence, and argues that Lawrence's own misgivings are exposed by the novel's sensational degeneration. *The Plumed Serpent* is marred, he thinks, by Lawrence's frantic efforts to convince himself that immersion in blood is preferable to abstraction into mind and spirit. Lawrence has damaged his thesis in advance by presenting the Mexicans as loathsome "lice-picking, down-dragging people," and by making Kate nauseously repudiate them. The ceremonial conclusion, in which the Aztec gods are re-embodied in Ramón and Cipriano, is therefore a confidence trick. Lawrence knows he is telling a lie, but he has to tell it ever more brazenly and to support it with ever grosser ritualized cruelty, in the hope of finally persuading himself to believe it. Kate, as Huxley sees it, is sacrificed to Lawrence's own queasy hypocrisy.

The same contrariety recurs in Huxley's preface to Merrild's memoir. To Huxley, New Mexico is a classical landscape, stark, starved, forbidding. To Lawrence, New Mexico is a romantic landscape, "nakedly religious." Huxley praises it because it is so healingly inhuman: "man is either absent (less than half a million people inhabit a territory twice the size of England and Wales) or, if present, seems oddly irrelevant." Human interference with the landscape has perversely made it less not more habitable: "by deforesting the lower slopes and overgrazing the pastures above the timber line, the settlers have succeeded . . . in increasing the area of desert and intensifying its aridity." Yet because it is inhuman, Huxley's desert is potentially divine. The silent sterile desert of the Southwest exemplifies, in his private religion, the boundlessness and emptiness of a godhead possessing no anthropomorphic attributes. It therefore eliminates human society. In his essay "Ozymandias" (collected in *Adonis and the Alphabet,* 1956) Huxley gives a cautionary description of the socialist commune at Llano which, like the military and aeronautic reservations in the area, polluted the sacrosanct emptiness of the desert and was therefore suppressed by the jealous spirit of the place. Only an abandoned silo and a ruined cow barn remain. Between 1942 and 1947, Huxley lived among this symbolic wreckage. The desert is an apt place for manifestations of faith, but it mocks them. Huxley is amused by the grotesque granitic solidity of Mormon architecture at Great Salt Lake, which hubristically defies the desert, and he wishes on the Tabernacle the same fate as the statue of the tyrant Ozymandias which molders in the waste in Shelley's poem. After the other monuments of the modern world are dust, he says in "Faith, Taste and History" (from the same 1956 volume), this obdurate object will still "be standing in the Western desert," inspiring in the "neo-Neolithic savages of post-atomic times" an "uncomprehending reverence and superstitious alarm." The smug expectation that the world is due to revert to savagery after a nuclear holocaust discloses another potentiality of Huxley's desert: it is dually a bleak heaven and a scorching hell, a hermitage and a laboratory of cosmic destruction, for it is the site of the first atomic explosion.

If used prudently, Huxley's vacant, dangerous desert can provoke a dazzling illumination. He proposes it as a psychic remedy. Excluding the affray of civilization, "blessedly non-human," it acts as "a spiritual restorative . . . an anti-hallucinant . . . a de-tensioner," since it discloses to human beings the limits of their power. The desert for Huxley is austere and eremetical. He rejoices in its desolation, which for him was a virtue of the entire continent: "the most wonderful thing about America is that . . . there are so few Americans," he says, reflecting contentedly that you can be eaten by a bear in New York State, or bitten by a rattlesnake in the Hollywood Hills, or die of thirst in the desert only 150 miles from Los Angeles. Hence Huxley's stoicism when his house in the Hollywood Hills burned down during a forest fire in 1961: he took it as nature's rebuke. He was being punished for imagining that he could take root in an alien, inimical landscape, for flattering himself that his belongings and his existence mattered. Auden's ideal landscape (as he says in the 1948 poem "In Praise of Limestone") is porous and populous, made of limestone because that is a stone to be carved and built with; Huxley's ideal landscape is sand and salt, shifting, malicious, scornful of human purposes.

Huxley attacks the pathetic fallacy, which asserts its ownership of nature by expending human sympathy on landscape. Romantic sentiment is thus the aesthetic version of the industrial exploitation of landscape, and the American desert is admirable because it resists this take-over: it contains no dancing daffodils or winsome flowers in crannied nooks to be collected, no rustic simpletons to patronize. Huxley disapproves of attempts to populate the desert, which violate the austere emptiness of the place. The socialist commune at Llano, he says, perished of its own internal contradictions when its members discovered (as Lawrence did at Taos) that "life in a community is life in a crowd."

Whereas Huxley's desert is a repudiation of society, Lawrence's was a concentrated re-creation of society, and this is why Huxley couldn't understand it. Lawrence went to the desert not to be alone but to excite those passionate, willful energies which are the agonizing life of human relationships. For this reason he always wanted company. The experiment wouldn't have worked in a Huxleyan solitude. Lawrence is forever proselytically seeking to extend his elective society, to engage new recruits. *Women in Love* ends with Birkin's obstinate theoretical insistence on union with a man as well as intimacy with a woman. Ursula objects that his desire to enjoy simultaneously two different kinds of love is false and impossible, but he won't believe her. Lawrence in New Mexico persisted in the same experiment, surrounding himself both with ravening women like Mabel and with blood brothers like Merrild and Gótzsche. When he invited the Danes to spend the winter at Lobo Ranch, Merrild demurred, fearing that they'd all get on each other's nerves, as had happened at Mabel's, but Lawrence insisted that they could be "a few men with honour and fearlessness and make a life together."

After leaving New Mexico, Huxley recalls, Lawrence talked of it "with a mixture of love and dislike; nostalgically longing to be back again in that ferociously virgin world of drought and storm, and at the same time resenting its alienness and lunar vacancy." But this converts Lawrence to Huxley's own classical and satirical aversion to romanticism. Lawrence, he says, found in New Mexico that "undiluted, the works of God are really too much of a good thing. . . . It is a terrible thing to fall into the hands of the Wordsworthian God." Wordsworth was in no danger of this among the homely lakes and maternal hillocks of his native district, but it could happen in New Mexico. Again Huxley is describing his own imagined desert, not Lawrence's. Huxley's argument that "what man has made of nature is often a great improvement on the original" is contradicted by Lawrence's determination in the desert to strip away (as he told Merrild) the "hygienic and shiny mucous paper" of civilization and "actually *touch* the country." Huxley's sojourn in the desert at Llano relied on hygienic fortification. Technological ingenuity redeemed a niggardly antagonistic nature and kept the environment at bay. Huxley irrigated the desert, conducting water into a sparse garden through a series of ditches, and installed a gasoline engine to generate electricity. Lawrence prohibited such cowardly gadgetry. He and the Danes had to fumigate, roof, carpenter, plaster, glaze, paint, whitewash, and curtain their derelict dwellings at Lobo Ranch. Instead of Huxley's canal relaying water down the mountain, Lawrence chopped holes in the ice on the creek with a hatchet to obtain water, or else melted snow on the stove. He approved of this primitive housekeeping because it betokened an adjustment of man to the elements, dispensing with machinery, and he rejoiced at his distance from "over-upholstered Europe."

Huxley wanted to be an anchorite, Lawrence a savage. Huxley's desert is an image of spiritual dessication, Lawrence's of sensual fulfillment. Huxley transfers Wordsworth to the tropics to demonstrate the fragility of romanticism and to enforce a penitential classicism, aware of nature's indifference or cruelty. Lawrence transfers Pan to America to regenerate an emasculated classical god and recover his romantic potency.

In his essay "Wordsworth in the Tropics" (collected in *Do What You Will,* 1929) Huxley dismisses romanticism as fond fair-weather sentimentality. Its conviction of the wise purposes and spiritual superintendence of nature can only be maintained in the temperate zone. Tropical nature, "under a vertical sun, and nourished by the equatorial rains," scorns Wordsworth's ingratiation. Huxley recommends the doting romantic to spend "a few weeks in Malaya or Borneo." That suggestion harks back to the itinerary of the tour described in *Jesting Pilate;* later, Huxley moves the location of his adversary classical nature from the Asian rain forests to the American desert.

The geographical change coincides with a spiritual conversion. Huxley acknowledged that the tendency of his novels was to transform satiric disgust into mystical enlightenment. The only way ahead for the skeptic is to collapse into faith. Geographically, the advance from satire to mysticism leads from the jungle to the desert. Huxley's jungles are a diabolical invention of the satirist. "The inhabitants of equatorial forests," he points out in the Wordsworth essay, "are all believers in devils." His deserts are a serene invention

Lawrence and Frieda baking bread on their ranch in New Mexico, 1924.
D. H. Lawrence Collection, Humanities Research Center Library,
The University of Texas at Austin, Austin, Texas.

of the mystic, places of faith not Manichean terror: hence the choice of a bitter salt lake as the Mormon holy land, or (as Huxley says in a 1962 *Encounter* essay on "Unpainted Landscapes") Holman Hunt's choice of the Dead Sea as the landscape in which to set his dehydrated, symbolically expiatory scapegoat. The satirist in Huxley salutes the desert as evidence of nature's gross bad taste. The lurid magenta mountains of Holman Hunt's painting are an accurate representation: "I have seen them in Palestine," Huxley says, "seen them again in California and Utah." In the essay on Wordsworth, Huxley suggests that a demon made nature in its own malign image; now in the 1962 essay nature is designed not by a devil but by a god with a weakness for the gaudy, fond of confecting "magenta mountains, vermilion crags, precipices stratified into the likeness of gigantic Neapolitan ices." The fear of the earlier essay has relaxed into a laughable monstrosity: "when the Almighty does go in for bad taste, the results are truly stupendous." But the mystic in Huxley values the desert, because it is a place of compulsory contemplation. In its emptiness there is nothing to do, nothing to look at, so the garrulous business of experiencing and observing is calmed into reflection on what Huxley calls "the essential mystery" of our incongruous presence on this planet.

Huxley's dismissal of romanticism is answered by Lawrence's essay "Pan in America." Lawrence, like Huxley, begins by quarreling with Wordsworth, who has emasculated Pan. The genius haunting classical landscape is for Lawrence not the devil imagined by Huxley but a lecherous, mischievous faun. Lawrence accuses Christianity of co-opting Pan and casting him as its cloven-hoofed, horned devil. The romantics revived his worship, but in doing so insulted him by making him respectable and neuter: "Lucy Gray, alas, was the form that William Wordsworth thought fit to give to the Great God Pan." Gods, however, are migratory. Pan escapes from Wordsworth's tame lakeland to America where, Lawrence announces, he is reincarnated as Walt Whitman. The lustful goat-god becomes the tutelary spirit of American transcendentalism, and is renamed "the

Oversoul, the Allness of everything." In America, Lawrence declares, "Pan is still alive."

Lawrence's criticism of Wordsworth differs markedly from Huxley's. For Huxley, Wordsworth's error was metaphysical: he made an alien nature amiable and knowable, and obscured the austere truth that human beings are the sentient victims of an insentient universe. For Lawrence, Wordsworth's error was moral: he made sensual nature feebly genteel. Huxley values the American desert because it mocks the pathetic fallacy; Lawrence values it because it recharges that vital relationship with nature which in England had become meekly "sweet-and-pure." Huxley's desert capsizes those metaphysical hutches which men build around themselves in their desperation to believe this insentient universe their home. But Lawrence in the desert recovers a sense of attachment to the universe. A tree on his ranch under the Rockies sends "shivers of energy" through him and he becomes "like unto the tree, more bristling and turpentiney," an emanation of Pan (Lawrence's thin, bearded face gave him the look of a neurasthenic satyr). In his turn he endows the tree with "a certain shade and alertness" from his own life. He thrills to the "resinous erectness" of the pine, and is revived by its "primitive savageness." His desert gives off vital sparks, whereas Huxley's is a parched mental space in which the cacti scientifically provoke changes in perception, not the raw transfusion of power Lawrence derives from the pine.

Lawrence believes that life consists in "a vivid relatedness between the man and the living universe that surrounds him," and he points to the totemic religion of the Indians at Taos as a case of such a union. To Huxley the beginning of wisdom was the understanding that there is no such animistic relationship. Science has shown the world to be "refreshingly other," atomized and blank. The only relationship with this void which Huxley permits is technological, because technology defensively extends human faculties and arms men against the inflictions of nature. Whereas Lawrence hoped primitive America would rise up against the mechanical United

States, for Huxley the United States has a technical obligation to subdue barbarous America. After Huxley went to live in California in 1938, the mystic and the satirist in him both yielded, as a later chapter will show, to the technocrat. Huxley's spiritual conversion in America was a conversion to technology, which first refutes satire by freeing us from soiling, demeaning physical nature, and then makes mystics of us by providing us with techniques for creating paradise. Huxley's heaven is a chemical compound, a drug brewed in a laboratory. The science-fiction novel *Island* gives the formula: "paradise . . . is symtrinitropsi-butyl-toluene, with an assortment of organic impurities." The vision-inducing drugs with which Huxley injected himself in California are a celestial technology, devices for rapidly translating the earthling into regions of hallucinogenic ecstasy. Mysticism is not a spiritual gift but a scientific technique, a "method of changing body chemistry." Embarked on an acid trip, the subject is like an electrical appliance "plugged in" or "turned on" to what Huxley, in a series of lectures at Santa Barbara in 1959, calls "unstructured transpersonal consciousness." The prodigies of parapsychology, extolled in one of these lectures, are a similar case of mental technology: telepathy is a miracle electronically institutionalized by the telephone.

Huxley's apostasy in California is virtually predicted by Lawrence in the essay transplanting Pan. Although Lawrence's primal America outlaws both idealism and machinery, he understands that the destiny of the United States is the transformation of idealism into mechanism. "The most idealist nations," he says, "invent the most machines." Because machines offer release from material cares, they are circumventions of life, and therefore they gratify the deathly spiritual idealist. Americans, in Lawrence's view, have an idealistic reluctance "to *do* anything": hence their armory of gadgets, which do things for them. They even leave killing to their appliances, which is why, when Lawrence was planning to murder Mabel, he disdained the use of a gun. Machines inhibit "the living stealth and preparedness with which one live thing approaches another." Guns allow you to shoot your prey from a comfortable distance, and spare you the ancient, guilty emotions of the hunt. Lawrence's Indians warm themselves at camp fires. Cutting trees and burning logs, they absorb into themselves the generative heat of nature. The white man, however, cossetted by appliances, warms himself by adjusting a radiator or checking a theromometer. Technology has estranged him from nature. He has locked up god inside his machines. Huxley's drugs would be, in Lawrence's terms, the most shameful evidence of this corruption, since they make an illusory god by chemical contrivance. Lawrence would have been equally scornful of Huxley's obsession with doctors. Medically, Lawrence was strictly homeopathic. When Merrild had a cold in the desert, Lawrence served him sage tea, which he believed moved the bowels and cleansed the blood. Huxley, on the other hand, consulted and befriended a cadre of American physicians, and permitted them to experiment on him. He retrained his sand-blind eyes in accordance with the ophthalmological therapy prescribed by "the pioneer of visual education" Dr. W. H. Bates, and he began taking mescaline to assist Dr. Humphrey Osmond, a psychiatrist from Saskatchewan, with his researches into schizophrenia. The correction of his vision enabled Huxley to dispense with one technological aid: having learned Bates's "art of seeing," he no longer needed spectacles. But he proceeded to adopt an alternative technology to correct his internal, subliminal vision: hence the recourse to hallucinogenic drugs.

Residence in America turns Huxley into Lawrence's deracinated modern man, abstracted from his own physical life, relying on engines to do the work of his body and on pseudo-scientific systems to do the work of his mind. Huxley's intellect became a faddish American contraption, a classificatory mechanism which coped automatically with the demands of human relationship. One of the medical authorities he favored, Dr. William H. Sheldon, had devised a temperamental typology which, like the Renaissance system of humors, reduced individuals to prisoners of their physical form. Huxley enthusiastically adopted this technique, and filed people in Sheldon's three categories as gutsy genial endomorphs, muscle-bound power-mad mesomorphs, or prickly brainy ectomorphs. On shopping expeditions Huxley rode the escalator at Ohrbach's in Los Angeles somatotyping passers-by, asking friends if they'd noticed "that marvellously somatotonic woman with the Aztec features."

In Huxley's America, an otherworldly mystical forsaking of works is made possible by mod. cons., while technology, outfitting the body with new time-saving appendages, diminishes Lawrence's life-struggle to a matter of mechanical adjustment. Huxley is living in Lawrence's automated hell of Uncle Samdom, where human beings are enchained by a fatal alliance between idealism and engineering. Lawrence's America is in turn discredited by Huxley, who calls it a wishful romantic dream, dishonestly cushioned by the science it pretends to reject. Lawrence began by describing America as "the pure landscape of futurity," but made that future from a recovery of the primitive American past. He has put Wells's time machine into reverse. Science fiction enabled Wells to visit the post-industrial future in the United States and to ascertain that it worked; Lawrence likewise visits the pre-industrial past in Mexico, and declares that to be a workable society. Both ventures, for Huxley, are self-deceiving, and in the change from one to the other millenarianism has declined into tourism. As Huxley says in *Beyond the Mexique Bay,* critics of society in the nineteenth century imagined lost paradises in the past or paradises regained in the future as corrections of contemporary errors: William Morris's feudalism on the one hand, Marx's revolutionary reckoning on the other. But in the twentieth century these prophetic projections frame a travel itinerary. Americans can take a train or an airplane, Huxley says, and visit the past in Mexico, the future in Russia or China. Lawrence considers himself an explorer (hence the fancied affinity with Columbus), but according to Huxley's argument he is only a tourist, dabbling with a primitivism to which he never resolves to commit himself.

If so, he is the last of the tourists to be treated in this book. He did try to live in New Mexico, but it proved to be no more than an expedient resting place in a harried, vagrant career. Before him, Mrs. Trollope and Kipling had attempted to settle in America, and had been rebuffed. Otherwise the writers dealt with so far travel through America, imaginatively alter it to suit their convenience— malevolently deforming it like Dickens, flirtatiously corrupting it like Wilde, taking inventory of its contents like Trollope, reconstituting it like Wells—and then discard it. The rest of this book will be about writers who go there as immigrants, not dilettantish tourists secure in the possession of a return ticket: Huxley again, Auden, and Isherwood. Until now, America has been a remote, impractical alternative with which the imagination trifles but which it always renounces. From now on, the choice of America is tantamount to the choice of life.

7

THEOLOGICAL AMERICA
W. H. Auden
in New York

As the Atlantic crossing becomes a rite of passage, so immigration inaugurates a process of conversion. Auden and Isherwood planned their journey to New York in January 1939 to formalize a change of faith. In moving to America they were repudiating a demoralized Europe, which had seemed during the Munich crisis of the previous summer to be ignominiously appeasing Hitler. Earlier, Auden and Isherwood had been proponents of social revolution. Like Lawrence before them in America, they saw themselves as saboteurs, and derived their literary personae from styles of political subversion. Auden saw the poet as a trained spy interrogating the evidence of human frailty; Isherwood saw the novelist as a conspirator conniving at the destruction of society by describing it with a merciless blandness. As literary travelers, their destinations had been battlegrounds. Between 1928 and 1934 they lived intermittently in Berlin, which, with its brawls between Nazis and communists, its homosexual bars and transvestite cabarets, was to them an incubator of revolution, a place where the disintegration of bourgeois morality could both be studied and enjoyed. Auden went to Spain during the civil war and broadcast propaganda for the Republican side. In 1938 he and Isherwood traveled to China, after the Japanese invasion. But the capitulation at Munich, shortly after their return from China, left them politically disenchanted. No longer expecting change in society, they resolved to concentrate instead on change inside the individual. From action they recoiled into meditation. Auden in New York turned from socialism to the existential Protestantism expounded by his mentor Reinhold Niebuhr, and Isherwood in California turned from socialism to yoga under the influence of his mentor Gerald Heard.

Europe during the 1930s had paralyzed writers by offering them two equally odious alternatives: the preciosity of the ivory tower or the belligerence of the barricades. Auden and Isherwood made their choice with an uneasy conscience. They pretended to place their art at the service of social reform, but were actually treasuring the lurid, pestilential detail of decay with a morbid, unpolitical aestheticism. Between these exclusive opposites—the futile composition of art for art's sake or the slavish composition of propaganda—there was, however, a possible compromise. Aldous Huxley, who had emigrated to America in April 1937, called it in a letter from Llano in 1945 "the alternative of spirituality." The scene of this option is America. Because it is immune to the stresses of European history, America doesn't require the artist either to become a political conscript or else remain a meretricious dilettante. America protects the artist's imaginative liberty because it allows him to explore his personal perceptual world without being accused of social irresponsibility. This is what Huxley means by the spiritual alternative. To Auden, Huxley, and Isherwood, America is a state of grace, a condition of freedom which they embrace by apprenticing themselves to strange new gods. Auden in America worships the austere Augustinian deity of Niebuhr, who has endowed man with the dangerous capacity for self-determination; Huxley venerates the subliminal gods men discover inside themselves when, with chemical assistance, they cleanse the doors of perception; Isherwood sits at the feet of saintly swamis and Vedantist gurus. America is interpreted theologically by Auden, psychedelically by Huxley, mystically by Isherwood.

In June 1940 Auden gave the commencement address at Smith College in Massachusetts and explained his migration to America as an existential act, the choice of a paradoxical and perilous freedom. Europe had suppressed this freedom. Mobilized for war, its societies had succumbed to a romantic malaise, sacrificing individual liberty to compulsory ideological dreams, like deluded characters in nineteenth-century novels turning away from a difficult prosaic reality toward the facile delights of fantasy. Europe was now a closed society, America by contrast bracingly open, still respecting what Auden called "voluntary behaviour."

This address, emphasizing American freedom, makes Auden's new home an existential country. Existentialism, insisting on the unique human possession of will and consciousness, makes this freedom a political and psychological challenge. Mental illness (according to Erich Fromm) is a panicky reaction against a freedom which human beings fear; the totalitarianism of the closed society is a similar cowardly betrayal of a freedom which thrives on controversy, a collective retreat into neurosis. To existential churchmen, freedom is a theological benison. God created man free, Niebuhr argued. Auden, paraphrasing him, said that grace is gratuitous, amazing because arbitrary. With Europe neurotically at war with itself, the guardian of this psychological, political, and theological freedom was America. Franklin Delano Roosevelt's was an existential presidency, encouraging Americans not to be afraid of their freedom. He told his subjects they had nothing to fear but fear itself; Eleanor Roosevelt in her autobiography admitted to having lied out of fear during her childhood, and persisted in the habit "until I reached the age when I realized there was nothing to fear."

At Smith, Auden said he had come to America to understand and act on his own freedom, and declared that the peculiarities of the American experience—its "historical discontinuity, its mixed population, and the arrival of the industrial revolution while the geographical frontier was still open"—made it an inspiriting, problematic case of the open society. His move there was a meditative reclusion.

He had absented himself from the European war in order "to understand what has come upon us, and why," and to do so he made himself an amateur theologian, reading Kierkegaard, Tillich, and Niebuhr.

Theology was in Auden's view better suited to the explanation of America than history. As yet, America had no history, because it had preserved its distance from the broils and intrigues of Europe. Wells saw the decision of America to enter history in 1917 as a secular incarnation, and Auden thinks of America's entry into the war after Pearl Harbor as a religious manifestation. The incarnation is the unexpected descent of grace into nature, of eternity into time: it is theology's redemption of history. America in both world wars rescues Europe from its self-engendered calamity much as God, by sending Christ into the world, had rescued man from the consequences of his sin. History is the dismaying record of secular error, theology the guarantee of divine superintendence, for theology discerns divine motivations behind historical disasters, and can show the fall from paradise to be fortunate after all. To Auden, the war from which he had exempted himself in 1939 revealed the bankruptcy of history. Man, left to his own godless ingenuity, had bred a monster. "It has taken Hitler," he said in a review of Niebuhr's *The Nature and Destiny of Man*, "to show us that liberalism is not self-supporting." With Hitler the devil materialized in human affairs. But if the devil still existed, it became necessary to postulate the continued existence of a god the liberals had condemned to death. Theology, the account of God's salvation of a miscreant world, intersects and arrests history. Niebuhr said that "the issue of Biblical religion is . . . how history is to overcome the tragic consequences of its false eternals." It overcomes them by turning into theology.

Auden's first works written in and about America—the operetta *Paul Bunyan* and the long reflective poem *New Year Letter* (both 1940), the verse-drama *The Age of Anxiety* (written between 1944 and 1946)—all concern the working of this theological atonement.

They survey American history between the rude natural society of the frontier on which Paul Bunyan the lumberjack flourishes and the mechanical urban society of New York in which the characters of *New Year Letter* and *The Age of Anxiety* live, and they find in that history a modern recurrence of the original loss and recovery of paradise which theology describes. Theology rearranges the tragedy of history into a divine comedy, and shows its traumas to be beneficent. Adam's fall is ultimately fortunate because his lapse prompts the mission of Christ, the second Adam. Man loses the paradise of Eden but regains a paradise within (the certainty of salvation and the soul's immortality) which is happier far than the bucolic idyll in which Adam and Eve luxuriated. Auden correspondingly sees America as a paradise lost when despoiled by industrialism but regained when the isolation and introversion which are in Niebuhr's terms "the tragic consequences" of industrial society turn into a benediction, stimulating men to invent private versions of the heaven Auden, following Henry James, called the Great Good Place. The loss of paradise occurs in *Paul Bunyan,* its restoration or reconstruction in *New Year Letter* and *The Age of Anxiety*.

The music for *Paul Bunyan* is by Benjamin Britten who, having left wartime England as a pacifist, lived with Auden in an artistic commune in Brooklyn Heights during 1939-40. The first performance of the operetta, at Columbia University in May 1941, was not a success, and Britten permitted no further productions until 1975. He found the work easy to forget because it is of little significance in his musical development, but the libretto is one of Auden's most important statements about America. The witty concentration and complication of Auden's text actually cramps Britten's music. The history of Paul the legendary lumberjack is narrated in a series of ballads, sparsely accompanied, and elsewhere music can do little but mock European operatic habits: a dog, for instance, yaps coloratura. Compared with the grunting, snoring, earthy English wood in Britten's later opera *A Midsummer Night's Dream,* the score is unresponsive to the American forest in which the action is set. Indeed, in its anticipation of the sea interludes in *Peter Grimes,* it often sounds more like nautical Suffolk than the pastoral Midwest. This shouldn't be surprising: whereas Auden in America embraced an alienation which was, he believed, the salutary destiny of the modern artist, living disconnected from community and prizing his rootlessness as a sign of existential freedom, Britten's brief period in America only convinced him of his ineradicable Englishness. In his address on receiving the first Aspen award in Colorado in 1964, Britten back-handedly thanked the United States for disclosing to him his personal imaginative England. He discovered Peter Grimes and the East Anglian landscape in California, after buying Crabbe's *Borough* in a Los Angeles bookshop during "the unhappy summer of 1941." This made him realize "where I belonged and what I lacked." He returned to England soon afterwards and rooted himself permanently "in the same small corner of East Anglia, near where I was born." His opera about that natal place, *Peter Grimes,* followed in 1945. *Paul Bunyan* was suppressed as a false start.

Auden always said, explaining his exile, that he loved his family but didn't want to live with them. Britten couldn't live without them: his Peter Grimes is maddened not fortified by his alienation. *Paul Bunyan* is about the rootlessness of America (its hero's job after all is cutting down trees), which Auden valued as an invigorating trial. When in 1940 his friends tried to lure him back to England, protesting that his imagination would perish unless nourished by its native soil, Auden admitted that "America may break one completely"—and in *Paul Bunyan* a quartet of defeated immigrants laments that "America can break your heart"—but "to attempt the most difficult seems to me the only thing worth while." The libretto of *Paul Bunyan* proposes deracination as a test which the composer fails.

Paul Bunyan is a jokey backwoods *Paradise Lost.* It is about America's loss of innocence, and also about mythology's loss of innocence. Auden pointed out in a *New York Times* article introducing the operetta that "America is unique in being the only country to create myths after the industrial revolution." Elsewhere, mythology is discredited by machinery, but America's late appearance in history allows it to combine two literary ages, the mythologically primitive and the mechanically modern. Its literature is all modern, but the subject of that literature, the struggle with nature in "an undeveloped continent with an open frontier and a savage climate," is mythological. The protagonists of American epic stalk deer or harpoon whales, or, like Bunyan, fell trees and level mountains. The puissance of the American epic hero is a mythic endowment but also a technological skill: "what Bunyan accomplishes as an individual is precisely what the lumbermen managed to accomplish as a team with the help of machinery." But because American myths are all about the industrial spoliation of nature (which is the reason for Lawrence's sulphurous denunciation of "classic American literature") they therefore record their own obsolescence. The operetta ends with Bunyan's withdrawal, because in clearing the wilderness he has created a democratic, scientific world which no longer believes in him.

Actually he is already redundant in the opera, in which he doesn't appear. His size rules out his physical presence, so he is represented by a megaphonic speaking voice offstage. Absence makes a god of him, supervising nature but not participating in it. Like F.D.R. in his radio fireside chats, Bunyan's relation with his subjects is mediated. He is not a person but a hortatory voice on the air waves. Auden's refusal to allow him to sing is also brilliantly apt. Lyricism is a human faculty. In *Paradise Lost* Adam and Eve sing canticles in praise of a God whose own idiom is crabbed, prolix, and sternly anti-lyrical. Bunyan's mode is rhetoric not song. Like Milton's God, he has theological truths to expound which lyricism would blur and soften.

As well as a god, Bunyan is an Adam who doesn't wait to be expelled from paradise but sets about deforesting it while still in residence. His felling of the trees is a harmless industrial correlative of Eve's consumption of the forbidden fruit. Chateaubriand in 1836 noted the element of primal aggression in the American lumberman's work. He remarks in his "Voyage en Amérique" that, because there was nothing old in America but the woods, the act of chopping down a tree is for the American the equivalent of patricide. Thoreau in his journal in 1855 reflects that "it is criminal to inflict an unnecessary injury on the tree that feeds or shadows us. Old trees are our parents, and our parents' parents, perchance." Nevertheless, the American is pledged to the destruction of that ancestral nature. Trollope on his tour in 1861 remarks that to the Kentucky farmers "a tree is simply an enemy" to be humbled. Bunyan in pillaging the wilderness is encouraging the American Adam to educate himself by falling. He says of the forest "it is America, but not yet." It won't be America until it falls from nature to culture and agriculture, until its virginity is plundered by revolutionaries and poetic dreamers, and Bunyan appeals for the aid of these "disturbers of public order" at the beginning of the work. The first symptom of this providential fall is the discontent of Johnny Inkslinger, Bunyan's book-keeper, who despises life on the frontier. His fractious intellectual ambition makes a rebellious Adam of him. He asks questions which God prohibits, but his impiety is virtuous idealism: he wants to be an artist, and the loggers' camp is no paradise to him but a miserable prison.

After the fall there will be the art Inkslinger longs for, and also wealth. Milton's justification of the fall is a metaphysical leap of faith: we must make ourselves believe that the paradise we will regain is preferable to the one we have forfeited. Auden's justification is more complacently economic. The fall is fortunate not because it immortalizes the soul but because it enriches the body. Only after the fall does America become the lucrative paradise for which Auden gives thanks in a 1963 poem about a money-making lecture-tour:

> God bless the U.S.A., so large,
> So friendly, and so rich.

Industry ravages nature but it creates money. The sufferings of the shanty boys in the forests are rewarded not by spiritual grace but by pots of gold. Auden's next operatic hero, Tom Rakewell in *The*

Rake's Progress (written with Chester Kallman for Stravinsky in 1948-49), is likewise an honorary American, despite the work's eighteenth-century English setting, for Rakewell shares Bunyan's faith in economic providence and a machine-made paradise. He invents a gimcrack engine which converts stones into bread, and declares that affluence will restore Eden:

> Thanks to this excellent device
> Man shall re-enter Paradise
> From which he once was driven.
> Secure from need, the cause of crime,
> The world shall for a second time
> Be similar to heaven.

Auden, who all his life congratulated himself on having been born into a family of British middle-class philistines and who in America proved himself a shrewd businessman, always securing top fees for lectures and poetry readings, maintained that America had spiritualized wealth. Money there was not a filthy bequest of the fall, but a sign of divine favor and paradisial plenitude. In Europe, Auden explained, money was polluted because it boasted of power. Europeans are selfish about wealth, because they covet it as a guarantee of freedom from the importunity of other people: they "feel they would like to have as much money themselves as possible, and other people to have as little as possible." Americans are more openhanded, because for them possessing money matters less than acquiring it. They dislike the idea of inheriting a family hoard because, as wealth is the token of success in one's personal struggle with an inimical nature, "the important thing is not to have money, but to have made it." The economic vice of Europeans, in Auden's view, is avarice, while that of Americans is waste.

In justifying the exploitation of the wild continent, *Paul Bunyan* directly contradicts Lawrence's reflections on the American past. Auden welcomes the urbanization of the forests; but Lawrence's study of American literature deplores "the horrid advance of civilization," and he himself, like Huck Finn escaping from the threat of adoption by Aunt Sally, was constantly lighting out for new, unsettled territories as civilization and its debilitating machinery caught up with him. At first in 1916 Lawrence intended to settle in Florida, then the following year decided that it would be necessary to go further west, "to California or the South Seas," in the search for a pristine frontier. He condemns the dispossession of the Indians, the ancestral inhabitants of America, by the white colonists. Auden, however, cheerfully defends the expropriation of Indian lands because, according to his industrious bourgeois ethic, the indigenous layabouts have to be rounded up and disposed of before a virgin land can become rich America. The Indians, he thought, deserved to be disinherited, because they had failed to turn natural resources to profitable use. The worst Auden could find to say of slavery was that it didn't pay: it was abolished because of its inefficiency, not because of its impropriety. Auden's comfortable advocacy of capitalist iniquities follows that of an earlier mercantile moralist, Trollope, who points out that Negroes were introduced into America because the white men couldn't work in the tropical heat, and the Indians wouldn't work at all. The shiftlessness of the Indians justifies their extermination, "which fate," Trollope notes, "must . . . attend all non-working people. As the soil of the world is required for increasing population, the non-working people must go."

Paul Bunyan studies the fall which made America Auden's bourgeois paradise from various overlapping points of view.

Chronologically, it is a fall from the timelessness or eternal repetition of myth into the diminished, consecutive world of history. A miniature representation of this fall is the calamity of Hel Helsen, the Swedish foreman. Helsen is a mythic character incongruously deposited in post-mythological history, an epic hero exiled in a democratic society. Bunyan says of him, "he was born a few hundred years too late. Today there is no place for him." As Bunyan withdraws, so Helsen falls. His cronies have warned him: "Take orders from Paul / Or you'll have a fall," but he insists on indulging his epic emotion of injured pride. The result, in this demeaningly democratic world, is a comic bout of fisticuffs. Knocked unconscious, Helsen, the antedeluvian epic hero, is laid to rest in a parodic funeral march. When he revives he is reincarnated as a sober, modest citizen. He forgets his feisty individuality, and joins in a partnership with Bunyan. He falls, like America, from epic outlawry to membership in society.

Generically, the fall can be seen another way. The chorus of farmers comments on the change in literary form implied by the progress of America in confiding,

> I hate to be a shanty-boy
> I want to be a farmer
> For I prefer life's comedy
> To life's crude melodrama.

The crude melodrama is the epic state of exposure to nature, comedy the cushioned later condition of shelter from nature. Comedy too is a social state (the farmer lives surrounded by his family, the shanty-boys suffer the privations of the bunk-house) which chastens melodramatic outlaws like Helsen and expels outsize melodramatic bogies like Bunyan.

Sexually, the fall leads from the rough masculine society of the pioneers to a world of marriage and child-raising. Kipling's epic America, from which women are excluded, has been disassembled.

Economically, the development is from forestry to farming and thence, by way of the locomotive and the telephone, to the urban world of corporate capitalism prophesied in Paul's farewell, when machinery will close the frontier.

Theologically, America falls from an age of totem and taboo, a superstitious pre-history in which Bunyan megaphonically directs the operations of a subject population, to an age of faith, invisible, internal, and voluntary. Paul is too totemic and anthropomorphic a god for this new age. His power lasts only until "external physical nature has been mastered." When the collective combat with the

environment gives way to the problem of individual human relations, Paul must disappear. God now, in this new world of existential Protestantism, is not a communal fetish but each man's private
possession—perhaps each man's invention. America undergoes the
same change. The rugged landscape has been subdued. The state is
now constituted by the acts and dreams of each of its citizens. As
Paul touchingly says at the end of the operetta,

> America is what you do,
> America is I and you,
> America is what you choose to make it.

America is the place of fearful freedom, of moral amateurism. Europeans make their moral decisions prescriptively, according to the tutelage of the law, but Americans, as Auden was fond of arguing, are
moral improvisers. Huck Finn's decision to save nigger Jim is for
Auden a characteristically American initiative, because it is not a
considered criticism of slavery and isn't intended as an admonition
to others. It is the inspiration of a moral amateur. It is that quantity
much admired by the existential psychologists and theologians of
the 1940s and '50s, an entirely gratuitous act; and it is into this paradise of extemporary mental freedom, where all experiences are novel
and therefore all actions must be daringly original, that Paul Bunyan
ushers America.

New Year Letter confers this new American freedom on art.
Releasing the poet from the partisanship which was obligatory in
Europe, America allows him to make his art an autonomous activity.
Poetry now has a charmed purposelessness, a quality it shares with
that Third Avenue bar in which The Age of Anxiety begins. Auden,
who after the 1930s liked to aver that "poetry makes nothing happen" and cannot foment revolution, calls the bar "an unprejudiced
space in which nothing particular ever happens." This is what makes
it symbolically American. In Europe, the poet's concern had to be
political states, but in America it can be those "autonomous completed states" which aren't political entities but the abstract inven-

tions of art. America permits the artist to relax into the recollection of "already lived experience." He no longer needs to live through his art, for he now knows that "Art is not life and cannot be / A midwife to society." He can admit that poetry is artificial, formulaic, inconsequential, which the Europe of the 1930s forbade him to do. This aesthetic retrenchment coincides with the protective domestication of *New Year Letter*: it is set in a Long Island cottage where, as the European war moves into Poland, Auden and his fellow refugee Elizabeth Mayer sit listening to a Buxtehude passacaglia. As refugees, they are no longer citizens. Having ceased to be the subjects of political authority, they now constitute a voluntary group convened in and by art. Their minds make "a *civitas* of sound." The city is now an aural, musical phenomenon.

The cottage on Long Island is an outpost of that new America envisaged by Paul Bunyan, in which individuals choose to establish relationships, rather than being constrained by membership of a tribe. Auden is referring to a cottage at Amityville, in the grounds of a sanatorium operated by Mrs. Mayer's husband, a physician who had fled from Hitler's Germany. This house was a shelter for artists in self-imposed exile: Britten and his companion, the tenor Peter Pears, lived here after their arrival in America in autumn 1939. Auden said of his own exile that he loved his family (which was England) but didn't want to live with it all his life. You can't choose to love your family: the emotion is inborn, compulsory. But in America you are free to select soul-mates and to fabricate your own voluntary world in their company. Auden's own experience confirmed his expectation of America: shortly after settling in New York, he met Chester Kallman, with whom he remained for the rest of his life.

Poetry has been domesticated in *New Year Letter*. America allows the poet to play games with his gift, instead of imagining himself an unacknowledged legislator of mankind: that role Auden from now on left to the secret police. America likewise domesticates the artistic tradition of Europe, which it folds up into a snug household. In Elizabeth Mayer's cottage, Schubert, Mozart

> And GLUCK and food and friendship made
> Our privileged community
> The real republic which must be
> The State all politicians claim.

America introjects the politics of Europe. The state now comprises one's friends, one's deeds, and one's record collection. There are two atlases, Auden argues, one the public domain which we all must democratically share, the other the inner space of privacy where each person is sovereign in the state which is the accretion of his acts and memories.

He migrates from one to the other, as he explained in the address at Smith, in order to reflect on what he has renounced. His sovereignty in the private realm of America is exercised in the recollection of what he has left behind in the imperiled public realm of Europe. Though the characters in *The Age of Anxiety* live in America, their memories are European, just as Auden and Elizabeth Mayer in *New Year Letter* meet as aliens in New York to talk

> Of friends who suffer in the torn
> Old Europe where we both were born.

But although this expanse of memory and already lived experience belongs to Europe, in growing up and working over it we exploit it as Americans, for the image Auden uses is that of the woodsman who

> patrols the forest tracts
> Planted in childhood, farms the belt
> Of doings memorized and felt.

Each of us is a Paul Bunyan. Our remembered past is supine nature, which left to itself "won't quite do," as Auden says in "City Without Walls." By toiling over it and shaping it retrospectively, we are behaving like Bunyan, enclosing, fertilizing, wrenching meaning from a stubborn landscape. Auden has made imagination cognate with industrialism, for both are exploitations of nature, and this enables him to welcome his alienation in America. Auden uproots himself by personal choice, but in the end all men will be uprooted by machines, and when this happens we will all be honorary Americans, for America is the "fully alienated land" in which no one belongs, in which all are refugees on

> An earth made common by the means
> Of hunger, money, and machines.

Poetry adapts itself to this alienated, industrialized, American world by becoming industrious, a demonstration of metrical and structural skill like a feat of engineering, an arrangement of squares and oblongs like architecture. The English Auden was a prophet. The American Auden is content to be a technician, and in this he is Paul Bunyan's successor. Bunyan's axe leveled nature. The technician's inventions now render nature obsolete.

New Year Letter, written immediately before the operetta text, establishes a lineage for Bunyan in describing the advent of economic man. Auden prided himself on being an aesthetic version of economic man, and brags in the preface to *The Dyer's Hand* that the essays collected therein were written for profit not delight, to pay the bills. Economic man's industriousness is a moral virtue. This "new *Anthropos*," Auden declares,

> Subjected earth to the control
> And moral choices of the soul.

The dual legatee of the Renaissance and the Reformation, forged from "LUTHER's faith and MONTAIGNE's doubt," economic man is a Protestant theologian, rescuing reason from the obfuscations of Catholicism and banishing the false necessity of famine and disease by making the earth fructify. Romanticism discredits economic man: Auden mentions the assaults on his prosaic probity by Blake, Rousseau, Kierkegaard, and Baudelaire. But though deposed in Europe, he flourishes in America where, as Auden's introduction to

Paul Bunyan argues, there is no enmity between romanticism and industrialism. Thus Auden can connect the frontier of *Paul Bunyan* with the urban setting of *New Year Letter,* for the towering individualist Paul lies behind the faceless toilers of the modern city as

> The neuter outline that's the plan
> And icon of Industrial Man.

Bunyan is an outline not a character because he is too godlike and omnipotent to be contained in a human action: he can't appear in the operetta. His successors, the men of the industrial age, are only outlines for the different reason that there is nothing to distinguish them from one another: they are merely statistics. American history is so telescoped that the two stages overlap. "The Commuter can't forget / The pioneer," Auden says, and he treats the mobility of modern Americans as evidence of the primitive nomadic impulse—Huck Finn's lighting out for the territory—which survives into an industrial society. Manufacturers shift their premises to the cheaper South, artists migrate east to New York, blacks to the North, the poor of the prairies to the West.

In Auden's paradoxical America, the frontier and the city overlap in time, and industrialism not only creates a mythology but generates an age of faith. The accumulation of lucre becomes a labor of spiritual qualification, and even the sleazy vileness of American society functions as a moral portent. The Great Good Place, in Henry James's story an amenable club, becomes in Auden an elective, private heaven, constructed in defiance of the Great Wrong Place which is contemporary America. Because America has disestablished the church, religious faith exists only as a result of personal choice, not as a natural and involuntary community. Each convertite devises his own version of the Good Place. America, as Paul Bunyan says, is what we choose to make it, and so is heaven. In Auden's view the mess of actual America serves to stimulate this personal quest for an ideal America. Industrialism abets faith rather than discrediting it. The horrors of the country—which Auden in the essay on James's *American Scene* lists as the jukeboxes, the un-nutritious salads, the neon signs and the radio commercials, the calibrated high kicks of the Rockettes—are allegorical admonitions, compelling the soul to postulate "by contrast . . . the Good Place" and to "desire it with sufficient desperation to stand a chance of arriving."

The bar on Third Avenue in *The Age of Anxiety* is the Wrong Place, but the characters go there to dream of the Good Place. They are a chance assembly—Rosetta the department-store buyer, Quant the clerk, Malin the airman, Emble the sailor—but they constitute together one of those elective communities of faith which are convened by Auden's America, since they're connected not by similarity of circumstance or by personal attraction but by the affinities of their dreams. The poem describes the construction and dispersal of their society. They meet at the bar, and are magnetized together as if each has overheard the others thinking; they retire together to a booth, and later adjourn to Rosetta's apartment. But the city which casually arranges their encounter also intervenes to divide them. Leaving Rosetta's place, Quant and Malin exchange addresses and promises to meet again, then part in the street and instantly forget each other. The city absorbs them, filing them away in different segments of itself. Malin travels south to Brooklyn on the subway while Quant walks east toward his home. The actuality in which they exist is crass and raucous, but the crooning of the jukebox, the rumble of the El, and the commercial persuasion of the radio only fortify their claustration in their dreams. The stage directions describing the banal doings of the bar are in dreary flatulent prose; the soliloquies of the characters are eccentric, introverted poetry. The night they spend together is an interlude of poetic reverie, but day recalls them to the prosaic business of work and war: they are "reclaimed by the actual world where time is real and in which, therefore, poetry can take no interest."

This division between the externality of the Wrong Place and the interior hermetic shelter of the Good Place, between grubby prose and eerie poetry, is one of the casualties New York inflicts on its inhabitants. The city is an imperious, grandiloquent public space behind which lie millions of miniature private spaces. It is a place of teeming crowds and of tormented loneliness. Individuals have to invent a secret society for themselves inside the crowd's anonymous profuseness by trusting, like the characters of the poem, to random meetings, brief encounters, elective affinities. New York is expert in arranging alienated, temporary relationships like those Auden describes. It is the home of the singles bar or the gay bar where the customer auditions candidates in the hope of finding someone to fit his or her ready-made fantasy, the home of computer dating and of narcissistic discothèques where people dance with their image of themselves not with their putative partners; it is the city of unrequited love and of requited self-love. Cities, as Auden says, dissociate "social or economic position and . . . private mental life." The New York in which his characters collide collectivizes people without relating them, because it deals only in quantities and can't recognize personal uniqueness. The soliloquies of these characters are their attempt to retrieve some individuality from the lonely crowd by the exercise of imagination, by making up a past for themselves as Rosetta does.

Auden's estimation of America as a hell in which one regains a personal heaven was shared by Aldous Huxley, who finds in California the same symptoms of the Wrong Place which Auden identifies in New York. In *The Age of Anxiety* the enemy of concentration is the droning insipid radio in the bar, peddling war bonds, issuing stertorous news bulletins, and advertising fatuous quizzes. The radio is determined to interrupt the communion between the characters, who leave their bar-stools and retire to a booth to escape from it. Huxley mentions this same importunate chatter of the radio in a metaphysical anthology which he compiled in 1946, *The Perennial Philosophy*. The mystic, he says, studies to create silence, as do Auden's communicants in the bar, but "the twentieth century is . . . the Age of Noise." The inescapable American radio is a pollution of the will, but its endless persuasive drivel only serves, Huxley believes, to strengthen the mystic's resistance. Its din paradoxically enforces the rule of silence. Quant in Auden's bar stops the radio by the exercise of mental telepathy. He points at it, and it shuts up. It falls silent because he has refused to listen to it. Huxley's radio makes more dangerous incursions, not only invading the mind with its noise but also seducing the ego by making it desire the tacky products it touts. But even here the mind can turn the Wrong Place inside out and make from it a replica of the Good Place. The radio exacerbates craving, turning its listeners into rabid consumers. The purpose of American advertising is to create appetites, to convince people that they need useless trinkets. The mystic on the other hand wants to regulate and subdue appetite, which is the source of human unease and folly. But the radio's incitements to desire at least warn Huxley that "desirelessness is the condition of deliverance and illumination." Consumerism is a spiritual malady. This is why Huxley when on mescaline trips was fond of frequenting the Californian equivalent of Auden's seedy bar, the World's Largest Drugstore in Los Angeles. The drugstore is the temple of false values, celebrating a profane consumerism and an idolatrous faith in redemption by gadgets. Huxley takes his visions into the drugstore because it is the vulgar hell inside which he concocts an alternative, chemical heaven.

New Year Letter charts Paul Bunyan's heredity. *The Age of Anxiety* describes his succession, exploring the anonymous, interior age of faith in which Paul is unavailing, the crowded privacy of the metropolis which replaces the superstitious solitude of the frontier. In *Paul Bunyan* all were immigrants. Now all are refugees. Both immigrant and refugee are for Auden premonitory figures in a world where people are uprooted by machinery and displaced by war. His housekeeper at his summer lodge outside Vienna was a refugee dispossessed by war, pauperized (as he recalls in an elegy written after her death in 1967) by the Czechs. Anxiety is an emotion invented by such people. A vague, disoriented unease, it is the most modern of emotions, the existential affliction of those who have been psychologically and territorially displaced and who no longer feel a connection with the world in which they find themselves.

Shortly after his arrival in New York in 1939 Auden wrote a song for a refugee whose country has been removed from the map:

> Say this city has ten million souls,
> Some are living in mansions, some are living in holes:
> Yet there's no place for us, my dear, yet there's no place for us.

The syncopated swing of these lines matches the refugee's predicament, for jazz, which Auden is mimicking, is the musical idiom of an enforced migration, the transposition of jungle sounds and rhythms to the industrial city. When in 1947 Leonard Bernstein began work on a symphony based on *The Age of Anxiety,* he cast Malin as a pianist playing febrile, neurotically unstable jazz. In the "Masque" section of the symphony, corresponding to the hectic festivity in Rosetta's apartment, the pianist disports himself with a frantic agility, fretting to suppress his own weariness and doubt. Jazz is anxious music, rhythmically frenetic and emotionally unbalanced. The virtuoso pianist must be by turns, Bernstein instructs, "nervous, sentimental, self-satisfied, vociferous." He is also a figure of instrumental alienation. Confronted by the mass of the orchestra, the soloist, in Bernstein's explication of the work, testifies to an existential division, the self's separation from reality. The piano plays beside the orchestra, and doesn't belong within it. The orchestra twice rebuffs it. When peremptory trumpets arrest the revelry in Rosetta's apartment, the piano continues, but the soloist is now alienated from his own instrument as well as from the orchestra: it's not the soloist playing but another piano somewhere else. The piano is also excluded from the solemn optimism of the epilogue, which is the revelation of faith. The soloist sits apart as an unoccupied spectator, watching the orchestra's spiritual recovery, Bernstein says, "as if on a cinema screen." This reference to the cinema recalls Lawrence's attack on alienatory damage done by the medium, which

turns people into observers of their own lives. In the original symphony, first performed in 1949, Bernstein condemned the pianist to
silence throughout the epilogue. Revising the work in 1965, he relented, and permitted the soloist a final confirmatory cadenza. But
not even this gesture of partisanship qualifies him for membership
in the orchestra. "The way is open," Bernstein says, "but, at the conclusion, is still stretching long before him."

The characters of *The Age of Anxiety* are theologically consoled in their depression and deracination. Anxiety, they realize, is
the longing of the expelled Adam for paradise. Quant tells the radio
that they are reversing history and restoring, in meditation, the state
of innocence from which *Paul Bunyan* industrially ejected them:
they are reformers founding "the Ganymede Club / For homesick
young angels."

Auden tried to apply this wisdom to his own life in New York,
and taught himself to rejoice in the city's alienatory brutality, brisk-
ness, and indifference. He regarded its disrespect for persons as an
exemplary modern moral trial. "You are forced to live here," he told
an interviewer in 1940, "as everyone will be forced to live." He even
took his work out into the brawling public space, in order to make
his isolation more piquant. He told the same interviewer that he
habitually wrote in a cafeteria during the mornings: "people pay no
attention to me. It's very satisfactory." New York made him learn a
set of mechanical skills which were both the life-saving aptitudes of
urban man and badges of existential courage. Cyril Connolly, who
visited Auden in New York in 1946, found him obsessed with the
cultivation of techniques for metropolitan survival. He prided himself on his negotiation of the snarled networks of the subway
system, and was punctilious about crossing streets directly the traffic
lights gave the starting signal. He insured himself against hold-ups
by always carrying a five-dollar bill to be handed over to any mugger
who might accost him. Auden had chosen to engage in a battle with
the mechanical city, and dreaded the accusation of incompetence.
His dictatorial ritualism in art and life develops from this sense of

the unrelenting pace and rigid agendas of modern mechanical New York. Mechanical skills become the poet's structural devices. The American Auden acclimatized the poem to the machine age by making it a contraption and himself a technician, expert in difficult rhyme-schemes and recondite stanza-forms.

Migration granted Auden a double alien status. Even after taking United States citizenship in 1946, he relished his disconnection from his adopted country, and claimed to be a New Yorker only, not an American. On his first return visit to England in 1945, he had made himself offensively alien in his native place. He went back as a captain in the American army, on the way to Germany where he was to inspect the psychological effects of bombing. The nature of the mission was calculated to annoy, since his defection in 1939 (about which outraged questions were asked in the House of Commons) still rankled. Auden caused universal offense by complaining how cold English houses were and ridiculing the penury of a rationed existence. Most outrageously of all, he contended that London hadn't been seriously damaged by bombing. Auden's rebarbativeness, which became progressively fouler and nastier over the years, was the sign of his refusal to allow himself to feel at home anywhere. Prizing his own precious freedom as an alien, he set about systematically alienating other people. Hence the tediously scatological conversation of his later years. When he returned to live in Oxford in 1972 he scandalized the sanctimonious diners at High Table in Christ Church by asking when they started masturbating or whether they peed in their bathroom sinks. He objected to the wash-basin in his college rooms because it was inconveniently high to double as a urinal, just as he declined to visit Japan because he was convinced that the toilet seats would be too small for his sagging rump. Why was he so insistently obscene? One of the reasons is jocularly theological. By talking dirty he was acquiescing in his own foul fallen nature, collaborating in that process whereby, in the individual life as well as in the American history of *Paul Bunyan*, we lose paradise in order to regain it. Filth to Auden was the humble uniform of humanity. He mistrusted cleanliness, which he thought impious. His advice to the students at Swarthmore College in Pennsylvania, where he taught between 1942 and 1945, was "Never forget you're a heel; . . . don't wash too much." Another reason for his scabrous manner was psychological: he embarrassed people in order to make them resent and disown him, provoking them to confirm his sorry alienation.

By a scrupulous domestic slovenliness he even alienated himself from the houses which should have been his private shelters. His untidiness was not negligence but imaginative policy. His ordure was absurdist in its madcap illogic. His house at Swarthmore contained a litter of gramophone records, bottles, and cigarette packets, but was otherwise unfurnished. He wrote at the dining-room table, and ate out. His costume was nonsensically contrived to alienate him from his body, as his domestic havoc alienated him from his surroundings. He padded down the street in carpet slippers, and hosted parties in a bathrobe. Rope held up his trousers. He reserved his socks for use as headgear during blizzards.

Residence in America also allowed Auden to enjoy a subtle alienation from the English language. England and America are divided by their common language. They share the words, but inflect them differently. America turns English into a foreign language, and this for Auden was not a disablement (as his friends assumed it would be when he left England in 1939) but the answer to a poet's dream. Poetry hopes to take the currency of everyday verbal exchange and make it rich and new. America does the poet's job for him. Auden therefore set about speaking American English, turning his native language into an awkward acquired idiom, flattening and clipping his vowels and cherishing local usages like "gotten." Being deprived of the word "gotten," he said in 1972, would be one of the sorrows of his return to England. His affectations were intended not to help him pass as an American but to alienate him from his English contemporaries. All of Auden's reflections on the difference between England and America take the form of literary criticism because he believes that national identity is defined and protected by linguistic quirks. An essay written for the *Anchor Review* in 1955 entitled "The Anglo-American Difference" examines this treacherous region between English and American usages, and admits that Auden's accentual oddities only confirm his dual alienation, from both England and America. He mimics the sounds Americans make because he can't naturally and unself-consciously belong to their linguistic community. "Any Englishman," he says, ". . . can learn to pronounce 'the letter *a* in psalm and calm . . . with the sound of *a* in candle,' to say *thumbtacks* instead of *drawing pins* or twenty-*of*-one instead of twenty-*to*-one, and discover that, in the Middle West, *bought* rhymes with *hot.*" But this mimicry won't make an American of him. Rhythm, pitch, vocal register will still betray him. America obliges the poet to remain outside the language he is using, like the soloist expelled from the orchestra in Bernstein's *Age of Anxiety*. Auden suggests his acquiescence in this linguistic alien status by going on, in the *Anchor Review* essay, to say that though his ear can recognize the difference between English and American poetic speech he can't explain it, because it is a matter of "fingering": a physical dexterity which is inborn and can't be learned.

Having trained himself to be an alien, Auden slyly shamed T. S. Eliot for pretending to belong to his adopted country. Eliot, after quitting America and taking British citizenship, assumed a fastidiously exact British pronunciation and comported himself like an owlish London stockbroker. Auden delighted in teasing the American cowering behind this English persona, and even declared that the opening line of *The Waste Land*, "April is the cruellest month," betrayed the poet's suppressed nationality. In England, April is damp but benign; only in America is it cruel, stirring a rank, pullulating vegetation with lashing rains. The English befriend nature, but Americans are convinced of its inhuman severity and intemperance. Auden even detected a covert Americanism in that reverence for tradition which was the mark of Eliot's adherence to Europe. He quotes in the *Anchor Review* Eliot's remark that "tradition cannot be inherited, and if you want it you must obtain it by great labour," and comments that no European critic could have made this statement. Though Eliot venerates European tradition, his assumption that it must be strenuously earned not atmospherically absorbed is, to Auden, American in its dutiful autodidacticism.

This exposure of Eliot's ambition to disappear into tradition implies Auden's own resistance to the encroachments of tradition, his pride in his alien status. In leaving England he did not jettison one tradition in order to subscribe to another. Both in England and America, he wrote in deliberate contravention of tradition. His orneriness derives from his suspicion that tradition means a relationship with others and membership in a society, enfeebling luxuries the alien cannot permit himself. The English poet, Auden points out, is traditionally a man talking to men, conversing with the society of his peers, whereas the American poet more usually talks to himself, or to a single intimate friend. While he lived in England, Auden often wrote like an American. The poems diagnosing the sickness of the '30s are prophetic and conspiratorial, the outcry of a voice in the wilderness and an address to the few sympathizers who can comprehend the subversive private language. Their strained self-reliant paranoia is a quality of the lonely American ego, not of the polite English professional. But after Auden went to live in America, his style became chattily English. Having forever alienated himself from the society of his peers, he began writing for them. The American Auden is increasingly a joker and a doodler, with a genius for frivolously aphoristic conversation in verse.

Garrulous ease is a quality both alien and offensive to Americans. Auden said in 1955 that "for a 'serious' poet to write light verse is frowned on in America." Again he is manuevering his way to imaginative freedom by agile self-contradiction, for in 1938, before the move to America, he had edited an *Oxford Book of Light Verse,* and claimed in his introduction that America was the current home of light verse. By light verse the Marxist Auden of 1938 meant folk poetry. His argument is that the industrial destruction of rural society in England has debauched popular verse: the ballad degenerates into the music-hall jingle. But in America, "under the conditions of frontier expansion and prospecting and railway development," folk poetry has remained alive. Industry there, as *Paul Bunyan* proclaims, is no enemy of myth and poetry. By light verse the Auden of 1955 meant, however, not proletarian legends but virtuoso doggerel, like the epigrammatic squibs he collected in various volumes as "Shorts," or the donnish clerihews called "Academic Graffiti." Idealistic American portentousness forbids the poet to say, as he would in Europe, that he writes "for fun." But it is precisely their own hedonistic triviality that Auden's American poems declare.

The freedom which Auden, in his sermon at Smith, had nominated as America's theological bounty, was at first, as discussion of the poems of the 1940s has shown, an existential tension. Later this stressful psychological self-solicitation loosened, in Auden's style of writing and of living, into a humorous crankiness. At first America seemed to have made him an introvert, estranged from community, anonymously scribbling in noisy cafeterias. Later, during the 1950s, it became clear that America was making him an eccentric. The eccentric is an introvert on the defensive, one who has turned his self-immersion into a defiant confrontation of the world, which he accepts only on his own mad or whimsical terms. This is the later Auden, clad in an armor of crotchets and faddish obsessions. Shambling about in carpet slippers with uncombed hair and clothes spotted by food stains, peevishly denouncing friends who were a minute late for an appointment, Auden was a symbolic New Yorker. For, while scrambling people into proximity, that city also separates them, incarcerating each inside his own fantasies. The subway cars are crowded, but the passengers don't talk to or even look at one another. If one of them talks, it is to conduct a long, angry conversation with himself. Physically collectivized, people are psychologically segregated. Emble in *The Age of Anxiety* wonders how you retrieve some individuality from the urban crowd in which you are jostled. The answer is to become mildly mad, to refuse to recognize the crowd's existence. Your eccentricity will be safely inconspicuous, because everyone else is just as crazily self-concentrated as you are.

Auden sees American literature as a charter of aliens' rights, a defense of deviant freedoms. Because the American poet isn't a citizen, he can't conceive of a character which is a public possession, and confers his own individual privacy even on a head of state. Tennyson's ode on Wellington's death, Auden says, is a poem about "a great public official figure," but Whitman's "When Lilacs Last in the Door-Yard Bloom'd" mourns Lincoln's death as if it were that of "some close personal friend." Orphans in English novels crave adoption into society, but their American counterparts flee from it. Oliver Twist ends ensconced in the Brownlow home where he belongs, but Huck Finn dodges away from Aunt Sally. Auden and Isherwood, leaving England together in 1939, were a paradoxical partnership of Huck and Oliver. Auden like Huck was running away from home: he loves his family but won't live with them. Isherwood's motives were those of Oliver. He is a vagrant for whom travel is not an escape from home but a quest for a rightful home. When first arriving in Germany in 1930 he told a customs official he was searching for a homeland, and hoped he might find it in Berlin.

Subtextually, American literature is for Auden a charter of homosexuals' rights. America through its literature dreams of a passionate blood-brotherhood. Huck, who escapes at the end of the novel from a rapaciously generous woman, has had a friendship with nigger Jim "far closer," Auden says, "than any enjoyed by Oliver." Melville's Ishmael is bound emotionally to Queequeg. Auden also quotes Whitman's longing for a comrade to accept his love and share his solitude. The latter point is significant. The male alliance is not to be familial and settled like a marriage. Whitman doesn't want a lover to live with, but a traveling companion on the open road. In accordance with the perilous existential American freedom Auden extolled at Smith, and in accordance with the promiscuous vagaries of homosexual freedom, these relationships are to be provisional and temporary, not heterosexually final like marriage. Huck and Ishmael have a nonchalant homosexual infidelity in their abandonment of their blood-brothers: Huck deserts Jim, Ishmael forgets Queequeg. America's social freedom allows a movement between classes and across territory which stratified, cramped England restricts. As a result, personal ties in America remain breezily casual, never becoming familial as they do in England, where everyone seems to be related if not by birth then by the homogenizing institutions of school, college, club, or adultery. "Impermanence is taken for granted" in all American relationships, Auden says. The country has learned from the informal, opportunistic, short-lived homosexual tenderness extolled in Auden's lullaby:

> Lay your sleeping head, my love,
> Human on my faithless arm.

Fidelity, Auden says in this poem, terminates at midnight.

Auden turns homosexual one-night stands into existential tests or theological reminders, especially appropriate to America, of the fragility and imperfection of all human couplings. Isherwood adapts one-night stands to his own new Californian religion by making them acts of arbitrary mystical worship. Speaking in a Gay Pride rally at Long Beach in 1975, he criticized the homosexual simulation of bourgeois marriage and praised "brief encounters" as "maybe . . . more marvellous than other forms of sexual relationship." Screwing around acts out the mystic's impartial adoration of all created things: "I don't see, theoretically, why there shouldn't be the most powerful sort of love, like St. Francis's, applied to one-night stands, where you really love a different person each night."

Given their faith in alienatory America and in the virtue of disposable relationships, it is fitting that America should so promptly have divorced Auden and Isherwood. In Europe they had been inseparable as travelers, literary collaborators, and occasional, fraternal lovers. America instantly divided them by presenting them with a series of choices which enabled them to discover their separate individualities. Auden remained in New York, while Isherwood traveled west to California. The city's grim regularity suited Auden the moralist and mock-theologian, who detested the solar optimism of California. During summer trips to Portugal or Germany during the '30s, Auden wrote indoors with the curtains drawn against the day, Isherwood outdoors stripped to the waist. Auden's preferred landscapes were mountainous and rainy, Isherwood's glaringly sunny and sandy. The climatic difference corresponds to a difference in literary vocation. The poet immures himself in hermetic cells or on inaccessible heights (Auden's New York was a man-made version of the Alps), while the novelist exposes himself to the brutal brilliance of the day. America enabled Auden and Isherwood to localize their fantasies, and shocked them into maturity by dividing them. Auden the muddling hierarch belonged in the geometrical chaos of New York, the city of anxiety. Isherwood advanced to the Pacific coast, where he found the hedonistic celebration of the body transvalued into an Oriental renunciation of physical cares.

New York, rigidly laid out in space on a numbered grid of streets, monitored in time by those flashing clocks on the tops of buildings, encouraged the punctilious ritualism of Auden, who didn't know whether to be hungry unless a clock instructed him, and invariably left dinner parties at 9 p.m. to go home to bed. Auden rejoiced in his enslavement to time, whereas California with its lotos-eating eternities of physical relaxation ignores time's passage. During his years in New York Auden pickled and prematurely aged himself. Time seismically furrowed his face, and the old Auden awaited his extinction with impatience. In 1971 he asked time to let him "bugger off quickly." Acquiescence in the process of his own physical decay has the same theological motive as his argument in *Paul Bunyan* that America can only become itself by aging and dying into life: time is the medium in which our fall ultimately turns fortunate. The ravages of time are wise and reconciliatory: "Time only knows the price we have to pay," as Auden says in the 1940 poem "If I Could Tell You." The self-repetitive social vices of Auden's old age—retelling stale anecdotes, dogmatic self-quotation—have a similarly orderly intention. They validate time by refusing to change, fossilizing in stasis. Auden chose to be boring rather than chafe against time's prolonged degeneration. In contrast, Isherwood in California has grown steadily younger. He writes about his past not to confirm his bondage to time but to cast it off. He still looks, in his seventy-fifth year, like an adolescent slightly wizened by exposure to the sun. Those bright, glacial eyes and that animated face contrast with the pockets of weary flesh which sagged from Auden's skull.

New Year Letter ventures a theological criticism of California. Describing the nomadic circulation of the American population, Auden mentions the rootless inhabitants of the prairies who drive in their jalopies

> To suffer further westward where
> The tolerant Pacific air
> Makes logic seem so silly, pain
> Subjective, what he seeks so vain
> The wanderer may die.

California is a false paradise, a place which discredits suffering rather than relieving it or understanding its moral uses. Eastern, urban man accepts his ills and anxieties, but the Californian pagan disparages them as subjective phantoms and lapses into otiose, suntanned enjoyment. The East is fallen, troubled, condemned by the curse laid on Adam to endless labor (Auden's middle-class puritanism liked a foul climate, which kept him indoors at work). New Yorkers are harried refugees from paradise, but Californians are still inside their verdant tropical Eden with nothing to do but bask in the brightness and tend their gardens, and this is why Auden's Protestant conscience censures them. In November 1947 he spent a week in Hollywood, staying at Stravinsky's house and planning *The Rake's Progress*. He steadfastly refused to go sightseeing, and recoiled in horror from the idea of the Pacific. He was persuaded to leave the house at night, after the sun was in retreat, for performances of a play and an opera. Otherwise, his only excursion was a trip to the doctor. He had complained of discomfort in his ears, and was sent off to have the impacted wax cleaned from the canals. In the paradise of youth and bronzed physical health, Auden seemed determined to cherish his own decrepitude and physical debility.

In Auden's compartmentalized year, summer was a problem because of his cantankerous dislike of the sun. During his first years in New York he passed the summer in a tar-paper shack on Fire Island. In 1948 he transferred his holiday to Ischia, and at last in 1958 he acquired an appropriately northern residence, a converted farmhouse at Kirchstetten, outside Vienna, where he spent half of each year for the rest of his life. Fire Island and Ischia were imaginatively unavailing because (as Auden says in "Good-Bye to the Mezzogiorno," the poem commemorating his abandonment of Ischia) the sun scorches away guilt and pampers a body which the moralist and theologian chasten. The European south, like the American West, is a place of blissful remission. The house at Kirchstetten restored symmetry to Auden's year because it wasn't a bucolic alternative to New York but a replica of the city. Auden in New York was confined to an apartment, a single squalid recess in the anonymous vastness of the city (in 1953 he settled at 77 St. Mark's Place in the East Village). In his Austrian villa he could relish the illusion of inhabiting a whole city. Criticizing the reforms of city planners in "Thanksgiving for a Habitat," a set of poems about the Kirchstetten house, Auden says that

> a pen
> for a rational animal
> is no fitting habitat for Adam's
> sovereign clone.

In New York he had his rational pen, in a rust-red brick tenement with a crumbling stoop, surrounded today by the detritus of the mechanical city—a grim den calling itself a cocktail lounge, boutiques of bizarrerie, a gay bath-house, and (opposite Auden's building) a cinema vending nostalgia, which is the way the age of anxiety has latterly devised of comforting its own sadness. In Austria, Auden had his sovereign domain, where he presided over three acres of land and a "conurbation of country lives," not as an anonymous member of the lonely crowd but with baronial pomp, in a street renamed in his honor.

The city and the house are comparable phenomena because they are both affronts to nature, which for the theological Auden "won't quite do," and must be fenced off from human society. Auden admired New York's contempt for nature. Other cities follow the meandering picturesque waywardness of nature; New York outlaws nature's zigzags and is austerely rectilinear. Other cities struggle along the face of the earth; New York upends itself, and lifts whole districts vertically to the sky inside its towering office- and apartment-blocks. Auden frequently declared that he preferred New York to London because New York at least wasn't provincial. One of the things he meant by this was that New York, a sliver of granite physically and mentally separate from the nature on either side of it, scorns the sentiment of locality. The meager nature it contains it segregates inside Central Park, as if to demarcate the difference between the habitats fit for humans engineered by architecture and the unkempt treacherous mess of the wild. London on the contrary is forever reneging, straggling back into nature, allowing itself to be bisected by a river, greening itself irrelevantly with lawns, parks, and forests. If New Yorkers make a garden they do so on the roofs of skyscrapers, to demonstrate their defiance of the earth. New York is proud to be a city, but London half-shamefully thinks of itself as a rural estate: this is why Auden called it provincial.

Architecture, Auden says in the prologue to "Thanksgiving for a Habitat," is a tribute to human superiority. Like theology, it is redemptive: for Auden "new styles of architecture" betokened "a change of heart." Buildings are an alternative to nature, and take umbrage at death. Cities declare man's theologically guaranteed immortality. Because cities are made by exclusion, they are also analogous to poems. A city is defined by walls which blockade it off from nature, and in "Ode to Terminus" Auden addresses the terminal god as the guardian of both urban and poetic form:

> God of walls, doors and reticence,
> . . . blessed is the City that thanks you
> for giving us games and grammar and metre.

Grammar and meter, like the city, are models of strict regularity. So are the crosswords which were Auden's hobby. Like the grid of the Manhattan streets, crosswords symbolize space ordered by right angles, and Auden's skill in completing them symbolizes time ordered and economized by technical ingenuity. Unfortunately, though, New York didn't produce crosswords worthy of itself, and Auden was reduced to solving those in the London Sunday papers. The imprecision of the clues in the *New York Times* crossword puzzle was, Auden maintained, the city's fatal flaw. In 1972, after he announced that he would in future spend his winters in Oxford, the *Times* invited him to write a farewell to New York for its Op-Ed page. He did so, and took the opportunity to denounce the paper's incompetent crossword puzzles, which drove him "up the wall with rage." Otherwise, he has no criticism to make of the city, so that his statement reads as if it is the improper crosswords which should be blamed for his departure.

The house in "Thanksgiving for a Habitat" resembles a city because it is a place of functional specialization. A city like New York disperses functions and allocates to each its zone: one area for garment factories, another for diamond merchants; downtown for finance, midtown for advertising; mutually exclusive ghettos for blacks, Jews, and homosexuals. The architecture of Auden's villa is similarly urban. The house is a city comprising separate chambers or precincts for the various friends who are the dedicatees of the poems. Louis MacNeice presides over creative work in the study, which Auden calls his cave of making. Chester Kallman occupies the sociable area of the living-room. Isherwood, the convert to yoga and

Californian religion, is relegated to the lavatory, because the mystic's obsession is the purification of his soiled physical existence. Like the city, the house ordains a division and distribution of labor. New York is segmented into areas reserved for specific functions. The house too contains one room for cooking, another for eating, one room for reading, another for sleeping, and so on. By devoting a separate poem to each room and offering each poem to a particular friend, Auden is domesticating his metropolis of elective affinities. The New York of *New Year Letter* and *The Age of Anxiety* is a chaos of rootless refugees who adhere by choice or chance, connected across empty urban distances by the automobile, the subway, and the telephone, since there is no natural neighborly community to enmesh them in customary relationships. The house at Kirchstetten is this New York in miniature: not a public space but a catacomb of separate privacies, a city rigged up from the elective affinities which link the poet to each of his friends without linking those friends to one another. Like New York, the house is an arbitrary selection from the global crowd of displaced persons.

Auden's compartmentalization of his territory derives its form from a political philosophy which in turn refers to the conditions of existence in New York. The philosophy is that of Auden's friend and fellow refugee Hannah Arendt, who had decamped from Germany during Hitler's persecution of the Jews. She met Auden in 1958, the year in which her lectures, *The Human Condition,* were published. Auden at once arrogated this book, paying it the compliment of treating it as his own: "every now and then, I come across a book which gives me the impression of having been especially written for me. . . . *The Human Condition* belongs to this small and select class." Its theories about the constitution of political order shape his understanding of New York and his organization of his domestic habitat.

Hannah Arendt's intention was to account for that "modern world alienation" which was both Auden's personal predicament and his poetic subject. Modern man, she says, has dually alienated himself, by retreating "from the earth into the universe, and from the world into the self." The two movements are congruent, and both are characteristically American. The country composed of immigrants and refugees who don't cohere into a natural community, who even owe their land to violent acts of expropriation, the country in which each man is an antisocial individualist (loneliness, the psychological cost of self-reliance, was for Auden the constant subject of American literature) is also the country which accomplishes the ultimate act of uprooting, removing man from his anchorage to the earth and sending him to the moon. To explain the process of alienation, Hannah Arendt contrasts classical and modern notions of political liberty. In the classical *polis,* the city of the Greeks which was a self-sufficient state, all men were political actors, united in their common access to the forum. The idiot in the classical definition is the unpolitical man, who fails to avail himself of his civic rights. Auden reprimanded the Stravinskys for a similar negligence when they admitted that they never bothered to vote. In the modern world we are merely the spectators of political acts performed by others, allegedly on our behalf. We now think of liberty not as the classical right to engage in political affairs but as an insurance against the government's interference. The classical community has been fragmented into a cell block of romantic privacies, each defending its boundary. Modern man's liberty is not his freedom to act but his freedom from the actions of others. The nineteenth century thinks of this retreat into privacy as a lyrical introversion; the twentieth century diagnoses it as a clinical symptom of alienation.

The alienated political state Hannah Arendt describes is Auden's New York. Mediterannean cities remain close to the classical form, because their inhabitants share the bustling common space of the market or the public square. Their living is done in the streets, and they retire home only to sleep. New York is a city of the modern, inward-turning, unsocial kind. For its fearful citizens the streets, as Auden says in "City Without Walls," are "lawless marches." Only tramps, toughs, and muggers live outdoors and prowl the nocturnal city. People of probity are inside and at an altitude in their residential skyscrapers, barricaded off from the anarchic public space, their doors chained and bolted, with guards on sentry duty downstairs in the foyer. Afraid of the wilderness outside their individual sanctuaries, New Yorkers have created Hannah Arendt's modern city in its most nervously alienated form. They have renounced their membership of the public space and retired to the safety of what Auden calls "numbered caves in enormous jails." Cities need walls to keep out the mess of nature, but in New York the purpose of walls is to keep out the city itself. People protect the integrity of their miniature private demesnes as vigilantly as they defend their bodies, because they perceive a similarity between the two. The apartment is the body's shelter, its armored exoskeleton.

New York divides its crowds into self-incarcerated solipsists, and their incommunicable dreams are Auden's subject. The woman at the fast-food counter in the poem "In Schrafft's" smiles with a motiveless rapture. A god has visited her, but the poet can't surmise why, and she won't tell. Auden's literary criticism invokes the city's decomposition of community to explain the social tensions in Shakespeare's *Coriolanus*. The modern world, he argues, foments a sectarian disaffection which is more introverted and therefore less efficiently organized than the radicalism of Shakespeare's plebeians: "if you went to Union Square," to search among New York's stump orators for a modern equivalent to Shakespeare's First Citizen, "you'd see plenty of dissatisfied 'radicals' but none with the . . . talent for action of Shakespeare's Citizen." Modern revolutionaries are not only alienated from society but alienated from each other by ideological dispute. The pacifists, Stalinists, and anarchists in Union Square would be too busy in mutual contention to "envisage any common scheme of political action." Auden was amused by a *New Yorker* cartoon which to him exemplified the psychological paradox of the lonely crowd. The cartoon "showed a little man struggling madly with a huge octopus issuing from a manhole. An utterly passive crowd surrounded him. On the fringe of the crowd two men . . . were walking by, ignorant of the cause of the disturbance. One . . .

turned to the other with the remark 'It doesn't take much to attract a crowd in New York.'" To Auden, the ancedote is, like the inexplicable beatitude of the customer in Schrafft's, a fable of the spirit's alienated and anonymous destiny in the city. Like the man with the octopus, each of us grapples with our fate or our demon in solitude, and other people either gape indifferently or ignore us altogether, like the supercilious passers-by.

Auden turns his Austrian house inside out, adjusting it both to Hannah Arendt's political theory and to the reality of New York, which has fragmented the public space we all share into a patchwork of nervously defended private terrains. Architectural megalomania belongs to an earlier state of civilization, when grandiose public spaces were a theater of power and a declaration of wealth. Now, Auden says, "only a press lord / could have built San Simeon," the Hispanic folly erected by William Randolph Hearst on the coast midway between San Francisco and Los Angeles. Aldous Huxley, who was an occasional guest at San Simeon, used it as a model for Stoyte's castle in *After Many a Summer*. Hearst's architecture is classical because ample and ceremonial, Auden's romantic because cellulated. The most characteristic niches of his house are places of romantic solitude not classical gregariousness. The bathroom, for instance, enshrines "the unclassical wonder of being / all by oneself." Huxley, Isherwood, and Auden all admired American bathrooms, but the adoptive Californians had spiritual reasons for doing so: the bathroom is a place of purification, in which acolytes lave away the physical filth scourged by Huxley the satirist and proceed to the mystical release of the spirit described by Isherwood. Auden's praise for the bathroom, however, follows the political science of Hannah Arendt and betrays the territorial anxiety of the adoptive New Yorker. Classical political man refused to conceal private physical functions, and bathed communally, but the bathroom in "Thanksgiving for a Habitat," lockable only from inside, testifies to the modern cult of privacy and its recognition that "to withdraw from the tribe at will / . . . is a sacrosanct / political right."

Migrating to America in 1939, Auden ejected himself from the national family and embraced a fearful existential freedom. He set himself to live and work according to the stark specifications of the modern world, alienated from his native community and even from his native language. England, however, remained his lost natal paradise, the cozy infancy from which maturity had debarred him:

> England to me is my own tongue,
> And what I did when I was young.

He therefore decided that it was the aptest place in which to spend his second childhood. Rejoicing in time's infliction and hastening its foreclosure, Auden looked forward to senility and did his best to advance it, behaving like an ungovernable, finicky baby, organizing his regime around regular mealtimes and early nights, re-creating in his apartment on St. Mark's Place the squalor of the nursery. Second childhood was to Auden satisfyingly symmetrical, a circular conclusion to life's pilgrimage. Theologically, it was a restoration of paradise, a return from the adult's alienated self-help to mindless incontinent uterine warmth. Psychologically, it was a renunciation of the sexual longing for bodies other than one's own and a return to the infant's enviable narcissism. In "A Lullaby" (1972), Auden curls up in bed, snuggles into his own body which is losing its virility and slackening into feminine flabbiness, and sings himself into gurgling oblivion. New York for Auden was the place to be adult in, the arduous world of work in which Adam and Eve find themselves outside the gates of Eden. England is the lost paradise of childhood and therefore the regained paradise of senility. Thus in 1972 Auden gave up his New York apartment and returned not to mother, but to alma mater. The Oxford college at which he had been an undergraduate, Christ Church, offered him the tenancy of a cottage inside its walls and inside the ancient walls of the city. He intended from now on to spend winters there and summers in Austria.

While packing to leave New York, he wrote a farewell to the city for the *New York Times*. His piece, published on March 18,

1972, contains the criticism of the paper's crosswords already referred to. It is Auden's last and slyest act of alienation, a series of barbed disclaimers in which he preserves his own freedom of maneuver by systematically causing offense. America for Auden was not home but an alternative to home and its enfeebling protective comforts. He can only exist in it by antagonizing it, warning it not to assume any claim on him and warning himself not to subside into the weak bliss of belonging. Therefore the valedictory piece in the *Times* begins with his refusal, even after having "lived more than half my life in the States," to "call myself an American." Though an American citizen, he treasures a spiritual alien status. The logic of this adversary position led him to adopt an equally offensive attitude in England. In America, he guarded his separateness by calling himself a New Yorker, relying on the reluctance of most Americans to consider the offshore island of Manhattan a part of their country. In England, he caused irritation by complacently referring to himself as an American and a foreigner. He declined to engage in Oxford chitchat about English politics, saying that as an alien it would be improper for him to have an opinion, and when it was rumored that he might be a candidate for the Poet Laureateship he pointed out that his adopted nationality made him ineligible, and indignantly denied that he would change his citizenship in order to qualify.

Though prepared to consider himself a New Yorker, he professed allegiance only to a specific, peripheral area of the city, so as to alienate the rest. The *Times* article slights the metropolitan pretensions of New York. Asked if he would miss the "cultural life" of the city, Auden's reply was "I have never taken part in it." His nannyish insistence on an early bedtime precluded outings to the theater or the movies, to concerts or opera. His cultural diversions were solitary vices, "reading, listening to records of classical music, and solving crossword puzzles," and he had no need of Lincoln Center or Carnegie Hall. The snub is sharpened as Auden withdraws further into his own seedy neighborhood. His New York, he declares, is not the affluent, official city but a down-at-heels village, the

Lower East Side. His fellow citizens are not the clerisy, among whose ranks he was photographed at the Gotham Book Mart in December 1948 during a reception for the visiting Sitwells, but the shopkeepers with whom, in dark glasses, carpet slippers, and laden with brown paperbags, he chose to be photographed for the *Times*. These local traders, who appear with him to illustrate the article, have a particular significance in Auden's New York, for they evince the ethnic separatism of the place. The clutter of uprooted nationalities Auden describes in the poems of the 1940s has not been smoothed into homogeneity. New York believes itself to be a melting pot, but Auden gives thanks that "it is nothing of the kind." In his neighborhood, Poles, Ukrainians, Italians, Jews, and Puerto Ricans remain defiantly distinct, and Auden confronts them as a solitary Wasp. New York remains the capital city of an alienated world. Extricating himself from it, Auden pretends that he will miss his "many dear friends," but he fondly names only the random collection of shopkeepers whose customer he has been. These are the minimal, alienated relationships to which the city dweller is condemned, lubricating commercial transactions with an exchange of formulaic cordialities: "Let me take this opportunity to thank in particular Abe and his co-workers in the liquor store; Abe the tobacconist; On Lok, my laundryman; Joseph, Bernard and Maurice in the grocery store at Ninth and Second Avenue; Harold the druggist; John, my mailman; Francy from whom I buy my newspaper, and Charles from whom I buy seeds for my Austrian garden." The city once spanned by elective affinities has narrowed into a zone of neighborhood shops.

Auden spent a disgruntled winter in Oxford, scrupulously alienating himself from the college community rather than relaxing into it, quizzing the costive dons of Christ Church about bed-wetting and peeing in wash-basins, stupefying himself with drink and morosely willing his own extinction. He had gone to America in 1939 to live; he returned to England in 1972 to die, welcoming his biological fate and behaving, even at his most scabrous, with what he considered theological propriety as he contemplated and gruesomely revelled in

Auden among the clerisy: at the Gotham Book Mart in 1948.
Lisa Larsen, *Life Magazine,* © 1948, Time Inc.

his imminent end. But death upset his ritualized schedule. It caught him between homes, as an alien in transit. After a summer at Kirchstetten, he died suddenly in Vienna in September, as he was about to return to Christ Church for the new academic year. Death when it came was not the doddering English decline into weak-sphinctered, infantile querulousness which he had expected. Instead it was abrupt, anonymous, American. He wasn't permitted to die at home, but collapsed in a hotel room after a poetry reading. Death didn't cajole him to sleep like an English nanny, but marked him down in the lonely crowd of the city and dispatched him with callous, merciful American efficiency.

Auden among his neighbors: with the mailman in St. Mark's Place, 1972.
Photographed by Karl Bissinger.

8

PSYCHEDELIC AMERICA
Aldous Huxley
in California

America turned Auden in on himself. Despairing of social change, he concentrated instead on changes of heart. Paradise has been lost. Going to America confirmed Auden's exclusion from it. He was ripping himself from his native place, sentencing himself to a career of daunting solitary labor. When in America paradise is regained, it is not in the form of the socialist millennium the English Auden dreamed of, but as a paradise within: the fearfully free world into which the characters of *Paul Bunyan* emerge; the incommunicable fantasies of the characters in *The Age of Anxiety*; the musical household of *New Year Letter* in which Auden listens to Buxtehude; the ecological niche he carves out for himself in Kirchstetten, or among the shopkeepers of the East Village.

America worked an equivalent change on Aldous Huxley. The English Huxley of the 1920s was a satirist, who longed not to improve the world outside him but to reprove and destroy it. Socialists dream of the millennium, satirists of the apocalypse. Satire is a recriminatory private dream of the day of judgment, when time at last will have a stop. That Shakespearean tag, used as the title of one of his novels, haunted Huxley. In a series of university lectures at Santa Barbara in 1959 he quoted it and remarked that it suggested to him "an entire philosophy." But satirists are not alone in believing that time must have a stop: so do mystics. The satirist halts time by force, consigning characters to a premature Armageddon. Hence the assassinations in Huxley's early novel *Point Counter Point*. The mystic stops time by floating out of it. We are all practicing mystics for a third of our lives, Huxley argued, because sleep is our daily liberation from the constraints of space and the lassitude of time.

Huxley's own personal development leads from satire to mysticism, and his move to America accentuates the change. Satire is a moral dead-end. The satirist will ultimately drive himself frantic in his helpless determination to punish the world. In any case he is bound to fail, because he is arrogating to himself that work of judgment which belongs to God. Swift imagines himself to be that vindictive God in his poem "The Day of Judgement," and Pope thrills to see "men not afraid of God afraid of me." But the satirist's only hope of satisfaction is to give up trying to be God and begin believing in God, to transform satiric disgust into mystical enlightenment. The mordant, dissipated atheists of *Those Barren Leaves* slump at the foot of the cross. The satiric California of *After Many a Summer* is a geriatric hell but also a mystical heaven devoted to the chemical and cosmetic abolition of death. Satire is Huxley's reaction to England, mysticism his response to America.

At the end of the tour described in *Jesting Pilate* (1926), which had taken him across America for the first time, he reflects on the difference between the satiric despair of Europe and the mystical ingenuousness of America. Europe denies values, America falsifies them. The European vice is nihilism, the American vice humbug.

But in exempting America from the European annihilation of morality, Huxley is already nominating it as a possible alternative, a mystical release from self-hating satire. Though Huxley on this first trip is offended by the mendacity of American advertising, the confusion and falsification of values to which the advertisements bear witness are only one logical step removed from the mystic's serene transvaluation of values. America is a satiric inferno which with a little encouragement might become a mystical paradise. Unlike Europe, which disparages the spirit, America even at its most commercially corrupt retains an innocent spirituality. Indeed its characteristic error, as Huxley sees it, is to garishly hybridize material goods and spiritual values. In 1926, this repelled him. Later, after he went to live there in 1937, it elated him, because it evinced America's unabashed, inane religiosity. In Asia, through which Huxley traveled before arriving in California in 1926, spirituality and material well-being are incompatible. Huxley blames penitential unworldly religious fanaticism for the human misery he finds in India, Burma, and Malaya. These societies condemn themselves to starvation, squalor, and pestilence because they are the craven servants of god and neglect their own economic betterment. But America triumphantly, even if absurdly, reconciles the spirit and the well-fed technologically pampered body. America makes religion a luxury, a leisured diversion, a smug thanksgiving for material affluence. The revivalist meetings Huxley observes in Los Angeles are syncopated masses, at which revelation is assisted by pipe organs, saxophones, and stunt men: "Hymns and the movies and Irving Berlin."

This is what Huxley means by the falsification of values. Auden argues that Americans transubstantialize wealth, turning filthy lucre into a divine benison. Money, according to this puritan theology, is a gift of grace, economic success the earthly equivalent of spiritual salvation. Huxley satirically derides this assumption in *Jesting Pilate*. He quotes a professor who opines that the plenty of America—its movie palaces, libidinal jazz bands, and pneumatic flappers, its gormandizers in restaurants—is the reward vouchsafed by Providence for the country's immaterial quest in search of "the Kingdom of God and His righteousness." Later Huxley was to understand the paradoxical justice of this argument. His mystical America depends on technology, which not only makes men religious by freeing them from their servitude to nature but grants them the means of transcendence: euphemistic morticians abolish death; the movies manufacture dreams; chemists synthesize the visionary potions with which Huxley experimented.

Jesting Pilate sees only America's falsification of values. But after he went to live in America, Huxley perceived this falsification as a transvaluation of values. The American institutions he mocks in *Jesting Pilate* are those he later returns to praise. For instance, the movies. Walking on the beach with Chaplin during this first visit, he is too absorbed in a mock-theological exploration of "the way of cinematographic salvation" to be tempted by the bathing beauties frolicking in the sun. The religious language is sarcastic. But two decades later, Huxley was solemnly convinced that the cinema offered a way of salvation, thanks to its powers of "vision-inducing phantasy." In his psychedelic treatise *Heaven and Hell* (1954) he acclaims the cinema as a visionary form which can distort and transform actuality, and finds this faculty exemplified in the disorienting close-ups of Walt Disney's *The Living Desert* or the prismatically fractured skyscrapers of Francis Thompson's *New York, New York*.

Huxley first interprets the cinema satirically, then transvalues it mystically. In Batavia in 1926, on the way to America, he goes to an open-air picture show, and marvels at America's exhibition of its violent imbecilities to the bemused Javanese. Hollywood neglects the political and spiritual superiority of the West, and makes global propaganda for Western silliness and criminality. The film Huxley sees represents America as a crude, instinctual, immature world of crooks and mental defectives. Huxley derives a satiric glee from this inadvertent treason. Smugly imagining itself to be glorifying the American way of life, Hollywood is actually, he says, inciting colonial insubordination in places like Batavia by advertising the vicious folly of the West. In Huxley's apocalyptic fantasy *Ape and Essence* (1948), Hollywood's distribution throughout the world of a treacherous parody of Western values is claimed as the devil's most ingenious satiric stratagem. The novel is set in a California populated by simian mutants, victims of nuclear radiation. The Arch-Vicar of the fiendish new religion practiced there praises Belial's sapience in confusing the world by persuading East and West "to take only the worst the other had to offer." The movies Huxley saw in Batavia are an item in this diabolical exchange. Instead of trading Western science for Eastern mysticism, the East imported the madness of the West, in the form of movies, nationalism, Marxism, and armaments, and the West in turn accepted the despotism and superstition of the East. Satire is mysticism inverted: heaven would have been established on earth, the Arch-Vicar says with dismay, if a rational synthesis of East and West had occurred. As it is, he flatters himself, mankind has "made the worst of both worlds."

But by 1959 the movies are an agent not of satiric subversion but of mystical uplift. In his Santa Barbara lectures Huxley pointed to Hollywood's gaudiest and most overblown statements, "the great coloured movies, the big spectaculars and the big coloured documentaries," as electrical actualizations of that visionary gleam which Wordsworth called "a light that never was on sea or land." That radiance still doesn't exist in nature. But it has been technically simulated by the cinema.

Jesting Pilate satirically connects the movie studios with the mortuaries of California. The "greenish-yellow" effulgence of the lamps in the studio Huxley visits "gives to living men and women the appearance of jaundiced corpses." Later, when Huxley's California has turned into a psychic laboratory working to cleanse perception and accelerate mental evolution, the analogy will have a different meaning. For the morticians, Huxley comes to realize, are engaged in the same battle against the depressing limits of human existence as the movie makers and the psychic researchers like Huxley's friend Timothy Leary. They are objecting to the humbling fact of mortality, transvaluing death cosmetically by embalming cadavers and calling them loved ones. Huxley likewise, during his first wife's final agony, transvalued death mystically, coaxing her to think herself out of her cancer-ridden, crippling body, to escape into a visionary eternity. The euphemisms of the mortuary, which at first seem odious to Huxley, turn into mystical truths. Institutions like Forest Lawn, by powdering over the evidence of physical torment and decay, by planting loved ones in landscapes of idyllic greenery from which crucifixes and all paraphernalia of religous suffering are outlawed, have extracted death's sting. The founder of Forest Lawn in Glendale, the model for the cemeteries in *After Many a Summer* and Evelyn Waugh's *The Loved One*, "prayerfully resolved" in 1917 to forbid all "customary signs of earthly death." Instead of physical loss, Forest Lawn emphasizes spiritual regeneration. It is not a morbid cemetery but a rural "memorial park." Death and satire are both disabled by its euphemisms, for death is the satirist's final sanction: his revenge on his characters is to execute them. When death loses its terror and ugliness, as it does at glib, glossy Forest Lawn, the satirist has no alternative but to renounce his weaponry of hate and study mysticism instead.

Huxley was gruesomely fascinated by an advertisement for "a firm of undertakers, or 'morticians,' as they are now more elegantly styled" which he found in the Chicago telephone directory in 1926. The proprietors were a smiling couple named Kalbfleisch, who prided themselves on their silky caskets, their sumptuous hearses, and their "grave, yet cheering, yet purposefully uplifting" service to their clients. Their sleek propaganda symbolizes for Huxley the American "revaluation of values." But at this stage he concentrates on the debauchery of language and travesty of devotional sentiment which that revaluation entails. The undertakers call themselves morticians because in a democratic society they have the right to be esteemed, and they dignify their sordid trade by calling it a "service," exploiting that word's Franciscan connotations of "self-sacrifice, abnegation, humility." This vulgar Babbitry sanctifies business, pretending to conduct it with the sublime disinterest which was once the prerogative of art or science.

Satirically partitioning the globe in *Jesting Pilate,* Huxley assigns to each continent its own style of spiritual error. Europe is the place of nihilism, which mistrusts all values. India is the place of mysticism, which overprizes spiritual values and in consequence condemns its population to material deprivation. America is the place of pharisaical egalitarianism, which has become a religion and requires that values be sacrificed to the professional self-esteem of undertakers like Kalbfleisch. Huxley blames the miseries of the East and the vulgarities of the West on the spiritual pretensions of mankind. The satirist is worried by the mixed state of mankind, its conjunction of ape and angel, and is forever inveighing against the pride of spirit which leads men to forget the shame of their material existences. Hindu spirituality disgusts Huxley, and he argues that India would be better off if it took more care over its material welfare. India dis-joins the two halves of the human equation, cleansing the spirit but allowing the insanitary body to fester. America, even more repellently, fuses them, turning gross material surfeit into a spiritual blessing, pretending that lowly material trades (like that of Kalbfleisch) are spiritual vocations. But later, Huxley interprets the contradiction in human nature differently. The satirist's vilification changes into the mystic's wonder. The American Huxley described mankind not as an obscene hybrid, with an angel's head and an ape's nether parts, but as a metaphysical paradox, a "multiple amphibian," nonchalantly inhabiting the incompatible worlds of spirit, intellect, and matter, just as an amphibious beast impartially thrives both on land and in the sea.

It is America which negotiates this change in Huxley from satirist to mystic. America heals the contradictions which enrage and sadden the satirist of *Jesting Pilate*. America humanizes Huxley, and it does so by inserting between the satirically polar worlds of spirit and matter the mediating agency of technology. The advances in sanitation, irrigation, pharmacology, social and psychological engineering which obsessed the later Huxley and with which he identified American civilization have a dual virtue: first they cleanse and correct the squalid body which disgusts the satirist; then they free it to concentrate on "The Other World" of spirit which Huxley in *Jesting Pilate* so harshly deprecates.

After their return from America in 1926, Huxley and his wife Maria alternated between London and Provence, until in 1937, in company with their friend Gerald Heard, the saintly pacifist who was to become Isherwood's mentor and yoga instructor in California, they returned to America. Huxley's plan was to tour the country, lecturing and researching a sociological book. This was a Wellsian project. Like H. G. Wells, he thought of America as a laboratory in which the society of the future was being experimentally constructed, and he wanted in particular to study techniques of educational and industrial organization. During the first year in America, while summering at Frieda Lawrence's ranch, he completed his Wellsian prescription for the future, *Ends and Means*. In 1938 a scenario he had submitted to one of the Hollywood studios was accepted, and he drove across the continent from the Hudson valley, where he was living in a farm cottage, to settle in Los Angeles.

At first he and Maria lived in Beverly Hills, then in Hollywood. In 1939, after Huxley had completed his first novel about California, *After Many a Summer,* they moved out to the ocean. Until 1942 they were at 701 Amalfi Drive, Pacific Palisades, in Santa Monica, across the canyon from the house in which Isherwood was eventually to live. Their landlord had filled the house at Santa Monica with grotesque cinematic gewgaws, and Huxley's attitude to this is characteristic of his imaginative stance in California, poised between satiric condescension and mystic detachment. He might have chosen the house as a garish specimen of Auden's Wrong Place. Inside the door was a facsimile of King Kong absconding with Fay Wray. The bar was garnished with jagged sawn-off Aztec motifs. Fairy lights festooned a mummified crocodile. Huxley satirically relished the house as "a source of amusement in a world filled with tedium." But the satirist by inhabiting the Wrong Place permits the mystic to conjure up the Good Place: Huxley's friends admired his serene indifference to the decor, and his lack of interest in changing it. When entertaining, the Huxleys neatly combined the two attitudes. Aldous led satirical tours of the monstrosities, while Maria prepared abstemious mystical repasts. She was repelled by the messy palpability of food, but turned satiric abhorrence into mystical fastidiousness, serving plates of string beans encircled by slices of banana, or starveling chicken portions from which she'd banished the drumsticks because, as she explained, "they looked so *gross*." Her mystical impracticality depended, like her husband's, on technology: these were science-fiction meals, abstract and unappetizing multiples of nutrients, which she gauged with a calorie counter.

The change California worked on Huxley can be registered by comparing his sarcastic enjoyment of the Santa Monica house with his attitude to a later house. Maria Huxley died in 1955. The next year Aldous married Laura Archera, a psychotherapist whose books of recipes for spiritual uplift—practical exercises for coping with stress and raising the level of consciousness—exemplify the Californian compact between technological self-help and mystical self-abnegation. With his new wife he moved to 3276 Deronda Drive, in the Hollywood Hills on the edge of Griffith Park. This house was destroyed by a brush fire in 1961. Aldous accepted the incineration of his possessions with the mystic's uncomplaining calm. He refused even to watch the progress of the blaze, and drove away with "a self-discipline worthy," as Isherwood put it, "of an Asian philosopher." Later he mystically blessed the fire for relieving him of the weight of his own past by destroying his archives. The loss, he told his friend Anita Loos, made him feel "extraordinarily clean!" His mystical imperturbability on this occasion wasn't without a certain spiritual conceit. Anxious to proclaim his imperviousness to worldly catastrophe, he was piqued when *Time* magazine reported that firemen had to prevent him from rushing tearfully into the flames to rescue his manuscripts, and wrote indignantly to the magazine correcting its version of events. The incident was, however, both a trial of Huxley's contemplative mysticism and a temptation to his satiric asperity, for the television cameras arrived at the burning house half an hour before the fire engines. Huxley angrily savored the justice of this, because it showed how technology had overtaken history in America: the cameras which translate the fire into a media event precede the engines which extinguish it.

The transvaluation of satire into mysticism is already implicit in Huxley's first Californian novel, *After Many a Summer* (1939). The subject is eternal life. The Hollywood magnate Jo Stoyte expends his fortune on the quest for personal immortality, and hopes to attain this state by technological means: he employs a physician, Obispo, to devise a preservative formula. Stoyte's ambition is native to California. He wants to arrest time, medically ensuring an eternity of physical gratification, just as the mystic mentally ejects himself from time into an eternity of meditative lassitude. Every sunbather on a Californian beach shares Stoyte's desire, lying entranced, empty-headed, and motionless for hours on end, as if willing the sun to stand still and blaze forever on his body. Sunbathing is a profession as selfless as the mystic's: the acolyte is enslaved to his tan. It is also a search for a perpetual youth, a personal immortality like that which Stoyte tries to purchase, since the bronzing of the body armors it against time, toughening and uncreasing the skin. Auden the moralist thought California the country of old men. It is the place, *New Year Letter* suggests, where people go to die, lulled into oblivion by the tolerant Pacific air. Senescent pilgrims hobble along the beach at Venice in Los Angeles, or sit in the disconsolate lobbies of retirement hotels playing interminable games of checkers. But for Huxley the mystic, California is the country of young men, the place where people go to be born a second time. The Oakland Museum in its collection of Californian painting has given institutional recognition to this rearrangement of chronology. The captions to its pictures assign three dates to each artist: birth, arrival in California, and death—that is, birth, rebirth, death.

About the Californian eternity the satirist and the mystic instantly differ. The satirist is impatient for a punitive end to time. He is convinced that time must have a stop, that after many a summer the swan (in Tennyson's lines from "Tithonus") must die. To the satirist, the indefinite extension of life is a horror not a miracle. The Struldbruggs in *Gulliver's Travels* are peeved by their inability to die, and experience immortality as a hellish protraction of boredom. In *After Many a Summer*, Propter the historian suggests to the millennially hopeful Peter Boone that eternal life would be a weary agony of entrapment in time. Only death, for the satirist, makes life worth living, because it promises eventual release. California is therefore engaged in an impious interference with the balance of nature.

Huxley the mystic is more sympathetic toward Obispo's experiments in evolutionary adjustment and genetic alteration, because he too frets to escape from time. The psychedelic drugs Huxley began to take during the 1950s opened mystical pockets in time. Huxley too, like Stoyte, half-longed to survive into the remote future, to study human evolution and verify his technological predictions. This is why he turned to science fiction, setting *Ape and Essence* in the year 2108. H. G. Wells in 1933 had already jokingly endowed Huxley with the elongated life coveted by Stoyte. In his futuristic dream-book *The Shape of Things To Come,* Wells promises that "changing biological conditions" will elasticize the human life-cycle. Looking back from the year 2106 (two years before the date of Huxley's Californian apocalypse), he allots hyperbolic death-dates to his contemporaries. Huxley's dates are given as 1894-2004. But time turned out to be less generous than Wells's eugenic prophecy, for Huxley died of cancer in 1963. Wells disapproved of Huxley for having given scientific progress a bad name in *Brave New World* (1932), and in *The Shape of Things To Come* calls him "one of the most brilliant of reactionary writers." The joke is that, by allowing Huxley to live until the age of 110, Wells grants him the benefit of the scientific modernity against which he had blasphemed.

Propter in *After Many a Summer* dismisses the eugenic millennium Obispo is trying to engineer. He is mystically intent on creating psychological not physiological eternity: a paradise within, a mental California on which time will have no claim. His eternity, he says, is a "timeless good." He deplores time as the medium in which evil proliferates. This mystical contempt for time as "the substance of evil" contrasts with Auden's ritualistic reverence for it as the substance of good, the medium in which man's fall is at last revealed to be fortunate. Auden viewed any interference with time as a sacrilege. Returning to England in 1972 he was aghast when, on the last Sunday in October, the clocks were put back to end daylight-saving. Unaware of the change, he arrived an hour early for a lunch engagement, and fussed for days afterwards over the impropriety of the hiccup in his routine. The conflict between Huxley's mystical loosening of time and Auden's ceremonial regimentation of it is stated in *After Many a Summer* when Jeremy Pordage, the English archivist imported by Stoyte, finds Propter's blather about eternities distasteful and proposes his own notion of time colonized, time socialized, time triumphantly occupied: "Why on earth couldn't people live their lives in a rational, civilized way? Why couldn't they take things as they came? Breakfast at nine, lunch at one-thirty, tea at five." Auden, like Pordage, insisted that he wouldn't know whether to be hungry unless he knew what time it was. Huxley the mystic would have considered this differently, as evidence that time and physical appetite are conspiring to enslave us.

California abets the mystic by confounding time, reshuffling history, giving the past a face lift. The Beverly Hills through which Pordage is driven on his way from the airport is a combination of museum, cemetery, and pantheon of world religions. Like a museum it equalizes all periods in time and all locations in space by jumbling together disparate architectural styles. Lutyens manors and Le Corbusier boxes abut on rococo pavilions and Mexican haciendas. Beverly Hills is a religious capital because each of these dwellings, mystically abstracted from the time and place in which it belongs, houses a divinity, a saint, a vacuous image—a movie star. Ginger Rogers, Stoyte's chauffeur points out, lives in a reproduction of a Tibetan lamasery. Beverly Hills is also a cemetery: Stoyte owns a landscaped resting place modeled on Forest Lawn at Glendale. But the cemetery is itself a museum of artistic effigies, containing replicas of the Tower of Pisa, the Taj Mahal, and the church at Stratford in which Shakespeare is buried.

Californian cemeteries like Stoyte's masquerade as museums because for them artistic reproduction is an earnest of physical resurrection. They promise their clients not the beatification of the spirit but the beautification of the body. Pordage at the mortuary inspects the "immortally athletic, indefatigably sexy" corpses and reflects that death has been vanquished not by freeing the spirit from the moribund body, as the older religions promise, but by preserving that body, injecting it with embalming fluids, painting over its pallor, twisting its rigid grimaces into the likeness of a smile. The cemeteries make good this promise of physical rather than spiritual salvation by exhibiting glossily new, eternally young versions of art works of which the originals are damaged or decaying. Art dies in Europe, and is born again in California. Forest Lawn at Glendale is Italy reproduced and therefore resurrected. It grants a stay of execution to works which time is steadily ruining, like Leonardo's "Last Supper" (which it has transferred from moldly egg tempera to the indestructibility of stained glass) or Ghiberti's bronze Baptistery doors from Florence. The reproduction is better than the original, because it has been saved from the incursions of time. Likewise, the cosmetically reified cadavers of Forest Lawn are an improvement on the living beings of whom they are facsimiles. This transubstantiation of a decrepit, time-bound body into a nubile loved one playing golf and tennis (as Pordage imagines) in some celestial country-club is matched by California's liberation of architectural styles from their imprisonment in history. The tinted corpse is better than the living creature, just as plastic flowers are an advance on the feeble organic actuality. Similarly, the parody of an architectural style in California is more to be admired than that style used with dull historical decorum in Europe. Stoyte's castle is not historically but platonically Gothic, as Pordage realizes. If it had been built in the thirteenth century, it would have had no choice but to be Gothic. Built in the twentieth century, with the advantage of modern engineering, its Gothicism is wanton, ideal, gratuitous.

Huxley's California warps time. Evolution there has been so accelerated that juvenility and senescence, the beginning of the world and its end, overlap. Stoyte's mistress Virginia (a hybrid of W. R. Hearst's protégée Marion Davies and Paulette Goddard, married at the time to Huxley's friend Chaplin) exemplifies this foreshortening of time. Like California itself, she has passed directly from barbarism to decadence. She is a playful, sensual savage, yet she lolls on antique furniture and rides a motor scooter. She goes shopping in a swimsuit topped by a fur coat. Because she is an animal, her nakedness is itself a costume. But her savagery is expensive, conspicuous consumption: she doesn't grow her own pelt, but robs other animals of theirs. Virginia's development is arrested mentally but physically extended into a luxurious excess. But just as satire has a way of transvaluing itself into mysticism, so a voluptuous materialism like Virginia's can turn into a cult of self-absorbed spirituality. Pordage wonders at the meditative rapture of the girls loitering outside drugstores in Los Angeles. They all seem to be silently praying: actually they are only masticating gum. They exist by stupid nature in that blissful, mindless state at which the mystic can only arrive by arduous self-discipline.

The gum-chewing girls sum up the problem of Huxley's California. Are they morons or ruminative mystics? Is California an indolent heaven of physical delectation like the Moslem paradise, or is it a hell of sulphurous unreality? Perhaps there is not even a difference between the two conditions. When Miranda in *The Tempest* first sees the bedraggled, treacherous courtiers, she salutes the brave new world which has such people in it. Prospero remarks sourly that it is new only to her. What she sees as heaven he knows to be hell. Huxley borrows the ambiguity when he calls his own nightmarish fantasy *Brave New World*. Wells's heavenly future of social engineering is to Huxley an oppressive hell. Hell after all may be preferable to heaven, because it is not so stupefyingly, statically perfect. This is why the rebel angels fell, and why Adam and Eve left the garden. Stoyte owns Watteau's "Departure from Cytherea" (actually in the Louvre), which raises this question of discomfiture in paradise and relates it to California. The picture shows the withdrawal of a group of lovers from a paradise of satiation. Stoyte watches them preparing "to set sail for some other paradise, doubtless yet more heartbreaking."

The psychological history of California is of paradise found, lost, chimerically regained. California caters to the dreams of successive generations of immigrants—gold diggers, chivalric squatters like Robert Louis Stevenson, the impoverished Okies Auden mentions, hippies, surfers, Zen-trained motorcycle-maintenance men. Its business is not only the satisfaction but the manufacture of dreams: Hollywood does the world's dreaming for it. But California is at the same time, as Isherwood says, "a tragic country—like Palestine, like every promised land," because it is strewn with the disappointments of those whose dreams have not come true. Perhaps its successes are even sadder than its failures. Those who do find El Dorado are liable to find that it doesn't content them. Like Watteau's Cythereans, they are sentenced to the misery of surfeit.

All travel, for Huxley, revolves inside this dismaying tragic cycle, with the feverish hope of the journey collapsing into the frustration of arrival. All travel is a version of travel to California, because every outing testifies to the frantic human quest for an unrealizable happiness. In *Along the Road,* a set of touristic essays published in 1925, Huxley the satirist makes travel an image of human moral folly. All journeys are returns to Eden, and are therefore doomed to fail. Tourists "set out, nourished on fables and fantastical hopes, to return, whether they avow it or not, disappointed." Travel is an existential ailment. The tourist never enjoys himself, but suffers inevitably from a sickening tedium, because "ennui is a holiday feeling," a disease of leisure. Nevertheless, the mystic stands by to rescue the bored, disgruntled satirist. The genuine traveler, Huxley says, will accept the infection of this ennui as a mark of his condition, an emblem (like the stark inhuman nature Huxley admired in the American Southwest) of his dissociation from a universe in which he doesn't belong, and learn to rejoice in a grim metaphysical freedom. Boredom is "the symbol of his liberty," an entranced state like that beyond time into which the mystic transports himself. Drug dreams are called trips because in Huxley's view they are psychedelic travel, tourism inside the head. Their visionary dreariness with its aching symptoms of withdrawal is the mood of all traveling.

Stoyte's Watteau is a map of Huxley's California. If the paradise in which one lives doesn't please, there are still chemical paradises within to be invented.

After Many a Summer satirically traduces the Californian paradise, but shows how mysticism might redeem it. Stoyte, though he longs for eternal life, is a broker in the deaths of others, since he owns a mortuary. Though California seems to offer the prolongation of life, this is an illusion fostered by the old and ailing. The blithe seasonless weather, the hypnotism of piped music, the bland enticements of television, all are preparations for death. California lulls one gradually into insentience, so that when death comes it is hardly noticed. Huxley was preoccupied by the rising average age of the world's population, and this is a problem focused on California. The lowered death-rate, he says in *The Human Situation,* is a biological disaster, because it will end in the overcrowding of the earth. As a satirist Huxley, like Stoyte, is in the mortuary business, reducing population for the greater good of humanity.

This doesn't mean that he approves of the tarted-up cadavers of Stoyte's Beverly Pantheon or Forest Lawn. In his view their prettifying of the corpse is an offense against evolutionary logic. Though the average age of the population is rising, old age has been abolished in America by what Huxley calls "the beauty industry," while Stoyte's cemetery and Obispo's laboratory are working at the abolition of death itself. Cosmetics, mud baths, paraffin wax, and plastic surgery turn hags back into nymphs: "the crone of the future," Huxley imagines, "will be golden, curly and cherry-lipped, neat-ankled and slender." The corpse of the future will be equally desirable, for Stoyte's cemetery has the policy of "injecting sex appeal into death." This is a satiric mockery of romantic mysticism. The romantics had made death an object of erotic yearning. Keats hoped to expire in a painless ecstasy; Wagner's Tristan and Isolde identify death with sexual consummation. Aimée in Waugh's Forest Lawn novel *The Loved One* is goaded to suicide at the mortuary by the Wagner excerpts she hears on the radio. The pulchritudinous stiffs of Forest Lawn turn a romantic dream into a necrophiliac fact. Huxley's evolutionary objection to California's cult of physical perfection and its burial customs recurs in his metaphysical digest *The Perennial Philosophy* (1946). Here he argues that man alone among natural species is capable of further evolutionary advance. Other species are "living fossils, capable only of degeneration and extinction," but humans have been challenged to a "cosmic intelligence test." Every other creature has failed the exam by choosing to assume the form most immediately convenient, but not ultimately best. Man alone has resisted this "present rapture of being perfect, but perfect on a low level of being." California, cosmetically pampering and chemically immortalizing the body, has frustrated evolutionary progress, and even made death into hedonistic self-indulgence.

Huxley's response to the Californian idealization of the body was the abstraction of the mind. In *After Many a Summer,* at the opening of the Stoyte Auditorium, the vaseline-voiced Dr. Mulge prates about "California . . . New Culture, richer science, higher spirituality." Huxley set himself to make good Mulge's boast, to turn California into a laboratory for psychic research. Discussing the drowsy torpor of Virginia, he distinguishes two Californian techniques for self-transfiguration. You can become "a mere body, strangely numbed or more than ordinarily sentient": this is Virginia's luxuriant way, and that of the sunbathers, of the movie stars who have no character but only luminous physical features, and of the loved ones at Forest Lawn. Or you can choose the cerebral alternative, and become "a state of impersonal mind, a mode of unindividualized consciousness," which is Huxley's meditative way. The two techniques are actually complementary. The vision-inducing drugs Huxley took are devices for changing the chemistry of the body which result in a dazzling transformation of the mind. Huxley's first experiment with mescaline was not until 1953, but already *After Many a Summer* points him toward the acid paradise which is that space of internal, unindividualized consciousness.

In Huxley's chemical heaven, a wearisome individuality will be renounced. So will literature. Propter, defining the Californian eternity in which the limits of the ego have been transcended, is also describing a state of consciousness which has no further use for literature. Good acts, he says, can't exist inside time because their special virtue is to liberate us from time and personality, from craving and revulsion, from all the "magnified projections of our personalities which we call our policies, our ideals, our religions" and to which literature (and the novel in particular) panders. Propter despises literature as an accumulation of facts and anecdotes unenlightened by a coordinating philosophy, and his scorn was increasingly shared by the American Huxley, who gave up the shoddy mimetic triviality of the novel and instead wrote half-mystical, half-technological treatises like *The Doors of Perception, Heaven and Hell,* and *Island.*

America makes the rejection of literature easier because it estranges the artist from the society he knows and thus baffles his imagination. Auden's friends warned him against America for this reason. But to Huxley, this was America's advantage. The 1959 Santa Barbara lectures triumphantly dispense with literature. Huxley first resolves character (on which the novel battens) into a metaphysical error, an "inspissated clot" which absurdly fancies itself an individual identity. Then he goes on to disestablish narrative and language. Both are preconscious vestiges of the race's infancy, from which the technological future will exempt us. Echoing Propter, Huxley calls "the story-telling faculty" a misuse of intelligence. The garrulous prattling which turns existence into an "endless serial" diverts schoolboys but oughtn't to bemuse adults. Words too are a casualty of evolution, relics of a prescientific understanding which could only subjugate the objects of the world by attaching names to them. Now that science has revealed the world to be "refreshingly other," indifferent to human sentiment, description is entrusted not to words but to numbers, formulae, equations. The technocrat knows the universe to be bleak, blank, atomized, unfeeling; but the mystic rejoices in that void and claims it as the region of Huxley's "unstructured transpersonal consciousness."

The loss of faith in literature is already evident in Huxley's second Californian novel, *Ape and Essence* (1948). The bestial, demonic California of this work, shattered and deformed by nuclear war, lays waste the cosmetic paradise of *After Many a Summer*. In the earlier novel the spirit is cheerfully merged in the body. Now the spirit is expunged and the body warped, not immortalized by make-up and embalmment but surgically adjusted: the priests of Belial in *Ape and Essence* earn entry to their caste by emasculation. Instead of the pagan cult of physical beauty exemplified by Virginia, there is the horror of mutant malformation in Loola, who thanks to the gamma rays has sprouted an extra set of nipples. The satiric assault the second novel makes on the first is summed up in the grave robbing by the mutant females. In *Ape and Essence* the beautified sleepers of *After Many a Summer* are exhumed and stripped of their clothes. One of the horned priests sports the uniform of a U.S.N. Rear-Admiral, "recently disinterred from Forest Lawn." Flossie, scavenging near the sepulchre of the movie star Hedda Boddy in the Hollywood Cemetery, retrieves a pair of nylons, greenishly discolored. Poole the scientist emerges from behind the tomb of Valentino.

In this ruined California, the cemeteries are a subterranean culture of antique finery, "the buried remains of *le confort moderne*," like the funereal treasures of the Egyptians. The graveyards, like the film studios, are images of world history collapsed into a grubby costume-wardrobe. Loola and her sister monsters loot the graves of the stars, and one of the priests discards a "pearl-grey jacket which once belonged to the Production Manager of Western-Shakespeare Pictures Incorporated" and dons the costume of "what remains of the Managing Director of the Golden Rule Brewing Corporation," whose tailoring is more conservative. So similar are the cemeteries and the studios that death is defined as a permanent affixation of make-up: the disinterred brewer's cheeks are still rouged, his lips "stitched into a perpetual smile." The studios are a graveyard of history, a wall-less museum of fallen masonry. *Ape and Essence* begins in one of the studios on the day of Gandhi's assassination. The futuristic fantasy which follows is a rejected scenario. The two parts are connected, for the studio in 1948 is an exact anticipation of the wrecked California of 2108: trailers trundle by carrying the detritus of the past—the door of an Italian cathedral, a pulpit by Niccolò Pisano. The studios, like the grave robbers, are pillagers of the past.

Huxley first planned *Ape and Essence* as a conventional novel, then changed its form to a mock-scenario. In doing so he was probably recalling a work discussed earlier in this book, the film of Wells's *Things To Come*, which he had seen in London in 1936. *Ape and Essence* uses those aerial perspectives which Wells considered to be the cinema's special prerogative: a view of southern California from fifty miles up plummets down to investigate devastated Los Angeles from a height of five miles; a montage of aerial views of London in 1800, 1900, and 1940 illustrates the disaster of overpopulation. The scenario also satirically suits form to content, enabling Huxley to use California's home-grown art against the state. Film is the form best able to represent the world's incendiary apocalypse, since it is a product of the same scientific revolution which has wrecked the world. The novel would be wasted on the beastly, inverted world of *Ape and Essence*. The creatures in it are not characters with private reserves of emotion and motive which the novel might explore, but only animals acting automatically on instinct, like the promiscuously rutting Loola. Character has been bred out of this world. All that remains of it is the obstinate "Fact of Personality" which makes Loola rebel against the shearing of her hair, and this isn't an individualizing force but an unconscious assertion. Love, for Poole, isn't the enraptured discovery of another individual but submission to "the warm, elastic Facts of Life." The scenario keeps a satiric distance, noting down automatic reactions, not speculating about motives. The internal life investigated by the novel is reducible in Poole's case to the "four seconds of moral conflict" which intervene before he submits to the in-heat mulattoes.

The scenario is a summary and dismissive mode. The narrator accepts no responsibility for what happens, but merely observes. This is why Isherwood calls himself a camera. The novel analyzes individual wills from within, but the camera can do no more than gape at the antic, inexplicable movements of bodies. Film studies its creatures clinically, as if in a laboratory, recording their responses to stimuli. As an art form, it embodies the calamitous "technological progress" which leads to the apocalyptic world of *Ape and Essence*. Love in the cinema, Auden said, always looks like "a natural effect caused by animal beauty." Whereas Huxley and Isherwood were both converted to the cinema in America, the new art form which Auden adopted there was opera. He considered the movies behavioristic: they insult that freedom which he so prized in America, and by reducing emotions to anatomical data they submerge spirit in matter. Opera for Auden declares the opposite, showing spirit triumphant over matter. The soaring voice's emergence from a barrel of flesh is a small miracle, a musical levitation. Auden sees opera as a theological form, and his passion for it coincides with his return to religion in America.

The cinema's materialistic suppression of spirit makes it a logical product of Huxley's pagan California. However, here too a transvaluation is at work. Satire first despoils the physical optimism of California. The fifth Earl of Gonister, who has abolished death, is at last discovered in *After Many a Summer*. But rather than being eternally young, he is a foul, senile "foetal ape." This undying ape begets the monsters of *Ape and Essence*, in whom the nature California divinizes is reduced to vicious minimum. The process, however, does not end here. The sophistic devils of *Ape and Essence* bless America precisely because it is so lewd, vile, and filthy, because its corruption announces the victory of their lord Belial. Huxley too recovers from satiric self-loathing by making hell a blueprint for heaven. The nature which offends the satirist can be disinfected by technology, and once that happens (as it does in Huxley's California) the satirist grows into a mystic. Now instead of scourging the body he blithely discards it. Huxley finds that American technology has discredited his satire. Hygiene and medical reform cleanse the body, the domestic comforts of America cosset it. Having disarmed the satirist, technology goes on to ease his advance to mysticism, by supplying him with the means of transcendence—chemically by taking drugs, electrically by watching films.

Huxley believed that this technological reclamation of nature was the spiritual meaning of California. In 1962 he planned a travel book about the state, but because by now California was for him a psychic territory in which technological developments assisted spiritual change, the book was to be a meditation not a journey, "a series of soliloquies having Far Western places as their source and excuse." He mentioned an itinerary in a letter to his son Matthew in 1963, proposing visits to "the kind of things (agri-business, new factories, lunatic asylums, scenery) which can be written about in the reflective travel book that I have in mind." This harks back to the Victorian inspection of institutional America. But the Victorians went to see institutions because, in their estimation, there was neither nature nor society in America. Huxley's intention is different: to him the West signifies the victory of technology over both nature and society.

This is why agri-business (the industrialization of agriculture) interested him. Bertrand Russell, visiting California in 1930, had attacked this trend as an example of America's homogenization of the physical world. For Russell, the Californian farmers have ceased to be superstitious servants of nature and become industrial manufacturers, turning the Garden of Hesperides into an orange factory. What for Russell was an impious meddling with nature is for Huxley a technological redemption of niggardly, inefficient nature. In 1953 he made an enthusiastic inspection of industrialized agriculture in northern California, and reported on the success of the mechanical cultivation of rice along the Sacramento River. He was equally impressed by agri-business in Washington, where a "million acres of barren plain" had been "irrigated by water pumped out of the Columbia River" to create farms which had virtually dispensed with farmers: "here one sees fields of peas, a mile square, with no human habitation in sight. People come out with machines three or four

times a season, to sow, weed, fertilize and finally reap—the final pro-
cedure involving the association of appropriate combines with mobile
refrigerating units, so that the product is deep-frozen the moment it
leaves the pod." Those dessicated frozen peas, like the meals served
by Huxley's first wife, suggest that a logical consequence of the satirist's disdain for nature and the mystic's calm superiority to it is an
anorexic dislike of food. The mystic's ideal diet would be technological, consisting entirely of pills.

Fertilizing barren plains, irrigating the desert, Huxley's technology is a domestication of miracle. Technology is an acceleration
of sluggish history, a triumph over human inertia and the improvidence of nature. Huxley was irritated by the slovenliness of the cotton
farmers of the American South. Refusing to change their habits fast
enough to accommodate the mechanical harvester, they were threatened with redundancy during the 1940s by another technological
novelty, a "synthetic fibre better and cheaper than cotton." The
southern farmers must be made, Huxley argued, to prefer "vegetables and health" to "corn mush, salt pork and pellagra," a disease
of malnutrition.

Auden's new friends in America were theologians like Niebuhr;
Isherwood's were Oriental mystics (most notably Swami Prabhavananda, a Hindu monk who had established a Vedantist center in
Hollywood); Huxley's were technocrats. "In this country I have been
associated," he said in 1938, ". . . mainly with doctors and astronomers." America for Huxley was the land of technology, and this
made it a spiritual realm. Europe in contrast began to seem crudely
materialistic. This opposition between Europe, where one is embedded in personality and social identity, and America, where one
is released into a contemplative existence at once scientific and mystical, creates a literary difficulty for Huxley. His problem always was,
as he admitted, the impossible task "of combining ideas and narrative." His novels tended to be hybrids of character in action and ideas
in exposition. Residence in America inclines him toward the immaterial intellectual extreme, away from the entrammeling literalism of

the novel. In a letter in 1942 he describes himself wandering between two worlds and getting the worst of both. Those worlds are the continents, Europe and America, but they are also incompatible intellectual ambitions. "Each requires," Huxley says, "that one should be whole-heartedly *there,* at the moment—with Micawber, as he is and for his own sake, while he is drinking his punch: with the Clear Light of the Void as it is and for its own sake, in an analogous way." Micawber from *David Copperfield* symbolizes the novel, feeding on the mindless superficial plenitude of life. Huxley impugns the form by associating it with such a shiftless, selfish character. Against Micawber, Huxley sets the mystical void, which is featureless and uneventful, and therefore inimical to the novel. Europe is Micawber's lavish kingdom, the desert of the American Southwest is the mystic's vacuum. Huxley's own fate is to belong to neither: "I have always tended to be somewhere else, in a world of analysis, unfavourable equally to Micawberish living, Tolstoyan arts and contemplative spirituality."

In Europe you live, in America you contemplate. Elsewhere, in contrast with the abstract mental freedom enjoyed by the mystic in his void, Huxley attaches the novel to the gravitational tug of the body. Novelists, he thought, ought to be men of Micawber's physical disposition, "burly genial fellows," florid, tough or tub-like. Huxley's own spindly vertiginous frame and his myopia were his disqualification for writing novels. "An emaciated fellow on stilts" like himself, he wrote to E. S. P. Hayes from Llano in 1945, was too far off the ground. He belonged in the rarefied ether of ideas, not on the horizontal plane of narrative.

Perhaps this is why Huxley so longed for film versions of his novels. At the end of his life he was negotiating with R.K.O. for the release of the rights to *Brave New World,* which that studio owned, and he tried to interest Stravinsky and Leonard Bernstein in writing music for a dramatized version. On the screen, the novel would lose its materialism and become insubstantial spirit. The imitation of life which Huxley thought so demeaning would turn into an electrical simulation of life, at once scientifically ingenious and mystically vivid. Huxley had both scientific and mystical reasons for admiring the cinema as an alternative to the novel. As a technological form, it was expert at the scientific study of nature. But as mescaline was a chemical inducement of vision, so Huxley saw the cinema as a mechanical simulation of vision. In collaboration with Isherwood he devised a film amalgamating the scientific and mystical potentialities of the form. The subject was to be a faith healer, a hybrid of scientist and mystic. But the studios vetoed the idea, fearing objections from the medical profession.

The psychedelic treatise *Heaven and Hell* includes a series of appendices on popular visionary art—fireworks, pageantry, magic lantern shows, and the cinema—emphasizing "the close dependence of such arts on technology." Illusion is fortified by science. Kircher's lantern is magic because "intense light plus transparent colour equals vision." Taking drugs, Huxley decomposes vision into biochemistry. Watching movies, he decomposes vision into electricity. Drugs are a technological aid because they save time, provoking a visionary elation instantaneously, as if at the flick of a switch, bypassing the mystic's patient labor of preparation. Movies likewise are vision mechanized. The technological abbreviation of time is important here too. Isherwood has often quoted (but never explained) a remark made to him by Robert Flaherty, whom he met first while working with the director Berthold Viertel in England and encountered again with Huxley in California. "Film," Flaherty said, "is the greatest possible distance between two points." The aphorism appeals to Isherwood because it implies a criticism of the novel's alacrity of narrative and suggests the mystic's painstaking organization of tedium. But for Huxley, as for H. G. Wells, the opposite is true. Film is a technological short-cut.

The cooperation between technology and vision excited Huxley in a short film by Francis Thompson, *New York, New York,* made in 1956. Thompson used distorting lenses to create a toppling, molten, dismantled New York, its skyscrapers reflected in and refracted by multiple prisms, hub caps, even spoons. To Huxley this suggested the mechanical nature of modern pictorial imagery. The forms of cubist painters "are identical with those obtained by photographing reflections in curved surfaces." But the succession of images is best represented by the dynamic, temporal art of the cinema, and can't be adjusted to the spatial form of painting. The images of the painters, Huxley argued, are like cinematic stills, deprived of the natural rhythm of succession. Representational painting is satisfactory in its static way, Huxley goes on, because it is imitating a nature which can't be predicted. We can never tell what any living thing will do next, so painting is right to pacify its subjects, catching them in repose, when for a brief while they are intelligible. But "in the non-representational art of reflections in a curved surface there is (given the laws of optics) a foreseeable element." Because reflection distortions behave and alter, as in Thompson's film, with logical predictability, non-representational forms should always, Huxley decides, be seen in motion. Representational movies aren't necessarily an improvement on representational painting, but "the non-representational movie seems more satisfactory than the non-representational picture." Cartoons would suit Huxley's criteria, because they don't photograph life as it inconsequentially happens but serially animate it, and one of Huxley's aborted projects was for a Disney cartoon version of *Alice in Wonderland,* a work of mathematical fantasy which would have exactly matched his theory of the mechanically visionary cinema.

Huxley's new friends in California were mostly scientists, he said. But because he was employed as a screen writer, he befriended numerous movie makers. As well, he knew mystics and missionaries like Krishnamurti the Indian theosophist. There is no contradiction in his belonging to such different coteries, for in his view the doctors, astronomers, theosophists, and movie stars were all engaged in the same, characteristically Californian activity. They were all intent on the technological actualization of heaven. Krishnamurti's technique for arriving there was meditative. The hot gospeller Aimée Semple McPherson favored spasms of frenzied rhetorical uplift.

Huxley's psychedelic city: a molten skyscraper from Francis Thompson's *New York, New York*, 1956. Creative Film Society, Reseda, California.

Edwin Hubble peered up into heaven through the telescopes of the Mount Wilson Observatory. Humphrey Osmond or Timothy Leary brewed potions to catapault the initiate into it. Chaplin, Goddard, Garbo, and the other movie stars of Huxley's acquaintance were already serenely enskied in it. Garbo, interpreting her own celebrity as an astral sanctity, commanded Huxley to write a treatment for her of the life of Francis of Assisi, in which she had cast herself as the saint.

Satirically, Huxley relished the occult quackery of it all. But mystically, he longed for it to prove true. This uneasy transvaluation occurs everywhere in his imaginative exploration of Los Angeles. As a satirist, he was a connoisseur of seedy vulgarity: he chuckled at the circumstances of his second marriage, in 1956, which took place in a drive-in chapel in Arizona, with a derelict cowboy recruited as witness. He relished the grime of his own satiric productions: in 1944 he told Isherwood that his new novel *Time Must Have a Stop* was "a curiously *trivial* story, told in great detail, with a certain amount of *squalor.*" The satirist's occupation is the detection of ordure. Fascinated by the irrigation system of Los Angeles, Huxley delighted in tracking down the city's sewage outlets. This was a satirist's triumph, for he'd located the orifices through which a pristine paradise flushed its bowels, and demonstrated that even angels were obliged to shit. A favorite spot was Redondo Beach, which an offshore sewage pipe often littered with a jetsam of soggy condoms. This beach is the

Huxley's psychedelic desert: an elf owl in a cactus from *The Living Desert* © 1953 Walt Disney Productions. Reproduced by permission of Walt Disney Productions. Courtesy of National Film Archive/Stills Library, London.

landing place of the rediscovers of America in *Ape and Essence,* but the sewer in 2108 is in ruins, and the sand no longer has its counterpane of soiled rubbers. The narrator recalls the magnitude of the elephantine drainpipe which evacuated the mess of Los Angeles, and touts sanitary engineering as the noblest achievement of civilization.

But sanitary engineering is also a technological reproof to satire. Machines conquer the satirist's disgust. This is what happened to Huxley's malodorous Redondo Beach: a sludge plant was installed to refine the excrement previously voided into the ocean. The bodily filth was transformed by the machines into fertile sweetness and methane fuel-light: the sludge activators marketed an "odourless solid" to farmers. Machines, Huxley complains in *Adonis and the Alphabet,* are rescuing humanity from the satirist. The American clothing industry has abolished dowdiness, American deodorants have abolished the atavistic human stench, American cemeteries have even abolished post-mortem putrefaction. Sewage systems, dry cleaning, hygiene, detergents, washable fabrics, DDT, and penicillin are all "technological victories over . . . dirt and that system of untouchability which dirt creates." Sanitary engineering prohibits satire and goes on, Huxley points out, to make saints of us all. In less healthy times, embracing lepers, kissing sores, and swallowing pus were activities reserved to self-mortifying mystics. Now soap, water, and asepsis have enabled us to conquer our revulsion and act with religious compassion toward the afflicted.

Huxley was fond of organizing excursions into the suburban waste-land of Los Angeles which had a similarly dual significance. In part these outings were mystic quests, in part self-satirizingly incongruous picnics. On one occasion he set out with Garbo to locate a medicinal spring in the Hollywood Hills. But a tramp (rather than the customary hermit) was guarding the source, and diverting its trickle of water into a dented tin bathtub. Another time, Aldous and Maria took a party to picnic in the dried-up, litter-strewn bed of the Los Angeles River. The company was a muddled selection from his various groups of friends: Chaplin, Goddard, and Garbo, Bertrand

Russell, Isherwood and Anita Loos, Krishnamurti and a band of acolytes. Ostentatious luxury jostled with faddishly abstemious religious ritual: Paulette Goddard brought thermos flasks of caviar and champagne; Garbo, dieting, carried her own garlands of vegetables; Krishnamurti and his crew trailed their own clattering array of pots and pans like a band of gypsies, because they couldn't eat from vessels polluted by animal flesh. Goddard was elegantly attired as a Mexican peasant, Garbo (to protect her anonymity) as a tramp, Krishnamurti and his followers wore saris. When the party was surprised by a sheriff and accused of trespassing, Huxley appeasingly pointed out the three movie stars. But the disjunction between personal identity and cinematic image affected by Garbo was only too successful. The sheriff looked closely at them and (Anita Loos reports) snarled, "Don't give me that! I seen them stars in the movies, and none of 'em belong in this outfit. Get out of here, you tramps." Off they scuttled, like a gaggle of holy mendicants.

The desert bordering Los Angeles was also absorbed into Huxley's ambiguous personal landscape. Satirically, it proclaimed the enmity of physical nature. But mystically, it exemplified the luminosity of divine nature. The agency connecting the two conditions is again technology, which reclaims the desert by irrigating it and thus makes Los Angeles ecologically possible. Huxley began by emphasizing the desert's hostility. Writing from Frieda Lawrence's ranch in New Mexico in 1937, he said that "human beings crawl about in this savage, empty vastness like irrelevant ticks—just not counting."

The notion of a landscape denuded of inhabitants is sourly gratifying to the satirist, serenely gratifying to the mystic. On a tour of the national parks in the 1950s, Huxley reflects that "all this enormous country we have crossed—Nevada, Utah, Idaho, Wyoming—is practically uninhabited." The desert has been mechanized, though not humanized. The "vast elevated plateaux" are "tilled almost without human hands, by means of huge machines." Nevada subsists on roulette, with "gambling machines in all the grocery stores, croupiers and crap-shooters in all the hotels, bars and restaurants." It is aptly purgatorial that gambling, an image of eternal human hope teased and defrauded by the inscrutable banditry of machines, should be confined to the waste-land of Nevada; apt too that this desert should be the place in which the end of the world is scientifically contrived. "At intervals, in the open desert," Huxley discovers "some installation of the Atomic Energy Commission, where they are manufacturing God knows what apocalyptic devices in the most absolute secrecy."

Yet because the desert is so satirically averse to human purposes, it becomes for Huxley a place of mystical initiation. During the death agony of his wife in 1955, he hypnotized her. The trance was a form of spiritual technology, intended to transport her to a visionary realm of light like that she had known in the Mojave Desert, where she "had lived with an abiding sense of divine immanence." In the desert, God is manifest in his absence. Huxley, hoping to turn Maria's physical death into an accession of spiritual life, appealed to the imagery of light with which her desert visions had been associated. Extinction he explained to her as a desert sunset, with the effulgence of joy and love in the west, vivid blue still overhead, and "the white light of pure Being" dazzling in the south.

The radiance into which hypnosis projected Maria resembled that other technologically conjured kingdom, "the mescalin world, where there were vast landscapes, mostly of the desert." The desert is nature at the creation, raw and denuded. Mescaline is a reversal of the initial terrible human fall from that primal state, a chemical fulfillment of America's promise to restore paradise. In 1956, during one of Huxley's mescaline experiments, he was injected with frenquel, which expelled him from his visionary delight and made him nauseously experience the fall, with sensations of dizziness and physical deconstellation. Then, after the frenquel wore off, the despair of this fall was vanquished again by the mescaline, and Huxley was restored to his psychedelic paradise.

Auden in America recovers paradise theologically, returning to the Anglican communion. Huxley's route back is physiological or psychedelic. Auden, reviewing the American past, applauds the forfeiture of Eden and the beginning of toilsome but lucrative human history. Huxley's last novel, *Island* (1962), also proposes a fall which is fortunate because economically profitable. Balin like Auden's Paul Bunyan argues that the island Pala should renounce its economic innocence and fall into history, industrially exploiting its natural resources and selling crude petroleum. For the islanders, the first temptation which makes them restive in Eden is the Sears Roebuck catalogue, teasing them with pictures of platform wedgies and dacron bras. But Huxley eventually discounts this Audenesque policy. Rather than cooperate in the loss of paradise and the long struggle toward its recovery, the islanders protect their innocence with mystic rites and hallucinatory drugs. Huxley was intrigued by the Oneida people, a sect in upstate New York during the nineteenth century, whose high-minded regime of male continence is commended in *Island*. Their yoga method of intercourse required the male to insert himself into the female and remain there meditatively motionless. Ranga in *Island* hails this coupling technique as "an organised attempt to regain that paradise" of infantile polymorphous perversity from which the genital obsessions of adulthood eject us. Auden's Good Place has retracted into the body. Drugs also solve the problem of the fall by allowing psychic innocence to be recovered at will. The Rani in *Island*, a mercenary revivalist, has engineered a chemical "marriage between heaven and hell." Huxley in America superimposes the Wrong Place of satire and the Good Place of mysticism. The Rani likewise has reduced heaven and hell to chemical compounds which are interchangeable. The spiritual potions react unpredictably—the moksha drug takes the tripper to heaven or hell, or to both, together or alternately, or with luck beyond either of them— and this variability of destination suggests Huxley's indeterminacy about America. Sometimes he reviles it as hell, sometimes he reveres it as heaven. According to the logic of the argument about the Good Place, if it is hell then that means it's the place where heaven must be constructed.

The psychedelic world disclosed by mescaline is in fact, as *The*

Doors of Perception (1954) and *Heaven and Hell* (1956) testify, a hallucinatory replica of western America. *Heaven and Hell* makes a psychedelic mirage of the map of America. Upending the continent, Huxley describes the westward thrust of exploration as a vertical excavation of psychic depths. He contrasts the sedate Old World of the conscious mind with the New Worlds of peyote-eating vision, "the not too distant Virginias and Carolinas of the personal subconscious and the vegetative soul; the Far West of the collective unconscious, with its flora of symbols, its tribes of aboriginal archetypes; and across another, vaster ocean, at the antipodes of everyday consciousness, the world of Visionary Experience." California in this description becomes a psychedelic El Dorado, a promised land in which the wealth coveted by the first settlers is now the symbol of a luxuriant irrationality, an "Other World of praeternatural light and praeternatural colour, of ideal gems and visionary gold." The acquisitive pioneers are now psychic researchers. The colonization of America has been treated before, by Wells, Lawrence, and Auden, as a scrambling pursuit of riches. Huxley turns it into the record of an individual mind's struggle to expand itself into a continental emptiness, to become "Mind at Large." The vacancy of western America is the space in which the mind recovers its lost, innocent amplitude. To release in oneself the capacities of Mind at Large is also to regain the "perceptual innocence of childhood," and this too is a mental event neatly adapted to California, which has never lost that innocence, and rejoices in a perpetual infancy.

Francis Thompson's lenses and prisms had fractured New York into a visionary geometry. Huxley's psychedelic stupors did the same for Los Angeles. In *The Doors of Perception* he describes driving across Sunset Boulevard as a passage through a Red Sea of traffic, the jumble of vehicles rearranged into a dazing symmetry. He enjoyed prowling in a state of doped elation through the shoddy treasury of the World's Largest Drugstore, imagining the tacky wares as the contents of his mind: "this suffocating interior of a dime-store ship was my own personal self; these gimcrack mobiles of tin and plastic were my personal contributions to the universe." Discussing radiance of color as an attribute of the visionary heaven, he defends the vulgar brightness of America as evidence not of coarse materialism but of spiritual craving, which commerce strains to satisfy. Yet in being so democratically distributed, the polychromatic spirit is debauched. Woolworth's, like the World's Largest Drugstore, is the purveyor of cut-price uplift, and Huxley regrets that "we have seen too much pure, bright colour at Woolworth's to find it intrinsically transporting." Rupert Brooke, in the third chapter of this book, identified Pater's Mona Lisa in the sky above New York, elusively winking as she commends a brand of pepsin chewing-gum. Huxley too finds the aureoles of the spirit world brightening the darkness in order to sell merchandise. Los Angeles is heaven in neon and at a discount.

Huxley prefers his chemical heaven to the drab human world. Initially America humanizes him, disarming his satire and transvaluing it into mysticism. But the agency which works this change is technology, and gradually Huxley's technological faith leads him toward a chilling dehumanization. Huxley the technocrat is a deathlier figure than Huxley the satirist, as the Santa Barbara prescriptions for *The Human Situation* disclose. The satirist wants to revenge himself on the demeaning human situation, the mystic to levitate out of it. But the technocrat, more alarmingly, wants to reform it. He regrets its fallibility, its inefficiency, and in the end deplores its humanity. In the lectures entitled *The Human Situation*, Huxley actually laments our "all too human world." Humanity for him is now a cosmic claustrophobia, like that which afflicts him in the World's Largest Drugstore: he suffers from "a sense of being boxed in a world where everything has a suffocating feeling of humanity, instead of being other than humanity." His own humanity embarrassed him. He was proud of his elongated skeletal frame, which he believed to be a grudging cerebrotonic concession to physical form. Given the choice, he'd rather have been a disembodied mind, a pure electronic intelligence like the robots he admires in *The Human Situation*.

Brave New World Revisited (published in 1959, the year of

the Santa Barbara lectures) admits this choice of dehumanization. Huxley warns against social and scientific tendencies which will actualize his brave new world sooner than he thought. But he had already allied himself with the nightmarish over-organized future of his fantasy by going to live in it. He had even borrowed the manipulative procedures of the brave new world for his own art.

Overpopulation, for instance, appalls him. He regrets the medical "death-control" which has lengthened life and congested California with the rejuvenated geriatrics who are fashioned into slick cadavers at Forest Lawn. But the satirist isn't constrained by the same medical ethics which have lowered the death rate. *Ape and Essence* solves the problem of overpopulation by sentencing the entire state of California to death. Huxley also enforces his own compulsory methods of birth control. *Brave New World Revisited* attacks behaviorism because it slights human individuality, but Huxley himself, living in California, had begun to doubt the value of this cherished individuality. Discussing "the problem of human nature" at Santa Barbara, he virtually denies that such a human nature exists. If it does, it is merely a sign of evolutionary backwardness. The satirist's contempt for human nature and the mystic's indifference to it come to the aid of the technocrat, in whose ideal future quarrelsomely different human beings will have become identical test-tube babies like those cultivated in the brave new world. Virginia and the gum-chewing girls in *After Many a Summer* already belong in this bland, unindividual future: they are simply appetizing bodies without minds to differentiate them. In the novels Huxley wrote in California, character either disappears into the vegetative peace of the body, as in Virginia's case, or else is chemically deconstructed. William Asquith Farnaby in *Island* takes drugs in order to cease being a person, and evaporates into a luminous, vacuous state of awareness.

In Huxley's California you can escape from a wearisome individuality either by evanescing into a mind like Farnaby or withdrawing into a body like Virginia. California persuaded Huxley that character is no more than an automatic reflex of physique. On the island of his last novel, education is grounded in neurotheology and physiology. Spotting gutsy endomorphs or mesomorphic muscle-men on the escalator at Ohrbach's, or categorizing himself as a cerebral ectomorph, Huxley reduces individuals to their physical exteriors. They can stay inside these bodies and be safely less than human like Virginia, or escape from them to be more than human like Farnaby or Huxley on their drug trips. California is a paradise because it grants human beings the freedom to be inhuman, either as psychedelically enlightened angels or as carnal animals.

The same mystical chemicals which dissolve personal individuality, lightening this obtuse "clot that one called 'I' " during Farnaby's acid trip in *Island,* also disparage literature. *The Genius and the Goddess* proposes a chemical decomposition of the novel. The pubic puppy love of Ruth is analyzed into its physical constituents. A "psycho-physical soup" clogs into "action-producing lumps of emotion and sentiment," abetted by glandular changes and the "thrill-solution" coursing out from her newly protuberant nipples. Literature merely panders to these "psycho-erectile capacities." Ruth paints her mouth and perfumes her body because she has been reading Wilde and Swinburne. *The Genius and the Goddess* begins with an assault on the novel. It is trivial because it is tidy, Rivers argues, and can never represent the unorganized chaos of existence. At Santa Barbara, Huxley complained that literature was devoted to the "awful humanization of nature." Poets speciously annex the external world to their own emotions, and novelists rearrange random bundles of atoms into the semblance of logical beings. The only art Huxley commends in these lectures is as bleak and blank as the atomized, unfeeling universe: the novels of Joyce and Lawrence, which in his view examine psychological change under laboratory conditions, as a chemical process; the music of Pierre Boulez, which fragments melody into rows of tuneless notes; the painting of Jackson Pollock, which declines to copy nature but flecks a canvas with dribbles of oil, the minimal and "atomic elements of form."

Island continues the assault on literature. The tropical zone not only refutes the cozy nature-sentiment of romanticism, but sets about the destruction of literature. Books perish, their paper rotted by heat or gnawed by insects, their glue melting. Farnaby welcomes the damage, and contends that literature is incompatible "with human integrity . . . philosophical truth . . . individual sanity and a decent social system, incompatible with everything except dualism, criminal lunacy, impossible aspiration and unnecessary guilt." Huxley's Californian heaven is a compound of science and mysticism, and literature is an enemy to both these mental realms. Dr. MacPhail in *Island* recalls his father's suspicion of poetry as "an autonomous universe" improperly positioned "between direct experience and the symbols of science." His ideal was "pure experimental science at one end of the spectrum, and pure experimental mysticism at the other." So was Huxley's. Lying between science and mysticism, literature is reduced to a fabrication of unreal experience, dismayingly inauthentic.

Brave New World Revisited further humbles literature by associating it with the mendacity of American mass communications and Madison Avenue advertising. Like the advertisers, literature deals neither in the true nor the false but in the unreal, the fictional, the irrelevant. America has come to resemble Huxley's brave new world because it uses art as a means of subliminal intrusion and manipulation. It conquers its citizens by entertaining them. American children, Huxley says, are "radio fodder and television fodder," so trained in submission that they warble singing commercials at their play. Jingles celebrating Rheingold beer or Pepsodent toothpaste are the nursery rhymes of today. Self-deluded and self-defrauded by residence in his brave new world, Huxley seems not to have realized that his own visionary mirages were a product of the same psychic interference which he denounced in American mass communications. He condemns the technical regimentation of human susceptibility as a crime against democracy, but by administering drugs to himself he was fiddling with his own sensory system, making himself the victim of a sinister chemical engineering. Reviewing the dictatorial uses of propaganda in *Brave New World Revisited,* Huxley remarks that Hitler understood how to control the masses by intoxicating their unconscious minds. But his own cleansing of the doors of perception is a benignly self-deranging version of this hypnosis. The subjects of fascism and of Madison Avenue, he says, have an idiotic suggestibility, but Huxley's own psychedelic afflatus is no more than an inspired suggestibility. Hitler injected the masses with the "active, extroverted drug" of "herd-poison." Huxley sedated himself with a passive, introverted, visionary equivalent.

America worked two changes on Huxley. It first turned him from a satirist into a mystic. Later it made both the satirist and the mystic adjuncts of a new American self, the technocrat. American technology, Huxley believed, has the task of saving prodigal humanity from disaster by reforming the species and reclaiming nature. Controlling population, devising new methods for irrigating the waste and cultivating food crops, technology is rescuing a crowded and depleted planet. Huxley saw evidence of this technological salvation everywhere in California, in combine harvesters, synthetic fibers and sewage-conversion units. The technocrat neither makes time punitively foreclose, like the satirist, nor dreamily eludes it, like the mystic, but simply alters its mechanism. Time, Huxley warns in the lectures at Santa Barbara, will drift entropically on toward destruction unless technology intervenes to speed it up—not, like satire, to hasten retribution, but to equip us with powers of survival which otherwise we wouldn't discover soon enough. As Huxley sees it, this technological takeover is happening in modern America. But technology can only rescue the world by dehumanizing it. If we are to be saved, Huxley argues, we must renounce our confused, helpless humanity, and the regressive literary imagination which clings to it.

Huxley in America advances steadily toward this dehumanization. First the satirist in him surrenders to the technocrat, who has sanitized the putrescent body. Hence Huxley's disgruntlement with the undecaying corpses of Forest Lawn, with the garment and beauty industries, with the sludge activator at Redondo Beach. Next the mystic capitulates, for the technocrat offers instant transcendence to the yearning mind. In California, religious experience can be extracted from the chemical secretions of cacti, from the cinema's mechanical conjurations of vision, even from drugstores and neon signs. The place Huxley designated as hell ends as his heaven. At first he enjoyed California's ghastliness, cheerfully exhibiting the horrors of his Santa Monica home, priding himself on his satiric or mystical immunity to his surroundings. But California revenged itself. The more sardonically he calculated his distance from it, the more insidiously it converted him to its scientific fads and religious crankery. At last, without noticing it, Huxley became a drugged subject of his own brave new world.

9

MYSTICAL AMERICA
Christopher Isherwood
in California

Isherwood went to America with Auden, and was befriended there by Huxley, in whose company he began writing for Hollywood and studying Oriental religion. But his experience of America diverges from theirs. Leaving Auden in New York to age as time's votary, encrusted with habits which harden sclerotically into rituals, Isherwood in the summer of 1939 traveled to California, where he has grown progressively younger, basking in the mystic's perpetual present and shedding selves by rewriting his past. Although his California overlaps on Huxley's, imaginatively it is a separate region. The mysticism Isherwood learned there is not a deconversion from satire, like Huxley's. Nor it is a parasite on technology: Isherwood has no need of psychedelic aids. Huxley's California is a place of intellectual treason, the extreme limit of the Western world, where the universal humanism of his Victorian ancestors sickens into a polymathically cranky alliance between science and superstition. Unencumbered by ideology, Isherwood's California is an agreeably temporary heaven, bright, clean, bland, and permissive.

Auden chose New York as the setting for a painful self-alienation. Sentencing himself to membership in the city's lonely crowd, he was scourging himself theologically, for his own good.

New York is a place for self-mortification. But Isherwood's moral style is more blithely self-indulgent and self-forgetful, and therefore suits hedonistic California, which licenses Isherwood's peculiar manner of self-deprecating narcissism. He has only one subject: himself. But he doesn't know himself. He writes autobiography in order to find out more about this stranger he happens to be. He edges toward the truth about himself by discarding the accretions of the past. California permits him to deny his past, because it is a state devoted to self-renewal, populated by migrants who are not the sorry displaced aliens of Auden's New York but people who have left behind them what they were and embarked on a career of self-regeneration. The books Isherwood has written in California are therefore emendations of and escapes from those he wrote in Europe. *Christopher and His Kind* (1977) rewrites the earlier autobiography *Lions and Shadows* (1938) and atones for its perjuries and its sexual coyness. Isherwood at the same time attempts to understand himself and irresponsibly escapes from himself by defaming the personae who have been his fictional aliases. The uncloseted, informal "Christopher" who is the subject of *Christopher and His Kind* disowns the evasive, mock-heterosexual "Herr Issyvoo" of the Berlin stories, the anodyne "William Bradshaw" (a code-identity concocted from Isherwood's vestigial middle names) of *Mr. Norris Changes Trains,* and the moralizing prig who is Isherwood in John van Druten's stage version of the Sally Bowles episode, *I Am a Camera.*

Driven in on themselves by exile, Auden and Isherwood spent their literary lives in America in meditation on their European pasts and in constant editorial interference with their early, pre-American texts. Auden maintained that a poem was never finished, only abandoned, and rewrote earlier works to adjust them to altered political opinions; Isherwood is still writing footnotes to *Lions and Shadows.* But Auden could only free himself from past selves by public acts of recantation. Hence his mutilations of juvenile poems which he considered politically dishonest. For Isherwood, self-negation is glibber and easier. He doesn't need to amputate a past identity, because he's not sure that he possesses any identity at all. His dubiety is the mood of California, which unsettles identity by disestablishing the past. Raymond Chandler's detective stories make both points about California. Because the citizens of Los Angeles are anonymous and pastless, they are all potential participants in a mystery. Identity in this transitory place is so tenuous that a name is a detachable label, and probably false. People being interrogated by Chandler's private eye Marlowe often ask him "Do you have a name?" The odd turn of phrase admits the possibility that he might not have one.

America confirmed Auden and Isherwood in their different styles of self-solicitation. But whereas Auden became a decrepit dogmatist, authorizing a single version of himself, prohibiting a biography, and requesting friends to burn his letters, Isherwood has disingenuously continued to re-create himself. His is a uniquely self-detached narcissism. He has the art, inculcated in him by the Vedantist mysticism of which he became an adept in California, of slipping out of his body and his mental attitudes and appraising them as if they belonged to someone else. This enables him to be at the same time frank and devious. Even the device of writing about himself in the third person is a formula for evasion: old Isherwood confronts young Christopher as a stranger, a quizzical object with impulses and intentions the novelist can't understand or regulate. Hence Isherwood's latter-day concentration on the sexual activities of the promiscuous Christopher. The body takes on a will of its own and becomes a character, but the record of its erotic spasms and seductive machinations discloses as little about its owner as would an inventory of his dinner menus.

Self-separation from the body is a talent cultivated by Oriental religion. The Swami in Isherwood's *A Meeting by the River* (1967) mocks his feeble Bengali body, and finds "the predicament of being obliged to live inside it" ludicrous. But it is also a condition of existence in hedonistic California. George in Isherwood's *A Single Man* (1964) apprehends himself, and is apprehended by the novelist, not as a person but as a wayward, incontinent body, its parts laboriously fitted together in the morning and wearily dispersed at night. Physique, in this bronzed paradise, has taken over from character as the source of identity. California exerts itself to instruct people in the proper use of the bodies which are both their property and their playthings. Campus bookstores sell volumes called operating manuals for male and female bodies, as if inhabiting a body were a technical skill, like driving a car or balancing on a surfboard. Isherwood himself jogs medicinally, "to shake things up," and George his single man limbers up at a gym, rejoicing in an "easy-going physical democracy."

Identity is variable in time and also scattered in space. Isherwood discards selves not only by revisiting and revising his past, but by traveling. One of the questions he and Auden debated to pass the time on trains during their Chinese expedition in 1938 was "Does a man become a different person in a different place?" Isherwood thinks so. Travel is a state of restless becoming, not static being. Isherwood condemns himself to perpetual motion, because while he is in transit he has no need of character or personal individuality. On the way to Berlin in 1929 he becomes "only a traveller, given over, mind and body, to the will of the dominant, eastward-speeding train." For the next ten years, he shuttled between London and Berlin, Bremen, Amsterdam, Brussels, Paris, and Copenhagen, with holidays in the south of France, Portugal, Athens, the Greek islands, and the Canaries, until the journey to China. Los Angeles, where he has lived since 1939, is the ideal location for Isherwood, because there anonymity and mobility collaborate to unsettle identity. The circuitry of the freeways and the shapeless sprawl of the city keep people forever on the move: they don't meet but slide by one another in parallel lanes, huddled inside their automobiles.

Geography confirms the discontinuity of Isherwood's selves. Settled in Los Angeles, he imagines his friends in London, occupied by the war and differently situated in time (it is night there), speaking of him as if he were dead. The body has voided these various selves, depositing them through times and places in the past, while it mystically reposes in an unchanging present. Lolling in the sea in *Down There on a Visit* (1962), Isherwood rejoices in an utter immersion in "now and here," and reflects that "even this body I'm floating in might as well be that of a teenage boy or a healthy old man—myself at seventeen or seventy; I would scarcely be aware of the difference." The body is ageless, because the only time it knows is the present tense of its itches and cravings, which demand immediate satisfaction, and this is why the Californian Isherwood so treasures and indulges it. For Auden, the youthful body is as defunct and irrecoverable as time past. In a poem saluting his Oxford tutor Nevill Coghill in 1965 he notes that

> now of the body
> I brashly came to my first
> tutorial in
> not a molecule remains.

But Isherwood believes that youthful form to be recoverable. The body doesn't age and degenerate steadily through time, but holds in equipoise inside itself the various periods of its existence. Isherwood re-experiences the past not only meditatively but physically, since all that survives of that past is the body. Because the body is constant and continuous through life, it is one of the mystic's agents in the defeat of time. All the stages of a life overlap in it. Time for the body is simultaneous not serial. When we feel energetic, we are young again; when we're exhausted, we're already old. Swimming, Isherwood can't tell whether he is seventeen or seventy. He wrote *A Single Man,* he has said, to demonstrate the "extraordinary variety of behaviour" of which the middle-aged are capable, suspended between rash youth and fatigued infirmity. George during the day in Los Angeles which the novel describes is both recklessly young (when he dashes into the ocean with his student Kenny) and desperately old (when he visits the dying Doris in the hospital). Isherwood's own dualistic face acts out this alternation: sometimes he looks tired, lined, and shriveled, like an ancient monk, but when he laughs he regains the face of an adolescent, with a shy smile and sparkling eyes.

An indeterminate nationality also gives Isherwood the freedom of different identities. He became an American citizen in 1946, but clings to the sense of foreignness, and remains, as he said in 1971, "extremely British." Auden too insisted on his foreignness, but with a different motive. Alienation was for him the stigma of modernity and a morose self-punishment. He wouldn't permit himself to belong to a community, because he believed he wasn't worthy of membership. Hence his studied alienation of himself from New York in his farewell to the city. Isherwood is not such a self-mortifier. He excludes himself in order to secure a point of vantage. He doesn't will himself to suffer like Auden, but chooses to observe the sufferings of others. He has an impish delight in belonging to a minority, because he tolerates no abrogation of his precious individuality. His symbolic hero is George, the homosexual Englishman in Los Angeles, whose singleness is the most important fact about him. Isherwood is glad to be homosexual, because it defines his differentness and guards him from the majority. He has said that, if his weren't the minority preference, he might change allegiance: "I should feel ill at ease, certainly, in a homosexual commune."

America and homosexuality have always been associated for Isherwood as defenses of his separateness. Early in his career he cast America as the continent of a hated normality, the realm of the majority which the conspirator must find a way around. During the 1920s he planned a novel called *The North-West Passage,* in which the northern circuit is the route taken by the neurotic hero Isherwood calls "the Truly Weak Man," who must avoid the shortcuts and compromises of life, brave the existential dangers of "the Test," and risk perishing in the blizzards. By contrast, "the Truly Strong Man travels straight acro·s the broad America of normal life, taking always the direct, reasonable route." This is the unswerving advance across the continent of Kipling's hero Cheyne in his locomotive. Isherwood, like Lawrence juggling itineraries in order to avoid New

York, favors the fugitive, seditious stratagem of the north-west passage because " 'America' is just what the truly weak man, the neurotic hero, dreads." He can enter it only by the rear.

Isherwood's memoir of his parents, *Kathleen and Frank* (1971), connects his change of citizenship with his repudiation of his genteel family. Isherwood writes about his parents to wrest himself from them, reversing a biological order. Instead of their child, he is, since he writes about himself in the third person, his own creation. America frees him because in going there he can dismantle the identity to which his family has fated him. For Lawrence, the significance of America lay in its dissolution of the old stable ego of European fiction. Isherwood in migrating also renounces the markers of character in the society and the novels of Europe, name and property. He discards the excrescent middle names with which he was burdened in homage to members of his family: "Christopher, from his schooldays on, groaned under the weight of his huge name and got an aggressive satisfaction from officially dropping the William and the Bradshaw when he became an American citizen." Those ancillary names were his camouflage in *Mr. Norris Changes Trains,* so in excising them he was also stripping away the pretenses of the older kind of novel, which traffics in character because the novelist shrinks from describing himself in his own person. At the same time, Isherwood transferred his inheritance—the mansion in which his mother lived, and the fortune due to him—to his younger brother. He even forged a new appearance for himself, to replace the one with which his parents genetically endowed him. Applying for a passport, he described his gray-blue eyes as "greenish grey" to spite his mother, who disliked green eyes.

Having detached himself from the suffocating embrace of his mother, he needed to repudiate his motherland as well. In taking American citizenship he did both at once. In America, he chose to live among his mother's class enemies. She despised the Manchester businessmen whose villas were proliferating around the family mansion. Isherwood excuses the malefactors by likening them to his new countrymen: they are "psychologically very close to a certain type of urban North American." America charms family bogies into harmlessness. Another stifling matriarch, Isherwood's sickly grandmother, has her second coming in California as a skunk. He remembers from childhood the medicinal stench of her flat and the moldy odor of her furs, and remarks that "in California, Christopher has found, most people take it for granted that the smell of a skunk is unpleasant. He has always liked it (in moderation); it reminds him so strongly of Emily." From his mother he inherits a fear of snakes which is Freudianly diagnosed as the symptom of "a repressed longing to submit to anal intercourse." This he overcomes when exposed to the slithering reptiles of California, and to flaunt his victory over a maternal inhibition he sets up housekeeping there "with a young man who kept non-venomous snakes as pets." This psychological parable recurs in *A Single Man* when Mrs. Strunk, George's neighbor, watches aghast as he plays with "harmless baby king-snakes."

Isherwood interprets his flight to America as a maneuver in a prolonged and deadly biological war between the Female (his castrating mother) and the Tyrant-Male, on whom she has vowed to revenge herself. He remembers his mother chiding his father (killed in action during the Great War) for reading Conrad's *Youth*, which she thought escapist. Conrad's maritime adventures, as the fourth chapter of this book implies, are epic, and therefore exclude women. Isherwood accounts for his mother's reprobation of *Youth* by arguing that "Man's basic threat to Woman is that he will run away from her; Woman's basic retort is that those who run away are children, not real men." This explains the motive for his escape to America (the country which in 1776 absconded from its motherland, and which has ever since been blamed by that spurned parent as an immature, unmannerly infant) and into the sexual prolongation and idealization of adolescence which he pointedly calls "boy-love." American citizenship and homosexuality both give notice of a refusal to be what his mother would estimate as a "real man."

For this reason, Isherwood's imaginary America could not include New York. He spent a few months there with Auden in 1939, but soon left for the west coast. New York, he found, was the embodiment of his trauma, not a relief from it. If the rotting, squalid family mansions described in *Kathleen and Frank* symbolize to Isherwood the fetid, contaminating possessiveness of his mother, then the architecture of New York incorporates the totemic, tyrannical authority of his father. "The skyscrapers," he reported, "are father-fixations." His account of his arrival in *Christopher and His Kind* makes these spectral parents the forbidding guardians of the harbor. The mother is the Statue of Liberty, the father the towers of lower Manhattan: Isherwood calls them respectively the Giantess and the Citadel. The Giantess no longer welcomes the immigrant but brandishes her torch threateningly. The jagged male Citadel of financial power and competitive aggression, bristling with ice and "flaunting its rude steel nudity," challenges the newcomer to combat. In contrast with the brutal phallic solidity of New York, Los Angeles is consoling because anonymous and impermanent. You can escape from your family there because it is a place of motorized transience, where not only relationships but even the landscape is fickle and unenduring.

Isherwood likes the tackiness and temporariness of Los Angeles. At first his reasons are psychological, but later he discovers a mystic moral in this rubbishly illusoriness. Los Angeles is a jerry-built paradise, the make-shift opposite of the eternal city. Towns in its suburbs, Isherwood remarks in an essay on the city in 1947, seem to have been run up overnight, and even the local industries are haunted by impermanence: "the aircraft perpetually becoming obsolete, the oil which must one day be exhausted, the movies which fill America's theatres for six months and are forgotten." His fondness for the shabby dereliction of the city isn't a patronizing reflex of disgust like Huxley's. For Isherwood, decrepitude isn't retributively pleasing (as it is for the satirist) but psychologically liberating: it confounds a past which is abhorrent because ancestral and familial. Explaining his affection for the seedy, dilapidated beach-

fronts of the Pacific—the stagnant canals of Venice, the inane carou-
sel on the pier at Santa Monica—he says that he prefers "the ignoble
ruins of the day before yesterday" to the "noble ruins of antiquity,"
because they impart a clean, bracing sense of time and its revenges.
None of this impromptu agglomeration was here a century ago,
probably none of it will be here a century hence, and "you won't be
here, either."

Geologically, Los Angeles is equally mutable. Along the cliffs
above the beach at Santa Monica the paths have slipped away, and
the palisades are carious and unsteady. Signs warn of landslides.
Isherwood's house juts out across Santa Monica canyon as if daring
this disaster. Rains annually wash away segments of the soft Hollywood Hills, and Augustus Parr the mystic in *Down There on a Visit*
jabs the hillsides with his walking stick to assist the process: the
mystic rejoices in unreality and infirmity, and longs for the decomposition of the world. Robert Louis Stevenson, writing about the
unstable hills of San Francisco, says they look unfinished, as if not
yet carved into their proper shape by rain and streams. To him
the geological volatility of California suggests the reckless youth of the
world, still "changeful and insecure." To Isherwood it implies the
world's weary age and its yearning for disintegration. In contrast
with Isherwood's mystic readiness for mud slides and earth tremors,
Huxley's approach to the problem is technocratic. Dr. Poole in *Ape
and Essence* attributes the debility of the soil to human parasitism,
and plans remedial action. He analyzes soil erosion and plant pathol-
ogy in the San Gabriel mountains, which have been denuded of
vegetation and furrowed into gullies, and satirically concludes that
Californians have poisoned their own land with "fungus bombs,
bacteria-bearing aerosols and the release of many virus-carrying
aphides."

The encroaching desert makes Los Angeles a place of dissolution, but because of the laving ocean it is also a place of purification.
With its laminated skies, manicured lawns, and glassy domestic
swimming pools, it has a pristine, vacuum-packed cleanliness which

Isherwood both psychologically and mystically admires. Psychologically, this hygiene represents America's cleansing of the grime and guilt of Europe. The celestial sanitariness of the American bathroom (where *A Single Man* begins) is a release from the tribal squalor of the English ancestral home. Isherwood in *Kathleen and Frank* recalls his childhood homes as places contaminated by history, stained by psychological anguish. Marple Hall is "a sick house . . . a psychic slum," which ought to be burned down. Its plumbing is a symbol of its ordurous condition: there was only one bathroom, and guests had to bathe in their bedrooms. Returning to visit his family in 1947, Isherwood contrasts the immemorial filth of England with the cellophane-wrapped, sterile health of America: "eight years in middle-class America, with its gleaming, hygienic kitchens, had made him dainty-minded, no doubt." His mother's kitchen range burned coal, which embedded dust in the carpet, and there was no vacuum cleaner to suck it out. He offered to present her with a vacuum cleaner, but she indignantly refused. She detested the present and its conveniences: grease and soot were the deposits of the past she venerated. The sordid family kitchen contained no refrigerator, and food was stored in a larder which doubled as a coal cellar. Isherwood set to work scouring and scrubbing.

Isherwood's prim cleanliness is one of the emblematic differences between himself and Auden. His house in California is a glass box with a white verandah, a monastic cubicle suspended in mid-air. Auden's apartment in New York was a cave of defilement. Auden in "The Novelist," a poem addressed to Isherwood, advises him of a professional obligation to investigate the grubby woes of men and be "among the Filthy filthy too." But filth was Auden's vocation, not Isherwood's. Isherwood trained himself as a novelist by studying medicine, and his attitude to the soiled world is clinical and rubber-gloved. In *Lions and Shadows* he remembers the operating theater at St. Thomas's Hospital in London as "an unnaturally clean kitchen." Auden during the 1930s moralized his own dinginess, scorning asepsis and declaring that disease is a manifestation of inner disquiets and dishonesty which can be cured only by a purification of motive. He believed himself to be immune to syphilis because his promiscuity was uncomplicated by guilt. Later, after his religious conversion, his squalor became penitential, the uniform of man's abject fallen state. Huxley was offended by American hygiene because it kept the satirist at bay. Auden too disdained hygiene because it sacrilegiously removed that self-disgust which to him was a theological virtue. Sex, he thought, "being metaphysically tainted, ought also to be physically unclean." His preferred activities were self-abasing, lubricated by sweat and invigorated by stench, like the session with the New York hustler in "The Platonic Blow."

California's scrupulosity about ablutions has a religious significance for Huxley and Isherwood. Huxley interprets it satirically, as evidence of the collapse of Christian morality. Hot baths are a victory over Christian self-loathing, which detested the body as the apparatus of sin and prohibited its exposure, even for cleaning purposes. Another Englishman in California, Alfred Hitchcock, like Huxley finds in this sanitariness a satiric clue to the erasure of guilt. Hitchcock confesses to a sinister daintiness in the bathroom: "When I take a bath, I put everything neatly back in its place. You wouldn't even know I'd been in the bathroom." He shares this anxiety with his malefactors—Janet Leigh in *Psycho* flushing the tell-tale scraps of paper down the lavatory, Anthony Perkins mopping up the bloody shower. This obsession with cleanliness is mystically interpreted by Isherwood. Scatology for him transforms itself into eschatology, sanitariness into sanctity. Hygiene is a spiritual discipline. Isherwood's biography of the mystic Ramakrishna justifies the dirty habits of the East as religious rites. Bathing in the Ganges is, he says, a holy act, so it is performed even by those who could wash more comfortably at home. Ramakrishna himself (in contrast with the sluttish housekeeping of Isherwood's mother) cooks in Ganges water, which purifies everything, and calls one of his acolytes "a clean new pot in which milk could be safely kept without turning sour." As Auden prescribed for the novelist a soiling apprenticeship among the filthy, so Ramakrishna, to humble his caste pride, cleans out a privy with his hands. Eastern dirt is clean to Isherwood because spiritually graced.

California has joined in the sacramental clean-ups of Ramakrishna's East, and now has a journal devoted to "water-consciousness." *Wet, The Magazine of Gourmet Bathing* is published in Venice, down the coast from Isherwood's Santa Monica, and explores "the biological, recreational, and spiritual aspects of water-use in our culture." The privy becomes an anchorite's cell, and mud baths, hot tubs, spas, and Jacuzzis its engines of purification. It is therefore apt that Auden, allocating the rooms of his house in "Thanksgiving for a Habitat," should assign Isherwood to the water closet. George in *A Single Man* reads Ruskin while defecating, and ruminates on the john about his buried past. Auden in the privy poem dedicated to Isherwood declares the posture of man excreting to be meditative, and commends Rodin for making his Thinker strain at stool. Auden's own excremental morality is that of the good bourgeois, whose bowel movements are metaphors of economic probity. Misers suffer from constipation, he points out, and banks have boxes for night deposits. But Isherwood's excremental morality is mystical. Emptying the body's wastes is a preliminary to the discarding of the body. George's defecation at the beginning of the day is balanced by the disposal of his dead body at the end of the day. Remembering the death of his mentor Gerald Heard, Isherwood has said that, after his stroke, Heard survived in a meditative paralysis, "aware of the body lying there, obviously irreparable and soon to be abandoned."

In Isherwood's city of the angels, dirt has been abolished and so has privacy. Angels are transparent, and the omnivorous curiosity of the suburban Angeleno is for Isherwood a gossipy variant of the saint's remorseless goodness. Houses, he notes, are arranged on unfenced communal lawns, "staring into each other's bedroom windows, without even a pretence of privacy." American curiosity is paradisial. Though never furtive or ill-meaning, it "can sometimes be merciless," because angels in totalitarian heaven can have no secrets. The snugly pretty suburbs of Philadelphia, to which Isherwood's hero retreats from Los Angeles in *The World in the Evening* (1954), are "a landscape without secrets, inhabited by people whose every word, thought and action would bear thorough investigation by the F.B.I." In Isherwood's suburban paradise, blandness is obligatory. Casual greetings are a litany, a ritual of responses as in a church service, enforcing an optimistic creed: "a reaffirmation of faith in the basic American dogma, that it is, always, a *Good* Morning," as George reflects. "Have a nice day," the Californian slogan uttered by bus drivers, waitresses, and bank tellers, has something faintly menacing about it, as do the signs on supermarket doors promising or perhaps admonishing the customer, "You're going to like it here." Not to have a good day, not to like it here, would be to confess your unworthiness to be in paradise.

The blithe frankness of Isherwood's American heaven contrasts with a preferred landscape of Auden's, the evasively private English village where the detective stories to which he was addicted are usually set. Described in the poem "Detective Story" and the essay "The Guilty Vicarage," Auden's imaginary village is a fugitive, innocuous hell, in which each house harbors a guilty secret. For this reason it entices the inquisitive, suspicious novelist. Isherwood, however, finds that the suburbs deter the novelist. In a world without secrets or privacy, there is no interior realm of character for him to explore. His trade can't be practiced in heaven. Isherwood can only write about the suburb of the angels by setting in it a character who is alien, both nationally and sexually, and whose singleness denotes his refusal to open his life to his inquisitorial neighbors. George deliberately conceals from the snooping Strunks next door the news of his lover's death in Ohio.

The novelist is unwelcome in paradise because his art depends on description and is therefore acquisitive and materialistic. California, on the contrary, is angelically negligent about property and possessions. In *The World in the Evening*, Stephen remembers a stained-glass window in a childhood home, which he used to peer through, "experiencing the pure pleasure of sensations which need no analysis." He tells his first wife about the window, and she (a novelist) remarks, "That's my idea of heaven, a place where you don't have to describe *anything.*" California is such a place. Description is disabled there, not only because the reality is stranger than fiction but because people don't seem to own their surroundings. They are not like Europeans, lovingly accumulating property of which novelists take laborious inventory. Their wealth is so abundant and so facilely acquired that they can afford to be dismissive about it. From Robinson Crusoe onwards, the European novelist is a compiler of stock lists, describing the treasures he can't own. California shames him, because its plenty discourages his acquisitiveness and purifies his materialism. Isherwood registers this change in himself in *Down There on a Visit*. Despite its opulence, this is not a world to be owned or lived in but a forbidding temple of the spirit, in which riches are symbolic gifts of grace. The Isherwood of *Down There on a Visit* is angelically detached from the place's spoils. He is laden with tribute—the preposterous salary from the movie studio, a convertible car, a furnished apartment hung with Renoir reproductions—in which he doesn't believe. Hence his generosity in disbursing money in restaurants, because he doesn't feel that it belongs to him; hence his feeling of being an imposter in his own car, or his refusal to imprint himself on his apartment by rearranging its layout. Like Hitchcock stealthily erasing his stains from the bathroom, Isherwood says "you'd find so little trace of me in the apartment that you'd have to look for my finger-prints in order to prove I lived there." Auden's domestic ordure implies the opposite attitude. Soiling and smudging things, allowing dribbles of egg to congeal on a shirt and so on, is the owner's assertion of his rights, his way of imposing his character on his environment. You only feel at home in your new apartment, Auden says, once you have shat there.

The proper habitation for the Californian angel, denuded of possessions and of personal identity, reduced to a saintly anonymity, is a motel room. To G. K. Chesterton, American hotels were the concentric circles of hell. Their sameness ("there is only one hotel in America," its pattern replicated and multiplied across the land) diminishes and dehumanizes their occupants, and the practice of paging guests in the foyers evokes, for Chesterton, drifting populations of lost creatures who will never be found, souls whirling in limbo. But for Isherwood this absence of difference and detail is the spiritual virtue of these institutions. The hotel receptionist in *The World in the Evening* is a discreet recording angel, validating the pretenses of the guilty fugitives who are his clients. Stephen has absconded from home after discovering his current wife fornicating at a party. He is the customary Isherwood hero, convinced (like his creator) of his own nonentity, yet agonizingly self-preoccupied, forever glancing sideways at mirrors to check that he is still there. Registering at the Los Angeles hotel, he reminds himself that "after all, I suppose I do actually exist. Anyhow, I seem to have a name, just like anybody else." The clerk, eyeing his signature, seems to be conferring an identity on Stephen the harassed transient.

Stephen flees to the hotel as to a confessional, and is tempted to disburden himself to the desk clerk as to "a doctor or a priest." George the single man likewise praises the motel room as an immaterial, penitential cell, an abstract apartment for a mystic to meditate in. When a patronizing easterner sneers at the unreality of American motel rooms, George replies with a paraphrase of Auden's argument that Americans are spirit beings accustomed to symbolic appurtenances, whose "life is all in the mind" and who despise the sentimental, antiquarian materialism of Europe. "An American motel-room," he says, "isn't *a* room in *an* hotel, it's *the* Room, definitely, period." America, where nature has its unorganic second coming in plastic, neon, and Styrofoam, has mystically "reduced the things of the material plane to mere symbolic conveniences" in order to free the mind. Europeans hate America because they are too craven, cupidinous, and romantically inefficient, too fond of "cathedrals and first editions and Paris models and vintage wines," to appreciate a world glossily reified. "We sleep in symbolic bedrooms, eat symbolic meals, are symbolically entertained," George boasts. He even manages to justify the un-nutritious gastronomy of America, where non-dairy toppings simulate cream and the national beverage of Coca-Cola is brewed from a secret chemical formula and flavored artificially. "We've retired," he says, "to live inside our advertisements, like hermits going into caves to contemplate." The motel room is a model of Plato's murky cave. Its occupants are electronically plugged into the world outside by the telephone and television, but they no longer belong in that world. Auden deplores American technology because it alienates people from one another and from society, mediating all human relations. The easier communication becomes, the more it contrives to stop people communicating, which is the plight of Auden's New Yorkers in *The Age of Anxiety* and *New Year Letter*. But for Isherwood this is technology's benison: it makes contemplatives of us all. The telephone obstructs intercourse. Each of us in our isolation is intimate with the plastic mouthpiece rather than with our interlocutor. Entertainment, George says, is also symbolic. People don't watch programs on television but worshipfully gape at television itself, admiring the medium which, like the telephone, consumes the messages it is supposed to transmit.

Isherwood's life-long fondness for the movies and his work as a Hollywood scriptwriter have the same contemplative justification. Recalling childhood trips to see Pearl White and the Keystone Cops, he admits to possessing "an indiscriminate appetite for *any* two-dimensional happening on a lighted screen in a dark theatre." For him, two dimensions are an improvement on three: the cinematic image is insubstantial and therefore mystical. The phantasmal light cast on a screen in the surrounding dark is mysticism's notion of the soul. Movies by translating persons into images make gods of them. Isherwood, helping the director Berthold Viertel to buy a Christmas present for Garbo in London in 1933, describes the disbelief of the shop assistant when he is asked to address the parcel to her in California: to him she is an "infinitely remote, two-dimensional deity."

The cinema, trading in illusion, makes do with two dimensions,

whereas the novel needs three, and must be solid, bulky, earthily actual. Isherwood's conviction of his own nonentity obliges him to
write novels which are not novels about a character who is not a
character. He can't be a novelist because, though fascinated by "the
outward appearance of people," he can only record how they look
and not what they feel. He is a solitary subject confronting a world
of engrossing but impenetrable objects. The cinema turns this disqualification into an advantage. Isherwood calls himself a camera
because the camera too is a sentient subject trained on a universe of
obtuse objects. In 1938-39 he and Auden planned a film about the
life of an American, in which the camera was to be the central character. The cinema rationalizes Isherwood's inadequacies of vision by
substituting neutral observation for the novelist's affectionate empathy, contenting itself with demonstrating (as *Lions and Shadows*
puts it) "how actions look in relation to each other; how much space
they occupy and how much time." The loss of a dimension is for
Isherwood a necessary concomitant of characterization. He argues
that "it is easier to remember a face if you imagine its two-dimensional
reflection in a mirror," and this is how he remembers his own face
and confirms his own existence: Don Bachardy's drawing for the
cover of *Down There on a Visit* shows middle-aged Isherwood interrogating the reflection of spry young Christopher.

Isherwood's first film work was with Viertel on *Little Friend* in
1933. The experience lies behind *Prater Violet*, written after Isherwood's move to California. In America the cinema became for Isherwood a mode of mystical abstraction, but in England during the '30s,
when he and Auden saw themselves as conspirators engineering the
overthrow of a social order, it was a mode of espionage. The director Bergmann, based on Viertel, salutes the film as an unpausing,
unapologizing medium, an "infernal machine" which once set in
motion regrets nothing, explains nothing, but "simply ripens to its
inevitable explosion," like the terrorist's time bomb. "I am a camera"
is the spy's incognito.

Adopting Bergmann's theory, Isherwood argues that the film's

Isherwood's self-detached narcissism: cover for *Down There on a Visit*
by Don Bachardy, 1962.

beauty is its fixed speed, which deprives the viewer of the liberty he enjoys with a book or a painting: "you have to look at it as the director wants you to look at it." The director is an absent but omnipresent tyrant. He is nowhere in the film but is therefore everywhere, and he constrains the audience as dictatorially as he does the actors. This is a replica of Isherwood's own self-detached narcissism: he is his own only character, yet he cancels himself out, treating himself as discourteously and dismissively as if he were someone else. It is also an anticipation of his Eastern religion, which disperses god throughout nature ubiquitously but invisibly. *Prater Violet* is not about the film which is being made, but about those who make it. Life lies behind the camera, not in front of it. Though trained on the world outside, the camera is, for Isherwood, an introspective instrument.

This is why Auden, in a series of short poems written in 1969, differentiates himself from Isherwood by declaring "I Am Not a Camera." The camera's unearned confidentiality suits the self-exposure of Isherwood but frightens the self-protective Auden. It trespasses on the privacy of those it studies, which doesn't worry Isherwood, in whose suburban commune secrets are not permitted, but disconcerts Auden, who in "Thanksgiving for a Habitat" fences off his own physical territory, marking a frontier thirty inches from his nose and warning that he can spit. Like Isherwood's glacial blue eyes, the camera is pitiless and surgical. For Auden it necessarily reduces emotions to "anatomical data." Lovers, he says, shut their eyes before they kiss, flinching from the rudeness of a mutual close-up. Auden even accuses the camera of creating sorrow, because it preserves a past we ought to be at liberty to live down. Isherwood grows by rewriting his past, and in this activity the camera, like the journals which are the sources of his autobiographical books, is an essential aid. But Auden grows by remorsefully suppressing his past, cancelling early indiscretions (hence his refusal to allow the Marxist poem "September 1st, 1939" into his later canon) rather than glorying in them.

In 1935 Auden was employed by the G.P.O. Film Unit in London, and wrote a narration for a documentary about the night mail to Scotland, but he never worked for Hollywood. An essay in *The Dyer's Hand* explains his objections. Reviewing the career of Anzia Yezierska, an immigrant to America from a Polish ghetto who has been lured "from Hester Street to Hollywood," he makes the screenwriter a symbolic victim of the age of anxiety. The writer conscripted by Hollywood is enfeebled by self-doubt. Miss Yezierska, removed from her obscurity by the Hollywood moguls, is plunged by the instantaneous abundance of riches "into the severest anxiety." Alarmed by her own success, she stops writing. Auden says that the drying-up of the creative power is a calamity to which the young American writer is peculiarly liable, and he explains it as a perverse self-defense. Hollywood appraises the writer as a property. He is expected to pay off those who have invested in him. If he can't reconcile himself to the new ambitions which the magnates implant in him, the only safety lies in not writing. Hollywood also offends against that work ethic which was an aesthetic rule for Auden, and foments anxiety by creating false needs. It encourages the writer to confuse the money he earns with the writing he does for love, not reward, and its luxuries promise a happiness which they can't deliver. Freedom from financial difficulty doesn't mean freedom from anxiety. Auden's comment on Isherwood's hack work for Hollywood concisely combines this existential reprimand with a middle-class philistine's envy of the rewards. Reversing Shakespeare's comment on his meretricious craft as an actor ("I have . . . sold cheap what is most dear"), he said to Isherwood, "You at least sell dear what is most cheap." The joke implies that Isherwood like Anzia Yezierska ought to repine, and accuses him of commercial sharp practice, inflating the price of his shoddy wares. But Auden is enough of a bourgeois to think that prostitution is nice work if you can get it.

In *Down There on a Visit* Isherwood preserves his integrity by insisting on the irrelevance of his wealth, and carelessly redistributing it. But in other moods he has ironically bragged of Hollywood's assault on that integrity. Gore Vidal remembers him at MGM in 1954 speciously supporting the studio's choice of Lana Turner for a film he'd written about the courtesan Diane de Poitiers. Isherwood's candidate had been Ingrid Bergman, but the moguls vetoed her as a moral reprobate because of her affair with Roberto Rossellini. Admitting to a paltry compromise, Isherwood warned Vidal, "Don't become a hack like me." The arch self-contempt is characteristic, but it contains an oblique truth. Isherwood plays at justifying his drudgery as an exercise in self-humiliation, a victory over professional self-conceit like Ramakrishna's manual cleansing of the privy.

But he has turned his indignity to his own account, and defends his toil as a mystical discipline. He enjoys script writing as "a tremendous holiday from the novel." More than this, it is a holiday from literature, a training in abstinence and abstraction like the meditative techniques of Zen, for its purpose is to dissolve the word and transform it into an image. Like transcendental meditation, it is a way of organizing silence. "You're always trying *not* to speak, trying to *show* it rather than *say* it," Isherwood explains. Obliged to visualize, the script writer submits to an enforced abstention: "you have to learn to stop relying on the word" and to think instead "in terms of possible silent sequences." Isherwood is pleased with his screenplay for the film of Carson McCullers's *Reflections in a Golden Eye,* which is "totally cinematic" because virtually silent. The novel frets to analyze the motives of its characters, but in the movies "the less you explain the better." Cinematic characters can afford to be "outrageously strange" (as Isherwood says of McCullers's people) and unpredictable, whereas those in novels must behave with psychological consistency. Isherwood admires the dislocations and emotional discontinuity of film, which conveys "the way that experience really happens to you" more accurately than the equable, consequential novel can. The gratuitousness of action in Antonioni's *La Notte* excites him for this reason: "the business with the rocket, and this strange, abrupt, bloodthirsty fight between the boys, which is suddenly over again, and she [Jeanne Moreau] wanders off, all this seemed to me quite extraordinary." The cinema represents the bewildering chaos of sensory experience yet, like the ambulatory Jeanne Moreau in *La Notte,* remains serenely indifferent to it. This makes the cinema a model of the mystic's conduct, abiding the world's vicissitudes, accepting the most ludicrous or calamitous of its shocks, but detached in self-contemplation. The accord between the formal possibilities of the cinema and the purposes of mysticism is so close that Isherwood even prepared a script based on the life of Buddha, which MGM for a time planned to produce.

Isherwood began his study of Vedanta soon after his arrival in California. The modern revival of Vedanta was the work of Ramakrishna and his disciples, one of whom, Vivekananda, visited the Chicago Parliament of Religions in 1893, seven years after the master's death, and later established missions in several American cities. The mission on Ivar Avenue in Hollywood was supervised by Swami Prabhavananda, who became Isherwood's instructor. Isherwood's conversion proceeded concurrently with Huxley's, but very differently. For instance, he never reconciled himself to Huxley's psychedelic drugs. In 1955, encouraged by Huxley, he bought some mescaline in a New York pharmacy, and in England later in the year went under its influence to Westminster Abbey in search of God. But God, to Isherwood's dismay, wasn't there. Perhaps drugs don't work on Isherwood because he is too retentive of self, too guardedly conscious. They offer to Huxley the bliss of self-obliteration; but Isherwood's meditative practices are a way of organizing and purifying the conscious self, not an attempt to expunge it. Huxley's unbelief is too corrosive to be borne, so he collapses from satiric skepticism into mystical credulity. Isherwood's progress was more hesitant and mistrustfully inductive. He was converted, he has said, because he couldn't bring himself not to believe in the Swami's belief. He works his way conscientiously through doubts which Huxley vanquishes instantaneously, because he fears the self-surrender which Huxley the satiric misanthrope longs for. His only subject is himself:

how can he therefore agree to renounce that degenerate, vexatious, but endearing self? When the conversion occurred, Isherwood astutely made sure that it was on his own terms. He presented the Swami with two objections to his acceptance into the faith: his enslavement to the false values of the movie studios, and his homosexuality. The Swami dialectically adjusted Vedanta to Isherwood's personal circumstances and insured him against self-sacrifice by arguing that the believer was a lotus on a dirty pond, pure despite the impurity of the world in which he lived, and countenancing homosexuality so long as carnal desires didn't obsessively disturb spiritual peace.

Once Isherwood's misgivings were appeased and he had ceased to disbelieve, he began re-imagining California in terms of his new faith. Aspects of this adaptation of California to Vedanta have already been mentioned: the slippery hills become an image of the world's illusoriness, the movies turn into an abstract, meditative form. In 1953 Isherwood and Prabhavananda published a translation of and commentary on the yoga aphorisms of Patanjali called *How To Know God*. The aphorisms are 1500 years old, but Isherwood's commentaries transplant them to the society and landscape of contemporary California. The final commentary quotes Vivekananda's account of the soul's travail through nature, which is an inadvertent allegorization of the western landscape. Vivekananda refers to a trackless desert where the soul loses its way, and its final destination in a sea which is "the ocean of perfection": the aspirant, that is, struggles through the aridity of Arizona and Nevada toward the cleansing Pacific. The hermit travels in the opposite direction, like Stephen in *The World in the Evening* flying east to Pennsylvania, renouncing the "dirty coast" and the treacherous "neon-mirage" of Los Angeles, welcoming the aloofness and vacancy of the inhuman desert. Desert and ocean are the dual realities of southern California, and they recur as symbolic demonstrations everywhere in the explications of Patanjali. Ablutions are acts of grace. Guilt is explained as a mud bath, clarity of consciousness as an unrippled pool, the mind as a lake whose wave motions can be controlled. Domestic swimming pools are islets of mental tranquility. When Stephen curses Los Angeles in *The World in the Evening,* he pleads for its swimming pools to be dried up.

Irrigation, which for Huxley proclaimed California's scientific victory over a niggardly dessicated nature, becomes in Isherwood an image of spiritual discipline. Goodness inflows, he says, like water released from a reservoir. Huxley is satirically gleeful about the geological instability of California, but Isherwood has the mystic's nonchalant attitude toward natural menaces. Living in a house perched on the edge of a canyon in a slide area, he seems to invite destruction by earth tremor. Glossing one of Patanjali's precepts, he says that spiritual retribution ought not to be confused with natural calamity, as happened in the ancient world, when earthquakes were interpreted as a divine judgment on sodomy. Combining both the peril of the San Andreas rift and the water problems of Los Angeles in his illustration, he says that "if you build your city on an earthquake fault, or neglect your dams or your agriculture, you will probably, but not certainly be visited with earthquakes, floods or famines. That has nothing whatever to do with the spiritual consequences of sin." Isherwood refuses to be apocalyptic about California, as Huxley is. He is concerned not with collective disasters, like the devastation of *Ape and Essence,* but with private destinies; not with Huxley's condemnation of the entire human race but with the "self-contained punishment" whereby sin creates obstacles to enlightenment. This is the case of his single man, mired in depression and regret, impatient for his own annihilation.

The yoga aphorisms indicate a further difference between Huxley and Isherwood over American technology. In Huxley's America, people have become adjuncts of machines, apprentices to gadgets. But this dehumanization is instructive. It may lead to a training of spiritual reaction which remakes the human organism as a contraption of spiritual engineering. Huxley mentions an Oriental friend ("a doctor by profession, a dervish by avocation") who has converted instinct into mechanical will and regimented his own heart-beat, metabolism, and respiration. These functions are no longer helplessly suffered, but can be induced and altered as if by flicking a switch. The body's capacities have become technical equipment. The mystic is a superior technocrat. Machines are tamed spirits. Huxley called applied science a "domesticated jinni": the mod. cons. of the American home are magic, powered by electricity. Spirits, conversely, are ghostly machines. After Huxley's death, his second wife communicated with him at séances, and she has compared the presiding medium to a spirit-telephone, transmitting messages from the ether.

Isherwood dislikes this reduction of the human being to a "psycho-spiritual instrument," which has resulted in the Californian equation between Zen and the art of motorcycle maintenance. For him, America's technological miracles are the detours of spiritual incapacity. Technology for Huxley is the extension of a physical into a spiritual power, but for Isherwood it is the denial of a mental power and a symptom of the West's self-impoverishment. "Instead of telepathy," he says, "we have the telephone, instead of levitation we have the helicopter, and instead of clairvoyance we have television." Although Huxley sees radio and television as malign devices which subliminally indoctrinate Americans, Isherwood in *Ramakrishna and His Disciples* identifies television as a Western equivalent of the Hindu mantra. The guru gives his disciples a series of holy names to repeat, and Isherwood proves the efficiency of this method of spiritual persuasion by pointing out that "a television advertisement can so permeate the consciousness of a community that the little children sing it in the streets."

Even negotiating the Los Angeles freeway system is a discipline for the mystic. Huxley, though too myopic to drive, was an accomplished navigator on the looping, labyrinthine system. The navigator's back seat is the perfect position for him: from there he can enjoy the sensation of commanding the car by remote control, employing the driver as his technological medium. He is the map-reading ghost in the rear of the machine. Isherwood's pleasure is in driving. George in *A Single Man* driving from Santa Monica to teach a class at San Tomas State College regards his mastery of the freeway as a credential of social membership, just as Auden in New York harped on alienated modern man's existential duty to decipher the subway system. The freeway therapeutically offers George both a contest of virile self-assertion and a meditative retreat from the self. At first he drives combatively, jockeying between lanes in a "mad metropolitan chariot race" which would have deterred Ben Hur. But as he continues, "some kind of autohypnosis exerts itself." He relaxes, and his reflexes do the work for him. The car is now driving him. The freeway changes from an epic chariot race into an undifferentiated Buddhist life-stream, "a river, sweeping in full flood towards its outlet with a soothing power." George is "like a master who has entrusted the driving of his car to a servant." But this self-detachment isn't like Huxley's manipulation of the car at two removes by navigating. George's body guides the machine, leaving his mind free to ponder and recoil "deep down inside himself." Isherwood's George on the freeway is performing his yoga exercises; Auden on the subway is like a god prowling subterraneously through nature, gloomily fraternizing with the grotesque species he has created:

> Scanning his fellow
> Subway passengers, he asks:
> "Can I really be
> the only one in this car
> who is glad to be alive?"

In 1939 Vedanta answered Isherwood's need for an alternative to the political ideologies of embattled Europe. His conversion was a deconversion from Europe. But increasingly he understands Vedanta not as an incident in his quarrel with home and family but a response to his adoptive society. As well as a response, Vedanta is a necessary mental protection against California. The lazy haze of the weather elides the differences between seasons, blurs time, and entices all creatures into slothful sleep. The euphemistic cemeteries "hospitably invite you," Isherwood says, "to the final act of relaxation." The lullaby of the climate is seconded by a seductive commercial hypnosis. Radio, billboards, movies, and newspapers "are for ever whispering in your ear," and in the yoga aphorisms their beguilements are described as mental impurities, an addictive reverie which is inimical to enlightenment. The blandishments of California must be resisted "firmly but not tensely," Isherwood advises.

Vedanta supplies the resistance, maintaining the mind's alertness. Huxley also sees this as an imperative, but his version of the problem is characteristically more sinister and psychedelic than Isherwood's. Isherwood is afraid of California because it's so enchanting, because its hedonism weakens the will and persuades you to "sign that seven-year contract, buy that house you don't really want, marry that girl you secretly despise." Huxley was alarmed by the hypnotic lure of California, but for him it is not a personal temptation as it is for Isherwood. Rather it flatters his satiric foresight by showing California to be an actualization of his brave new world. In 1957 he was amused to hear that a penal institution in Tulare County, California, had experimented with miniature loudspeakers under the pillows of volunteer prisoners. Into these during the night was repeated an inspirational homily on moral living. Huxley had described this "sleep-teaching" twenty-five years earlier, in *Brave New World*, where it is called Hypnopaedia. California seeks to make all its inhabitants as meekly suggestive as sleepers. "As the Buddhists insist," Huxley says in *Brave New World Revisited*, "most of us are half asleep all the time and go through life as somnambulists obeying somebody else's suggestions. Enlightenment is total awakeness. The word 'Buddha' can be described as 'The Wake.'" California has made a philosophy from comatose mental inertia. Its jargon extols an anesthetized bliss which is variously described as "mellowing out," "going with the flow," "staying loose," or being "laid back." Isherwood declares that salvation in Los Angeles depends on "the art of staying awake." Vedanta is his counter-soporific.

Huxley's California is a hell in which one constructs a phantasmal heaven. Though Isherwood's attitude is similar, it is more affectionately inflected. In the essay on Los Angeles he contributed to *Horizon* in 1947, he devises an itinerary for a visiting satirist: "In order to get the worst possible first impression of Los Angeles one should arrive there by bus, preferably in summer and on a Saturday night. That is what I did." Like Huxley, he is virtually recommending the most dismaying route of entry into what he calls "the Unpromising Land." Since then he has relented. Whereas Huxley apocalyptically punishes California in *Ape and Essence*, Isherwood, who is at once so merciless and so indulgent about his personal infractions, comes to prize it for its faults. His talent for self-flattering self-excoriation is shared by America, and this is one of the reasons why he likes it. His own version of Huxley's contention that one lives in America because it is so awful is melioristic and ironically self-reproachful. He defends America by calling it the place "where the mistakes are being made—and made first, so we're going to get the answers first." America is no longer a laboratory of social experiment (as it was for Wells), but of instructive calamity. "I feel it's marvellous the way we talk about our failings," Isherwood says. He is referring to America, but he might be referring to himself. He adores America because it shares his obsession with self-criticism. But for Isherwood as for his adopted country, self-criticism is not a sign of satirical self-dislike, but an ostentatious luxury which only the most invincible egotist can afford. Isherwood, who in his volumes of autobiography delights in his own frailties and sexual truancies, fondly translates the social vices of Los Angeles—its impermanence and anonymity, its sprawl and its sluggishness, its infatuation with cinematic illusions—into mystical virtues.

Because he is devoted to the follies of the place, and adroit at twisting them to moral and spiritual advantage, he resents facile criticism of California like Evelyn Waugh's *The Loved One*. He worked with Terry Southern on the script of the film version, but admits to detesting the book's snobbery. Waugh's novel is an affront to Isherwood's mystical California, because its satirical objections to the funeral practices of California are part of a doctrinal quarrel with America. Huxley and Isherwood joke about Forest Lawn, but secretly approve of it, Huxley because its abolition of death makes it an outlandish institute for psychic research, Isherwood because its propaganda hints at a reincarnatory mysticism. Recommending *After Many a Summer* in his 1947 essay on Los Angeles, Isherwood mentions one of the mortuary's advertisements, "in which a charming, well-groomed elderly lady (presumably risen from the dead) assured the public: 'It's better at Forest Lawn. *I speak from experience.*'" Waugh the Catholic dogmatist is, however, alarmed by the heresy of California's new religions. *The Loved One* reproves California in the hope of reclaiming it for orthodoxy. This is why Isherwood dislikes it, and why it is so inefficient as satire.

California is immune to Waugh's satire because its truths are stranger than his most wounding fictions. In the implausible reality of Los Angeles, Waugh's exaggerations—a street called Via Dolorosa, a studio hack called Lorenzo Medici—are harmless. The only way Waugh can subdue the unruly, fictitious actuality of California is to import codes of honor and gentility which California itself has never recognized. His characters are therefore English expatriates, constrained by the rules of clubmanship and fearful of social disgrace. The novel harries those who betray the club: Sir Francis, ignominiously fired by the studio; Dennis Barlow, who falls from respectability by taking a job in a pets' mortuary; or the scene designer who goes native, wears ready-made shoes, a belt instead of braces, an open-necked shirt, eats at a drugstore, shakes cocktails for a living, and has to be repatriated by the Cricket Club. But even the club's disdainful police force is powerless in relaxed, opportunistic California. Dennis at the end of the novel pockets the money subscribed by the club to pay for his return passage, but tricks his sponsors by blackmailing Joyboy the mortician for a similar amount. The satirist can threaten the penalty of "exclusion from British society," but in California that is hardly a deterrent.

Waugh wants to make a colony of California. The opening of

the novel, which camouflages Hollywood as a barbarous imperial outpost, is a good joke but a frustrated one, because it confesses a longing to change the subject into an easier, more abject target. One of the cricketers sadly admits this in lamenting Dennis's decline from the composition of verse to the incineration of pets: "in Africa, if a white man is disgracing himself and letting down his people the authorities pack him off home. We haven't any such rights here, unfortunately." Waugh derides the funeral practices of California in order to prosecute the new religions of the place, to which Huxley and Isherwood had been converted. Again, as with the colonial presumption about Hollywood society, the satire is an outraged defense of orthodoxy against innovation. Waugh's Californians are heretics, schismatics, rebels against his grand design to incorporate America into the universal empire of the Catholic Church.

An article written for *Life* in 1949, the year after *The Loved One,* proposes this imperial stratagem as a solution to the problem of American classlessness. Waugh is distressed because Americans disown their Catholic heritage, and argues that they do so out of social embarrassment. The second and third generations of Catholic immigrants regard their religion as a social handicap and "associate it with the smell of garlic and olive oil and grandfather muttering over foreign language newspapers." Catholicism in America can be saved only by a recovery of social esteem. Waugh pleads for the constitution of a Catholic gentry, which will be at home in country clubs and social registers. This wishful thinking lies behind *The Loved One,* whose characters will neither behave genteelly nor acknowledge the authority of Waugh's Catholicism. The heroine Aimée, a cosmetician at Whispering Glades (Waugh's name for Forest Lawn), has no religion because she is progressive, but relies on the mystic counsels of the fraudulent Guru Brahmin, like Isherwood with his Swami. Dennis intends to set up shop as a nonsectarian pastor, specializing in funerals.

Whispering Glades enrages Waugh because it impiously denies death. This, however, is its value for Huxley and Isherwood, to whom it suggests that death is only a metaphor for a change in consciousness. Hypnotizing his dying wife, Huxley told her that pain is death in life but death is an accession of new life, because it relieves the body from its travails. The death of Isherwood's single man is the improbable result of a failure in the brain's circuitry: a cerebral event, not a moral penalty. Aimée's mother was a convert to "New Thought and wouldn't have it that there was such a thing as death." When death comes for Aimée, it is chemically self-administered (she injects herself with cyanide at the mortuary), and she is goaded to it by the ecstatic venery of the Wagner excerpts she hears on the radio. The hostess at Whispering Glades rebukes Dennis for being afraid of death, and promises that advance reservation of a burial plot will take care of all morbid emotion, since he will then have an investment in his own demise. The cemetery proscribes floral crosses because they are tokens of suffering. In an article for *The Tablet* in 1947, Waugh listed other orthodox objections to Forest Lawn. It obstructs the natural retributive process of decay, and sends its embalmed customers "straight from the Slumber Room to Paradise," bypassing any state of penance; and its admissions policy is illogical: suicides are welcome (Sir Francis in *The Loved One* is accepted into Whispering Glades after hanging himself), whereas under Waugh's older religious dispensation they would have lain at a crossroads, impaled.

Isherwood has his revenge on Waugh's doctrinal chastisement of California. The script he and Southern wrote for Tony Richardson's film sabotages the novel. Travestied, *The Loved One* becomes a parable in praise of the Californian accord between mysticism and mechanism. Waugh's plot is suppressed. Instead, a scientific boy wonder who launches space rockets from the pets' cemetery inspires the Blessed Reverend, the founder of Whispering Glades, to offer his clients a technological resurrection: bodies will be disinterred and fired into space. The lucrative acres of the mortuary will then be free for development as an amusement park. The first customer to be loaded onto a missile is the luckless Aimée. Isherwood and Southern

Aimée's space-burial from *The Loved One* ©1965 Metro-Goldwyn-Mayer.
Reproduced by permission of Metro-Goldwyn-Mayer.
Courtesy of National Film Archive/Stills Library, London.

warp Waugh's satire into a surreal, mock-mystical comedy. In the
yoga aphorisms Isherwood says, "instead of levitation we have the
helicopter." The film reunites technological miracle and mystical
prodigy: the Blessed Reverend travels by helicopter, and the mummified corpses he sends into space have likewise been freed not only
from mortality but from gravity, reclaimed as orbiting angels.

This revision of Waugh coincides with Isherwood's criticism of
Huxley's Forest Lawn novel. The 1947 essay on Los Angeles commends *After Many a Summer*. By 1964 it is a classic, and George
teaches it to his seminar of dullards in *A Single Man*. The class's in-

quest on the novel yields a series of propositions, impartially listed by Isherwood. George ventures no opinion, and allows his students to reveal themselves in formulating a criticism of Huxley. Their findings are California's repudiation of Huxley's interpretation of it, and a cover for Isherwood's own reservations about the novel. The students are innocents who can comprehend neither detestation of the world nor transfiguration of it. They are therefore equally critical of Huxley's satire ("This novel is clever but cynical. Huxley should dwell more on the warm human emotions") and of the spirituality into which satire is transvalued ("This novel is arid and abstract mysticism. What do we need eternity for, anyway?"). They have no need of the idea of eternity because, as healthy Californian animals, they are too busy enjoying the actuality of eternity. They also sense the bad faith which makes the mysticism an alibi for satiric misanthropy ("Mr. Propter shouldn't have said the ego is unreal; this proves that he has no faith in human nature"), a vengeful etherealization of the human world ("He wants to get rid of people and make the world safe for animals and spirits") and a retreat from a physical existence which disgusts Huxley (two of the propositions concern the carnal inadequacy of the characters: "Mr. Propter has no sex-life. This makes him unconvincing as a character," and "Mr. Pordage's sex-life is unconvincing").

With much of this the noncommittal Isherwood might be presumed to agree. His own California is a placid sensual heaven, not Huxley's psychedelic mirage. George's students, criticizing Propter's argument that time is the medium in which evil proliferates, use one of Isherwood's images, the laving ocean: "To say time is evil because evil happens in time is like saying the ocean is a fish because fish happen in the ocean." Huxley's time hastens toward putrefaction. The fifth Earl in *After Many a Summer* seeks immortality but wizens into a foetal ape. Isherwood's time is the benign medium in which we live down our past and outgrow our errors. As Isherwood in California has grown backwards, rewriting the past to cast it off, so George's utopian suburb is a place for second childhoods, a "beautifully ordered nursery-community where Senior Citizens (*old*, in our Country of the Bland, has become nearly as dirty a word as kike or nigger) are eased into senility, retaught their childhood games." Isherwood's final affectionate revenge on Huxley is to show the indifference of the students to the novel's imprecations. California is angelically unscathed by satire, and the students misread Huxley's nemesis as a gospel of blithe self-content: "This novel is a wonderful spiritual sermon. It teaches us that we aren't meant to pry into the mysteries of life. We mustn't tamper with eternity."

The novel in which these misgivings about Huxley are expressed is itself an answer to *After Many a Summer*. *A Single Man* is a discreet "spiritual sermon" confiding Isherwood's own mystical perception of California and testing the effect this new religion has on the incorrigibly worldly form of the novel. The moping, solitary hero, hurling himself at the end of a dreary day into a drunken frolic with one of his students and afterwards abruptly expiring, is Isherwood's version of the saint. He has said that *A Single Man* demonstrates the disequilibrium of middle age, which alternates like George between riotous youth and decrepit exhaustion, and is therefore always unpredictable. But this unpredictability is also a prerequisite of sainthood. In an essay on the religious novel, Isherwood says that the saint bemuses the novelist because he always acts disinterestedly and therefore gratuitously. The novelist is trained to follow behavior back to its origins in self-serving "fear, vanity, or desire." But the saint has none of these blameworthy motives, and "his every action is a genuine act of free will." Therefore "you can never predict what he will do next." George clings to the selfish vices the saint has overcome, but he acts with the saint's stunning spontaneity. His day is a succession of impromptu, impetuous, inconsequential detours: escaping from Doris's hospital room, driving through the hills, escaping from Charlotte's house, groggily surfing with Kenny, masturbating, inexplicably dying. Living from moment to moment episodically, he is both staying loose, as the Californian should do, and also acting 'without attachment to the fruits of an act," which, as Isherwood says in his life of Ramakrishna, is the Bhagavad-Gita's counsel.

"We are to perform every action as though it were a ritual, of which the value is symbolic," unperturbed by the consequences, which "we dedicate to god." This is Ramakrishna's teaching, and George behaves in accordance with it. Because he acts in a ritualized stupor, rather than calculating consequences and determining his own future, he is not a conventional novelistic character. What he does is no guide to what he is. He acts with sublime self-detachment, and is so neglectful of the querulous self that he seems not to be a character at all. This is why the title of the novel is not his name but the mere fact of his singleness. Isherwood is both paying tribute to the healing anonymity of California, where people are free to lose their identities or remake them, and referring to one of the monastic renunciations demanded by the Ramakrishna Order, which requires initiates to abandon their names as a symbol of their passage beyond personal identity. In England, Isherwood's hero would be George, classified by a name, relegated to a past. In California, he is merely a single man, and not even his singleness is remarkable. Isherwood himself in moving to California shed a pair of names, William and Bradshaw. The acknowledgments to his study of Ramakrishna comically catch some fellow acolytes sloughing off their humdrum hereditary labels to be exotically rebaptized: "I have had constant help from John Yale (now Swami Vidyatmananda)" and "I must also thank . . . Ursula Bond (Pravrajika Anandaprana)." Ramakrishna himself signalized his accession to a new state of being by assuming that name and ceasing to call himself Gadadhar. In *A Single Man* George's acquisition of a name, which in a European novel would be the instigation of character, is an afterthought. It happens after a long process of assemblage, after the shambling body which hauls itself out of bed has defecated, washed, and dressed itself, because the wearing of a name is a concession to the society outside. Other people must be able to fix a tag of identity to this body, but the body doesn't need one for conducting its relation with itself. It adopts a name for the same cautionary, cowardly reason that it covers its nakedness or shaves its beard.

The body wears a name for purposes of social intercourse, but

310

not a character. Visiting the hospital, George is horrified by the same process at work backwards: Doris is no longer a person, only a malfunctioning body. He too at the end of the novel lapses into a disposable body, dead garbage to be carted away. This tenuousness of identity is both the prescription of a mystical attitude and a sharp glimpse of Californian manners. Europeans are uneasy with Californian familiarity: its instant recourse to first names, its omission of patronymics in introductions. Californians think this is because the visitors are too punctiliously formal. Actually it is because they dread the spiritual democracy into which George has merged himself. The zany individualism of California, with its cults of self-development and ideologies of spiritual growth, is a contradiction of personal individuality. Forcibly individualizing themselves, these people have ended looking exactly the same, like the sunbathers with their indistinguishably perfect bodies. Not even George's singleness can make an individual of him, because everyone else is equally single. He enjoys in his personal existence that saintly characterlessness he praises in Californian motel rooms.

Character retracts into body. In the Californian morning at the beginning of the novel, waking up is a primal experience of life, a first awakening to self-recognition: "waking up begins with saying *am* and *now*." George is the first man in the world, like Adam awaking in Eden. The initial shock of immediacy leads him to postulate an I to whom these sensations belong, and to gradually elaborate a language. At once, because time in California is so foreshortened and Eden overlaps with Armageddon, there is a lapse into the fallen state of disease and dissipation. The primal I, later to become George, senses the arthritic twinges and nauseous spasms which constrict it and shuffles off to empy its bladder, check its obesity, and put itself together as a "live dying creature."

This disappearance of character into body is at once a fact of Isherwood's California and a discipline of Vedanta. Physiology, he explains in the study of Ramakrishna, abuts on spirituality, just as sanitariness is next to sanctity. Mystical events, for Huxley technological feats, are for Isherwood physical manifestations. Hindu physiology, for instance, directs spiritual energy up the spine from the base where it is stored. "Om," the mystic syllable, is a happening inside the body: its correct pronunciation, Isherwood says, exercises "all possible positions of the throat, mouth and tongue." Hinduism spiritualizes "gross physical organs"—navel, heart, throat—as lotus-formed centers of consciousness. The body is the seat of self-definition, and therefore in Ramakrishna's definition it impedes enlightenment. Egotistic illusion is physically experienced as what Isherwood calls "the body-idea." The perception that "I have a body" is an admission that "I am I, and therefore other than Brahman." But though the body is a prison, it must not be harmed. Suicide is forbidden because for a Hindu birth in a human body is a metaphysical privilege, earned only after many rebirths in inferior forms. And the body equips its inhabitant with the means of extricating himself, by meditation. To this end, Isherwood recommends sexual reversal. Distinction of gender is a fallacy deriving from "the body-idea" and "the idea of ego." The devotee should therefore think himself into membership of the opposite sex, and Isherwood even proposes transvestism as a useful technique for crossing the putative border between male and female. Indirectly, this justifies George's homosexuality. The single man in a suburb of heterosexual incubators at least hasn't convinced himself that sex will make him immortal by proxy. He understands the fickleness of sexual contact and the vagaries of desire. Hence the finicky masturbatory scenario he devises, conjoining first Kenny and the Mexican tennis player, then replacing the giggly Kenny with the Mexican's blond opponent. Futilely spilling his seed, he is closer to wisdom than the procreating Strunks next door.

But this assiduous, solipsistic service to the body's wants is also an attribute of Isherwood's Americans, who punish the body in the hope of perfecting it, slimming, deodorizing, depilating, and jogging it, or working on its tan. Americans are Adams trying to render their bodies antiseptically unfallen again. Their hedonism is disinterested, even prayerful. The mystic's plight of entrapment in a body corresponds to the cinema's formal condition of confinement to bodies. The cinema can't probe beneath the flesh to investigate thought and motive as the novel can. Instead it transcribes the movements of bodies. Isherwood imposes this cinematic externality on his own narrative in following the jerkily unpremeditated actions of George. He is no longer the novelist mining the heart or brain of his character, but the cinematographer tracking the bulk of the character's carcass.

Isherwood is evasive about George's death, introducing it as a supposition, a wild improbability which might all the same be possible. The uncertainty again has a religious implication. Mysticism makes death a metaphor. In the life of Ramakrishna, Isherwood calls sadhana, "the supreme act of ego-surrender . . . through which God is known," a condition "as appalling as death itself; a leap into the utter void." George's demise is a vault of faith into the unknown, a renunciation of the troublesome individuality which constitutes his singleness, an abrupt graduation to enlightenment. Because Isherwood can't follow him there, he can't be sure what has happened. The mystical virtue of this death is confirmed by the fact that it occurs in America, for Isherwood, struggling away from his family in *Kathleen and Frank*, vows to die somewhere else, not, if he can help it, at home. Auden went home to die, celebrating the biological circularity which had turned the old man into a puling, messy big baby. Isherwood can't conceive of his own death as a gradual shuffling into senility like Auden's. His life is a perpetual present, the tense of youthful California and of Ramakrishna's beatitude. Isherwood sums up Ramakrishna's gospel in one word, *"Now."* Ramakrishna neither laments the past nor fears nor anticipates the future, but exists "in continuous contact with that which is eternally present. God's existence has no relation to past or future; it is always as of *now*." Hence the death Isherwood proposes for George and by implication for himself is an instantaneous electrical disconnection. The brain is blacked out, the power line of the lungs cut, and there is no time for the "skeleton crew" of arterial engineers to rig up a new circuitry.

313

America's traditional offer of rebirth to the immigrant has been revised. Now it promises him death. The choice of America is not the choice of life but the choice of self-extinction. With the death of the single man, this book ends. In retrospect, it seems to have described a progressive contraction: from the anatomies of American society over which the Victorians labor to Isherwood's identification of America with his own self-rejuvenating physical anatomy. Or perhaps it has been a progressive etherealization: from the Victorian criticism of Americans as unmannerly brutes to the modern celebration of them as a race of angels—Auden's existential refugees, no longer rooted in the earth, Huxley's robots, Isherwood's sun-tanned transcendental meditators. The first half of this book is about American society. The Victorians and later Kipling excavate the institutional foundations of that society, the aesthetes try to reform it, Wells and Lawrence foment revolutions in it. Thereafter, America is not a place of social action and adventure, as the different missions of Wilde and Brooke, Kipling and Stevenson, Wells and Lawrence make it, but of claustration and reclusion. America is no longer a society, but a moral or mental retreat—for Auden a country of lonely, displaced people, with a foreign policy embodying an unrequited love for the world, for Huxley a satiric hell which drugs and machines can convert into heaven, for Isherwood a place, like Ramakrishna's sadhana, of blissful nonentity.

Through time, this is how the process of imagining America has developed and controverted itself. But, as the joke has it, in America geography takes the place of history, and if the different images of America unfolded by this book are distributed through space, another, less morbid and introverted conclusion suggests itself. Each writer here discussed discovers a personal America for himself. Each version is new, and each contradicts all the others. The Victorians deplore America because it has not yet attained the social nicety and complication which the novelist values. But the aesthetes admire its undress and don't want it to dwindle into a civilization, while Kipling finds in its barbarity an invigorating epic heroism. Wells's America strains toward a scientific future, Lawrence's exhumes a mythical past. Auden's New York is a vertical city for a hieratic moralist to live in, Isherwood's Los Angeles a horizontal city for a mystic, whose vision is of the chaotic, thronging democracy of all created things. But Isherwood's Los Angeles is not the same place as Huxley's. Isherwood's city is an illusory fabrication in two dimensions, Huxley's a monument to technology's suppression of arid, antagonistic nature. America is ample and generous enough to tolerate all these impositions on it, and versatile and various enough to adapt to all these transformations of it. The moral of this book, like that of America, lies not in its unity but in its diversity.

INDEX